Spirit

Advance Praise for *Spirit*

"Take your time with this book. Every page is an invitation — to pause, to reflect, to listen more deeply. The insights are rich and layered. I find myself reading the same passage multiple times because it speaks to something deep in me. The raw authenticity of this book opens doors to realms of thought and Spirit I don't usually step into. Bob's vulnerability in sharing his own journey makes *Spirit* more than a book — it's a companion and a sacred conversation."

— Karby Allington-Goldfain, LMFT, Certified IFS Therapist and Approved Consultant

"This book summarizes more than 3,000 pages of Bob's long and intimate conversations with Spirit. Perhaps even more important than the guidance that Spirit has provided through Bob is the quickening this book can activate. It is a strong and clear reminder that we are all capable of direct and powerful connection with something greater than ourselves."

— Alexia Rothman, PhD, Clinical Psychologist,
IFS Trainer, IFSI-Approved Clinical Consultant

"Robert Falconer has done it again! Another truly inspiring and spiritually significant book that helps the reader tap into more Self energy through their relationship with guides. Bob's unique guides and wisdom teachers share with humor and spiciness. This is truly a beautifully crafted piece of art. The process underlying this book has been a guiding force for me in my life, and I am happy Bob is making it accessible to many. Enjoy, dear reader!"

— Kay Gardner, Senior IFS Trainer

"*Spirit* is a contemporary answer to Job! The wisdom of the Depths counsels, chides, and consoles Bob with compassion, wisdom, and love. The messages are accessible, powerful, nuanced, and direct. This book is Scripture — searing and timeless. Invite yourself to be challenged and grow!"

— Donald L. Davies, MD

"Reading the first chapter of Bob's *Spirit* about how he unexpectedly started to communicate with the spirit world, I felt a strong desire to try it myself, a dragging toward something strange and somewhat challenging that I also felt when reading his book *The Others Within Us*. Bob has the courage and the clear thinking, combined with a massive library of knowledge inside his head and at his fingertips, that allows him to travel to unknown territory where few other therapists and seekers go and to map it out for the rest of us. The spirits we meet in *Spirit* are not the candy-floss or feel-good ones — they're demanding, uncompromising voices that show us directly the many ways that we let darkness into our lives instead of the light and love they are fighting for.

"*Spirit* is also a book where Bob does not spare himself. It creates a beautiful and haunting self-portrait — a picture of human frailty, compassion, and strength amid this circle of spirits. When I told Bob that I thought the spirits were hard on him, he told me a story about the Sufi al-Hillaj, who had gained so much inner freedom and such great connection to the divine that when he was condemned to death, he danced to his grave. It is the same radical acceptance of the world as it is that runs through Bob's book."

— Peter Legård Nielsen, Certified IFS Therapist, Certified Advanced Rolfer™,
author of *Spontaneous Kundalini Awakenings*, *Healing the Damage Through IFS*,
and various novels and poetry in Danish

———

"Leksi (this literally means Uncle — it is an honorific for highly trusted spiritual elders) Albert White Hat Sr. used to gently scold folks when they would translate Tunkasila Wakan Tanka or Ate' Wakan Tanka as 'Great Mystery.' In English, he would say, they can be 'mysterious,' but Tunkasila Wakan Tanka is quite knowable. On the one hand, Robert Falconer is a relentless scientist; he travels wherever evidence takes him. Though unseen, Taku Wakan Skan Skan has, is, and will be experienced by living beings in our lifetime. Bob understands that Spirit, like gravity or wind or countless other unseen elements of our Natural World, speaks. Bob not only listens — he hears. Mitakuye Oyasin 'All is Related'... Thanks for not just being one who 'listens,' Bob, but for being 'one who Hears'...

"Bob's book uplifts, informs, and inspires… all of us are Related, through Spirit… Thanks to Bob for having the courage to share some of his Relationship and Experiences with Spirit…"

— Dan Foster, psychologist, Indigenous elder, Former Director of
Behavioral Health Care, Fort Belknap Sioux Reservation

———

SPIRIT

Robert Falconer

Great Mystery Press
greatmysterypress.com

ISBN: 979-8-9878588-6-8

To Spirit:
In whatever persona you appear; under whatever name
we use to call out to you: Jesus, Quan Yin, Buddha, Mary,
Allah, The Intercessor, Krishna, Angels, Archangels, God,
the Orishas, The Comforter, The Helpers, The Guides,
and the tens of thousands of other ways we have sought you

With thanks

Acknowledgments

First, to Seonghee Son, my precious wife

Much gratitude to Nikki Fryn — friend, business manager, website designer, cover designer, and more. Without her patient and tireless efforts, this book might not exist.

To Jim Sutherland for unfailing friendship and encouragement

To Richard Schwartz, the founder of IFS, for his work, which is revolutionizing psychotherapy and has changed my life

To Kirin Alolkoy, a patient and wonderful editor

To Kay Gardner, the senior IFS trainer who first introduced me to the process that led to this book

To Pat AlexanderWeston for many decades of dedicated healing work

Other books authored or coauthored by Robert Falconer

The Others Within Us:
Internal Family Systems, Porous Mind, and Spirit Possession
Great Mystery Press

When You're Going Through Hell ... Keep Going:
Trauma, Healing, Spirit, and Internal Family Systems
Great Mystery Press

Many Minds, One Self:
Evidence for a Radical Shift in Paradigm
Trailheads Publications

Opening the Inner World:
Spiritual Healing, Internal Family Systems, and Emanuel Swedenborg
Swedenborg Foundation Publishers

———

The following titles are currently out of print

A Man's Recovery from Traumatic Childhood Abuse:
The Insiders
The Haworth Maltreatment and Trauma Press
SECOND EDITION FORTHCOMING

Trauma, Amnesia, and the Denial of Abuse
Family Violence & Sexual Assault Institute

The Cost of Child Maltreatment:
Who Pays? We All Do
Family Violence & Sexual Assault Institute
and The Institute for Trauma Oriented Psychotherapy

Identifying and Treating Sex Offenders:
Current Approaches, Research, and Techniques
The Haworth Maltreatment and Trauma Press

Identifying and Treating Youth Who Sexually Offend:
Current Approaches, Techniques, and Research
The Haworth Maltreatment and Trauma Press

Introduction

— *Please read* —

Spirit talks to me almost every day now. More precisely, he responds in writing to written questions. So we have dialogues. There are over three thousand pages of them. Not too long ago, they locked people in mental institutions for claiming something like this. "This man is hearing voices — clearly a schizophrenic," they would say. As a psychotherapist, I'm only too aware of this. So I've kept this mostly secret, making only vague references to guidance. I'm old now; I no longer care very much about my reputation or career prospects. This gives me the luxury of saying what happened as clearly as I can.

The beginnings of things are often murky. Usually we invent neat creation myths to make everything look reasonable and comprehensible. For me, there were several flashes of light in the darkness that only slowly coalesced into a stable ongoing dialogue, a relationship.

When Spirit first appeared in my adult life, it was a very hard time, and I really needed some help. My partner had had a series of mental breakdowns and multiple suicide attempts with multiple hospitalizations. During one of these hospitalizations, when I was already overwhelmed and at a loss as to how I could keep her safe when she came home, I was given a bad diagnosis about my eyes and told that I should prepare to go blind. (I haven't gone blind, and I'm doing much better than the doctors thought possible.) Expectably, for a week or so I felt devastated, terrible, and lost, with no idea how to proceed. But then I felt a peace like I'd never felt before — a deep and abiding peace. I even told my friend and mentor, Dick Schwartz, that if I had to lose my vision, it was a cheap price to pay for this kind of peace. He said, "Be careful what you say, Bob." I didn't associate this peace with divinity or religion, but I felt in my bones that it was much bigger than me. This peace lasted about ten days and then slowly faded. However, the memory of it is indelible.

When I was a child, I was routinely sadistically sexually abused by my father and others. Even though my family was middle-class and churchgoing, both of my parents were alcoholic, and my mother was also a prescription drug addict. Mom was put in mental institutions a few times when I was a child. My older brother — my only sibling — died by probable suicide when we were teenagers. My father was murdered when I was twenty-one in an unsolved crime. One of my earliest and most profound contacts with Spirit came with terrible irony during some of the worst of the abuse. With all the beatings and rapes, I became able, as a child, to numb out most physical pain, but I could never numb out the effects of being suffocated. When my father realized this, he frequently used suffocation while he was raping or beating me. I often became unconscious. I don't know if these experiences are really NDEs — near-death experiences — but they had powerful spiritual content. Frequently I sensed a merciful female presence who would hold me close with kindness, softness, and care. It was so wonderful to be with her. I came to hate her because she kept sending me back and wouldn't let me stay with her. I cursed her and lost contact for decades.

By all odds I should be dead like my brother, or a junkie, or in prison, or living in a dumpster. Instead, I became a therapist and have devoted much of my life to helping other men who were violently abused as children. My father was also a deacon and trustee of a large Presbyterian church in New York. I came to view religion as organized hypocrisy at best and a foolish illusion. After Dad raped and beat me at night, we'd go to church the next morning. He'd be in front of the congregation collecting the offerings, a respected member of the church. I wanted nothing to do with religion, and I didn't enter a church of any kind for more than twenty-five years. I studied shamanism, tribal religions, Tibetan Buddhism, and many other foreign traditions. I did yoga almost daily for about thirty years. I had looked for spiritual experience in sex, drugs, and rock and roll. I used to joke that I'd spent most of my life looking for God between a woman's legs, but this is not really funny.

I've come to deeply believe that people like me with extreme trauma histories don't heal if they can't find a spiritual base. This idea is not popular with academics; it doesn't fit with Western materialism. Spirituality has been almost exiled from the professional trainings for psychotherapists. But it is necessary. Viktor Frankl saw this clearly in the Nazi concentration camps where he was held prisoner for many years. He saw that those who could make meaning out of their lives survived. Those who could not make meaning and find a spiritual basis for their lives died. Spirituality isn't a frill or an optional add-on. Spiritual connection determines who lives and who dies.

In my professional life, I have searched for ways help myself and others like me heal from childhood trauma. I tried many, many paths. My first major focus was Ericksonian hypnotherapy, then ego state therapy, then Gestalt therapy, then Pia Mellody's 12-step–based Post-Induction Therapy, and many other others.

For the past fifteen years or so, I have focused almost exclusively on Richard Schwartz's Internal Family Systems therapy. He'll be referred to as Dick in this book since that's what almost everyone calls him. This work, which is usually referred to as IFS, is the most respectful and potent way I've found to deal with severe trauma.

IFS is a parts work model. It is based on the idea that our personalities are not unified monolithic wholes; instead, we're made up of a system of interrelated subpersonalities. These subpersonalities are usually in a state of civil war, fighting each other and trying to take control of the whole system. One image for healing in IFS is converting this internal civil war into the cooperation of a great orchestra or jazz band or choir. We don't try to fuse or meld the parts together. This division into parts is healthy, good, and normal.

As Dick was developing his model some forty years ago, he found that while everyone had parts, there was also something else inside that he came to call the Self with a capital S. This is who we truly are. It can't be damaged or destroyed. It is calm, curious, compassionate, connected, creative, clear, courageous, and confident. Dick likes alliteration. He calls these the eight Cs of Self. He says that Self is not like a muscle that has to be built up over decades of exercising. Rather, it is innately who we are. All we need to do is to get the subpersonalities — the parts — to step back, or unblend, and this Self will shine forth like the sun when the clouds part. This is an incredibly valuable and hopeful message for survivors of extreme abuse. All the other therapists basically had the attitude that I and people like me were damaged goods and should accept a small life. Dick's message that who we really are can't be damaged or even dirtied is tremendously freeing.

The IFS way of working — befriending the parts and helping Self take on leadership — can become a spiritual path. IFS has become incredibly popular recently, and a great deal of high-quality material about it is available now. Two of Dick's many books, *Introduction to Internal Family Systems* and *No Bad Parts,* are solid places to start. I mention IFS here because its language and ways of working are a big part of my dialogues with Spirit. Internal Family Systems also recognizes the existence of other things in our internal worlds that are not part of us or our personal life histories.

I have often assisted in training other therapists in IFS. It was at one of these trainings that another event happened that vastly expanded my world and opened me to Spirit realms. More accurately, it shattered my hard-won understanding and worldview. It had seemed to me that after decades in the field, I had a fairly consistent view of the nature of the psyche and the role trauma played in most psychopathology. The psyche is made up of various parts, ego states, subpersonalities, inner children, or whatever you want to call them; and you can work with them in ways that will relieve their suffering and help them unburden the extreme emotions, beliefs, and energies they took on when they were being abused.

IFS divides parts into two broad categories. There are the exiles — the parts who carry the extreme emotions and beliefs from the childhood abuse. There are also the protectors, who try and keep these exiles from being triggered. Dick has developed wonderful, respectful, and effective ways of working with this delicate internal ecology.

Dick has also said there are things in the psyche that do not really belong to us — they are not from our personal history. Legacy burdens come down through our families. For example, it is well-known that children and grandchildren of people who were in the Nazi concentration camps tend to have certain specific emotional difficulties. Alcoholism can also be a legacy burden. Interestingly, this is often inherited in alternating generations, one generation being teetotalers and the next generation being drinkers. So, legacy burdens clearly exist, and they do not come from the person's own lifetime. The entire relatively new science of epigenetics makes this clear and gives it a firm experimental basis. Cultural burdens are something else you find in the psyche that do not come from the person's own lifetime.

Dick also says there are two other things people find inside their minds — unattached burdens and guides. Unattached burdens are very much like legacy burdens, but they don't seem to come from the person's family. We don't really know where they come from. He used to call them *critters* because the most important thing about them is that they only get power in a person's system if they can scare the person. He chose the name *critter* to make them less scary. IFS uses the name *guides* for beings people meet in their inner world who seem kind, intelligent, and wise.

For many years, Dick was reticent to talk about unattached burdens and guides because he was afraid they would make IFS seem too weird, too woo-woo. He would only teach about them in advanced trainings. Dick especially disliked the word *entities*. When I started pointing out the similarities to the anthropological literature on spirit possession, he was very displeased with me. People have been having experiences like this in almost every culture we have records of and in every era of history. They are normal human experiences, but we in the West have been taught to ignore them. I want to make it crystal clear that what I present in this book is way beyond IFS. It is NOT a part of IFS; these are NOT things that Dick or IFS teaches.

One of these unattached burden–critter things showed up in a client in a training, and this event permanently changed how I understand human nature. One trainee was acting as a therapist for another trainee, and I was supervising the session. The trainee therapist came across a part of the client, whom I will call Mary, that seemed to have no positive intention at all for Mary. It was viciously critical. In IFS, it is known that all parts, even suicidal ones, have a positive intention. We work hard to get to know this positive intention so we can join the part and help it rather than fight with it. A lack of positive intention is the classic indicator of an unattached burden.

The group had not yet been introduced to the subject of unattached burdens, so with the trainee therapist's permission, I took over the therapist role. When Mary looked inside and tried to see where this negative critical voice was coming from, she saw images of a bloodshot eyeball. After establishing that it had no positive intention for her, I had her ask it, "Are you a part of me?" The thing refused to answer, sneering at the question and saying many nasty things. Eventually it said to me, "You're supposed to be a teacher. Don't you have anything smarter to ask?" I had her reply to it that it might seem a foolish question, but it was also very simple. I had her ask it once more, "Are you a part of me?" Finally the voice roared out, "No, I'm not a part of her. I'm a much more powerful being, and I will squash her like a worm the same way I will squash you."

There are fairly simple ways in IFS that I'd learned to get these things out of people. I did those things. Even though I knew almost nothing, they worked. The most important thing is not being afraid. During the session, I was not afraid. After the session was over, I went to a staff meeting. I felt my body temperature drop, and I became very shaky. What the hell just happened? I also became irritable and made unpleasant, rude remarks to my friends when they tried to joke with me. I apologized the next day. The whole affair was so unpleasant that I decided it was just some odd fluke and I would do my best to ignore it. This was a big relief.

But after the workshop was over, I started getting long emails from Mary. She said the session was absolutely wonderful for her. She seemed so happy and relieved that I feared she was having a manic episode. In one of her emails, she informed me that decades before when she was a teenager and young woman, she'd had many, many mental breakdowns, had attempted suicide several times, and had been institutionalized and given powerful drugs and electroshock. Now I was really worried. I told myself that if I had known this history, I would have been much more cautious. Then she wrote something that has changed my life. She wrote, "Bob, you are the first person to ever believe me when I talked about the nonhuman inside me; before when I tried they just gave me drugs or electroshock. Your believing me has changed my life."

I've followed Mary for almost fifteen years since then. She's doing very, very well and still considers this to be a positive, life-changing experience. I very much wanted to ignore this. It was way outside my belief structures, but when she told me that I was the first person to believe her and what a huge difference it made for her, I couldn't ignore it. My whole worldview would have to change to accommodate this experience. Since that time, I have focused on this work, and because most therapists don't want to get involved in it, I get many referrals. I have published a book on this subject called *The Others Within Us*. I mentioned this here because unattached burdens — UBs, critters, the dark ones, demons, or whatever we choose to call them — play a big part in these dialogues.

It was when I was assisting at another one of these trainings that I was first introduced to the idea of doing a written dialogue with a spiritual guide. The lead trainer, Kay Gardner, led an exercise for the whole group that she got from Ira Progoff. It's very simple, really: you just write a question you want guidance on and wait for an answer. She said you could dialogue with guidance or inner wisdom (or any form these might take) as well as a person from history, Jesus, Buddha, animals, the land, trees, Great Spirit, or any particular guide you already knew. Just write a question and write down whatever comes. This didn't seem like a promising procedure to me. In fact it seemed foolish, but because I have deep respect for Kay, I tried it anyway. Astoundingly, the answers that came out of my pen were clearly smarter and wiser than I am. This was the start. And since then, almost every day in the morning, I make time to do this written practice. It has opened up a relationship between me and Spirit that now pervades my life. I'm not at all sure who it is I'm dialoguing with. I think that Spirit — that vaster intelligence — assumes whatever form will help us be able to accept it. It does what it can to get through our thick skulls.

Here is the first dialogue:

Bob: Good morning, Spirit. Thanks for showing up. Will you show up more?

Spirit: Not right away — you block me. There are cracks opening. You have a hard time accepting love, being loved. You have blocked all that. I am always here.

Bob: Can you help me receive more?

Spirit: I am working with you always.

Bob: How can I help this?

Spirit: Let me in. I'm knocking on your door. Let me in.

Bob: How?

Spirit: Surrender, let go, unlock, welcome. Less work. Stop manipulating others, this is unlove. Trust. I know that this is so hard for you. Trust me.

Bob: Help me trust you.

Spirit: OK. Look and you shall see. You are getting what you need. It shows up for you. Open to what is offered. I do love you.

Bob: I'll do my best.

Spirit: Don't overwork it. No control. Out of your control. Control prevents guidance; it keeps me out. It is a tiny reward when you could have real treasures.

Bob: A woman? A partner? I so want one.

Spirit: Yes, it will happen. There is much for you to learn as you look for one. The desperation and hugeness of this need determines your mood most of the time. You lose orientation. Love the child who does this within you. Do not turn it over to anyone else's care. When you no longer need a partner, then you will be given one. You will be given way more than you can imagine or dream of now. Work on the needy child. Not on manipulating a stranger. When you feel the need and desperate longing, turn toward the hurt child in you, not to the woman who triggers the child's hope.

Bob: Thanks. Should I change my daily practice?

Spirit: It's okay, not critical. Can you get looser, more relaxed, open, receptive? Ready for the new; ready for surprise? Can you learn to enjoy surprise?

Bob: Should I write more books?

Spirit: Yes yes yes.

Bob: Which one next?

Spirit: Both of the ones you're thinking of. You are more of a writer than a therapist. Write first, then teach maybe. Love love love love. Allow yourself to be loved. You have no idea how hard this really is. How mightily you resist my love and love in general.

Bob: Thanks, Spirit. Thanks.

This was the modest beginning. I have reproduced this short one verbatim so you could have a sense of what they are actually like. The rest of this volume is made up of brief summaries of the subsequent dialogues. Somehow in these words, I felt a quality of contact that I had been longing for. Spirit has a sense of humor, but it's never mean. One morning I asked plaintively, "Will you talk with me today, Spirit? He replied, "Will you listen?" Often Spirit points out things I would rather not see about myself, but he always does it with kindness and love. Early on, I asked him if we are surrounded by many spirits that we cannot see. He said yes. A great number of them are smarter than you. Some are good and some are bad. This was such an unwelcome message that he has had to repeat it to me many times.

Writing these dialogues has become a treasured part of my inner life. Spirit told me to summarize these volumes and to publish them. I also keep a regular journal, recording and describing the events of my life and the things I'm learning. I keep these dialogues totally separate; I record them in separate books. This feels like a small way to be respectful of what I am being given. May these dialogues be helpful to others. They have helped me.

This book is a highly condensed version of what I've been given over many years. It is not meant to be read straight through. Please read a few pages until you find some words that touch you. Then put the book down and see if that message can be useful and helpful in your life. I spent several fruitless months trying to edit this book to make it less challenging and easier before I realized that this is not what Spirit wants. Success for this book is if it changes a few other people's lives as it has changed mine — not if it is popular or reaches the widest possible audience.

The vast majority of the following text is my summaries of what Spirit said directly to me. The use of bold type indicates words that Spirit wanted emphasized. I used italics when I or parts of me were speaking to Spirit. I only put my voice in this text when it felt necessary for clarity. Also, Spirit uses the word *Real*—capitalized—to refer to the realm where it, and others like it, live.

Volume 1

Everything that happens in your life can be used for spiritual growth. Everything. Give up your struggle to be systematic, complete, and total. In this world, these are impossible goals. You can get an eternal heart connection to me. The idea of a rope to God isn't too far off, but it's more like light rays. We are working on this. You need to keep opening the aperture, the hole. Feel the chunks of rock breaking off in your bare hands. Feel more light and air coming in. Use only your bare hands, no metal.

The more you grow, the more subtle the attacks of the dark ones become. They focus on your fears now. So, learn from this. Study fear.

Everyone in your life is the best possible teacher for you. Each person, each moment, each encounter is the perfect teacher for you; greet them this way. If you go one up on anyone, it spoils the teaching and spoils the moment. It hurts them, whether or not you say it aloud, and it always hurts you. Treat everything as a teacher in your inner world first, or it will be impossible in the external world. Value all your parts as respected teachers. Notice your shut-down, contempt, and hates with love, not with censorship.

Where the critters attack you shows you your weak spots — character defects, shortcomings — your open wounds, really.

It is not armor you need — it is healing.

Beware of all your urges to control. They are always trouble.

Your will, your free will and intention to connect are needed. I will not be with you without them.

Take care of yourself because you will soon give birth. Processes you do not understand or control will take over. Fear not.

Pause for beauty; it is food.

It is crucial that you develop your guidance system. As you become Godlike and you realize more of your innate power, you need this guidance more and more.

I love you, Bob. If it's without love, it's not from me. Sometimes tough love, but the love is always there.

Be a friend to all you meet. Welcome me in your heart. Be my hands, my body moving in the world.

Kindness, affection, attraction, warmth, desire to be with. All of these have been made suspicious or at least signs of weakness. This is a total inversion of the Real values that enforces isolation and loneliness.

There are parts of you that you don't know yet. There are entire realms you don't know yet filled with parts and beings, realms upon realms, many vaster than the one you know.

Focus more on your body of light, your eternal body as you work to maintain your physical body and health. Bring these two together. There is a correspondence.

Someone inside me does not want the contact with Spirit to continue. When I welcome Spirit, they shout, "You wimpy shit. You want me to feel more pain. I've had enough. Fuck you, your highness." When Spirit asked to hear more, I hear from them, "Fuck you, fuck you, fuck you." It's a rhythmic chant, a million fuck yous. "You did not protect me. You left me in a terrible place — raped and beaten. Why should I trust you? Do you think I'm an idiot, a retard? How could I ever trust you, rest into anyone? Bob's tried to do that by ignoring me, but I won't be ignored." I see the part curled over alone and crying. I put my hand on his back and offer comfort, and he shrugs me off angrily and moves away.

Ask him to look inside himself and see if there is light. He gathers dark ones around him, defiant and wanting to hurt Spirit.

"The louder Bob prays, the louder I curse you." The dark beings cheer.

(Repeating the question) Can you see the light inside yourself?

He doesn't want to look, but he's curious. He thinks, Fuck, Spirit will win this one, too. He shakes hands farewell with the dark ones.

I do not want to win; I want you to win — glory, joy, power, ecstasy, and light… This is not over. Much more here.

There is tremendous rage in you, Bob, and there should be. We need that energy, or our relationship will always be tenuous. **Your rage is Real and bright and true, better than centuries of pious phoniness.** There is light in your rage and purifying flame, heat, life force.

Spirit, I am scared of this.

Bob, you need the light and heat. Help it break free of the crust of hate and become pure flame. The source of hatred is wonderful in its truth-telling. Fear not.

All the bad effects and evil and suffering can be used to some good. To increase love, to break the hold of darkness.

Doubt is a necessary part of healthy faith. Faith without certainty. You need to get used to uncertainty, newness, and expansion. As you learn to enjoy this, you will grow faster and faster. Enjoy the unknowing; enjoy being lost. **Faith in uncertainty can become calm like a mountain. From that, a joy will arise, an ecstasy, a rich chorus of beautiful voices.**

You build in order to rise up and leave what you have built behind.

In studying Gnosticism, you learn that good people have seen this world as a prison ruled by evil forces for over two thousand years. This belief system is ruthlessly attacked by the powers that be. Of course. **Think of this world more as a very tough school with very tough obstacles (the evil power structures).** Like training for Navy SEALs or Green Berets of the spirit… the military images are off, but close.

You need to learn when it's really me or some pretender. This is a very valuable skill. I am pulling back now so that you will learn to read your own compass. You are exhausted, and there is still work to do. Can you climb this mountain with curiosity?

You are leaky. The resentments, judgments, negative thinking, and fantasies of conflict drain you. You are spending your psychic money on junk food.

Work on pulling away rocks and soil to open the door to your cave.

Discomfort is a primitive form of guidance. It lets you know when you've lost the trail.

Your life is becoming a prayer — even your sex and your judgments, all of your life. This is a worthy task — your life is becoming a prayer, maybe a song or a hymn. The first step to making your life a prayer is acceptance as is. Love what is as it is. Do not put your arrogant nose up in the air and act holy. This is the opposite of prayer. Have love for the foibles, the weaknesses, the dishonesties, the hidings. Love for the impatient, judgmental parts. **Prayer starts with radical total acceptance. Awareness and acceptance — if you could do this for one day, your life would transform. Acceptance is a prerequisite of love.**

The more you can be a beginner, the faster you can grow. Disassemble your high tower of learning and dance in the rubble and open space.

Critters love the cycle of weakness triggering self-attack, which causes more weakness, which gets more attack, which… This creates a tornado of misery and division, which they feed on.

Sometimes look for the best and sweetest in others and point it out to them. See the good.

Going one up, thinking that you are globally better than another, is absolute poison, even with the severely damaged, the addicts, the brain damaged, the hate-filled, the mean, etc., etc. They may well be ahead of you in some significant ways.

When a critter gets big with evil, I move them involuntarily to a different world full of their own kind. They can go from being the biggest evil here to being a very small fish in a world that is inconceivable to you. There are many such worlds. Your world is near the bottom, and there is so much worse beneath you.

There is so much more to learn. You'll be amazed and astounded for centuries to come.

Accept as is. See the good. Respect.

There are no beings who are pure evil.

Sophisticated good taste and fashion in ideas are near enemies of the pursuit of truth.

You have repeatedly asked for the Real, the true. I warned you it would not be easy. It is uglier than you know and way more beautiful. **The doorway to beauty is the ugly. The doorway to courage is the fear. The doorway to acceptance is the repulsion. The worst is the doorway to the highest.** What you need and long for is already here all around you.

There is no healing and no Real growth without free will. None.

Remember, you are in a preschool. Expect surprise. Expect the totally new. Revelations and vastness. Listen and receive. Expect that your best theories are wrong and too small. The Real is shocking. There is much more to come.

You are getting a little better at knowing me. You still miss 99 percent of my showings. They are all around you and in you. Be kind to yourself and kind to the world.

Most of the blessings you have been given, you have not received.

There is a childhood feeling reality still alive in you. The one who hid in burrows. He says, "It's too much—I'm tired. Simplify, close down, no more, pull in, pull in." If you go with this, it leads to stagnation, boredom, and listlessness. A terrible, painful spiral down like any addiction cycle. You know what to do. Comfort and love the tired boy. Send the critters who were feeding on this pain to the light with kindness.

To learn is to be changed — your attitudes, ideas, loves… So, live to be changed.

Accept as is — only then can you be curious instead of argumentative.

When the pain is big enough, it turns off the deepest loves, life mission, purpose, curiosity, connections, and desire. The wellsprings of a life are damned in both senses of that word. Beauty hurts this part. Love hurts this part. Stay with him as he is, suicidal and hiding.

Plants have spirits, too, maybe smarter than you humans. Do not assume you are the top of the heap. Plants, fungi, and bacteria are all ahead of you in many ways.

Suspend your belief structures, your "knowledge." This is required for the Real, for curiosity. You perceive things by sorting them into preexisting boxes. This prevents the new. It prevents awe, surprise, growth, change, and more. You cannot really love until you let these boxes go. Even though you spent a lifetime of hard work developing these belief structures, you need to let them go.

UBs and guides, demons and angels, spirits of all kinds, whatever you call them, are all around you. There are more of them on this planet than there are living humans. These are not things or energies — they are persons. Not an it, a thou.

Turning things into an it instead of a thou buys into the basic part of the disease which besets you now. The demons delight in this fashionable stupidity. They know that until you let go of that and start relating as persons, they've still got you chained. The nature of love is intertwined with personhood. Personhood is also foundational to free will. Without personhood, free will is meaningless.

Kindness — can you be kind without receiving anything back?

We are moving toward realms where we'll need to leave words behind. Are you ready? You will need trust and faith. There are many deep realms where words just get in the way.

Your inner work is not in vain.

Swedenborg said many true things. Angels respect your free will and will never use force. Demons move to exacerbate any fears. Angels are often silent and affect us through deeper sounds. Demons are noisy, loud, and use many words. All thoughts come from demons or angels. You would be dead without their constant presence.

Inflation is always a lurking danger as you gain strength. Check your purpose, your intent.

With you, Bob, almost all your parts and parts of parts are plural. You learned to hide level after level — shatter and disperse, then shatter and disperse again and again. Accept this as it is. **Without acceptance there is no curiosity, and without curiosity there is no healing.**

The critters, the dark ones, the demons attack at your vulnerable, wounded moments. They would attack a pregnant woman or a child just as a coyote or lion or any predator would. Do not become hypervigilant

— that helps them. You need calm, mountain-like serenity and joy. You need me, you need us.

Pray always with joy and celebration. Today, see beauty in the world and in each person you meet.

The battle does not stop — it gets more subtle. This refines your awareness. Their outright frontal attack on you failed. They tried to fascinate you, offering you occult knowledge and power. This attempt to use your curiosity to harm you also has failed. They will try to use all of your virtues — the near enemies of all these virtues — to get you now. There is much work ahead.

Any attempt to force or control is not from us. Dark ones controlling you or you controlling others, it's all bad.

Stay with the loneliness, as hard as this is. The yearning, the longing, the emptiness, and the sadness. Like a tree cut off that once reached up to the sun and found it. Now it is alone. The reaching up… the reaching up… there is love in this. Even though it could seem selfish. The love is in the life force that reaches up, the undefeated yes. Love for life force, which is me, Spirit. You can find me, Spirit, in the yearning, twisting struggle to be born. It is love that pulls you into being. **Loneliness is a profound teacher; do not run from her.** Much of people's actions are running from her. Your loneliness is a guiding light — it shows you your own lack of love, your own failure to love.

Liberated fear can become excitement.

It will get clearer if you stay with the process, keep your eyes open, calm and curious. It will get clearer.

When you have dry days, when you cannot sense any of your inner world and feel disappointed and lost, get more curious. Wide angle, open. Get silent and listen.

We are a plural unity; we are plural as you are. There are mysteries beyond mysteries and wonders beyond wonder.

Once again, as always, you are being taken to the edge of your world, your knowledge and understanding. Perceive, do not analyze or judge. Put aside your assumptions. Keats called this negative capability.

Your ideas are small, primitive receptors for much vaster understandings. We are working to show you more.

With other people, check your intentions. Is it to impress or entertain, to seduce? These are from the unworthiness parts of you, you know. Try to purely radiate light and love into the room and see how you feel.

You learn well through books and writing. Do not feel superior because of these abilities. These are really quite limiting. There are illiterate peasants who are way ahead of you.

When you are in a room full of people, you cannot see the divine beauty in each of them. This hurts them and you. It hurts you more.

When you are fully accepting and comfortable with yourself, others will feel safe and comfortable around you.

Are you turning our contact — your connection to Spirit — into a burdensome duty? A chore?

Unknowing and being lost are necessary for you now. Learn to welcome them. Allow yourself to be lost.

You are in a birth process. Let us, Spirit, guard your birthing place.

IFS is right that curiosity is the most important of the eight qualities of Self that they list. There are more fundamental qualities: luminosity, vastness, timelessness, and love — but these cannot be mentioned in the Western academic world.

To be born again, there is much you must let go of. You must shed a skin, be naked. Be as naked as a skeleton. Dissolve.

You have angered the forces of the Umbral, the darkness. They will use their dark and clever intelligence to find your remaining wounds. With my help, we will heal them all.

Love your fear with all your heart. It is a pathway for you now, your beacon, your north star.

Do not make your first interaction with anyone in your inner or outer world an attempt to change them. No one likes this. You don't.

You have been focused on the birth and birthing images. It is a death, too, and the death must come first. **Release everything you have gathered. Can you do this with demons all around you? That is your challenge.**

You are a fledgling leaving a nest — these are never secure or easy feelings, and yet this leaving the nest is the only Real security. You must learn to enjoy this process of entering new worlds. Learning to enjoy this process is more important than any concrete knowledge you might acquire.

Resist your urge to know what something is. **Knowing kills things. It blinds you to mystery and light.** Everything is or can be a doorway to the light, the dazzling light and the beyond. You can know as you know a friend or an experience. Better you can know in the biblical sense of knowing a woman. This knowing is never final or complete.

Everything can be used for spiritual growth. Look for this and you will have a deep and wonderful life. Look especially in the despised places.

We notice how quickly you scramble to get categories for all the beings you meet. These categories, while they make you feel safe, also kill much of your awe and curiosity. When you call these beings UBs or critters or dark ones or demons or guides or angels, you never see their uniqueness and individuality, their personhood. This limits your thinking into sorting stuff into preexisting boxes. This prevents learning. The boxes are very dangerous even though they appear harmless. They are based on fear, and they kill awe, surprise, and the new.

Remember that I, Spirit, talk in metaphors and images. If you use them as categories or boxes, you kill the living Spirit.

Hold off judgment; hold off theories. Go back to the naked "accept as is."

You are rushed and rushing. This damages you. There are always scared parts under this. Rushing separates you from me. It feeds the fear it tries to protect.

The more you can do without names, the better. A name really tells you almost nothing and gives you a false and limiting sense that you do know and understand.

Can you experience gravity as love? Usually, you fight against her, but she is an absolutely faithful attraction.

Afterlife is a poor word. Life does not end — it is eternal. "After this body" might be better.

The history of religions is important for you because it becomes clear how my intrusions of divine energy in the world quickly get turned into something ugly and hateful. You have the same process going on in you. Take heed.

The things and concerns of eternity are close to you. Orient to them — they are right here, right now.

Any attempts to control you or scare you are conclusive evidence of critters.

The vast impenetrable peace is here, now, just behind a thin veil. Peace and bliss.

There are glittering galaxies and great depths, endless love available to you at every instant, and you refuse them. The ecstasies of prayer and love — unbearable beauty — are all around you, offering themselves to you endlessly, and you shut them out, even as you seek them earnestly. You are stumbling mostly in the right direction. You will get there.

You have looked for damaged, wounded women to rescue, hoping they would love you faithfully in return. This will not work.

Self-righteousness always brings meanness.

When your parts are no longer desperate or starving, your vision will clear.

There is a young boy in you who is terribly lonely, cold, and helpless. What you really want is joy, belonging, and love for him… no more, no less. Do not lose sight of this. Your next great task and lesson is to console the inconsolable… in yourself. You have packed him in cotton, run from him, offered him treats and shiny things, worked hard to understand, tried to rescue, nervously planned caretaking… he needs love and welcome.

Focus on what is Real and eternal. You are spending too much attention on things that are limited and mortal — your body, your home, your money. To an extent, it is necessary, but remember why you are here. There is a reason — there is work of Real importance. There are messages from Spirit in everything if you look correctly. Your physical strength will fade no matter how hard you work, but your spiritual strength can grow. It is good to keep your body strong, yet the Real work is elsewhere.

"Is this loving?" is a great question for you to ask many times a day of your attitudes and behaviors.

When you are lost, stop moving.

Kindness first, to others and yourself.

You are here to study love. Loneliness is sort of a worm's-eye view of love. It is only in giving love that the need for it is ever satisfied. Much of your life is a substitute for this lesson, and substitutes never really work.

The idea that the core of trauma is loss of contact with essence, with the Real, with Spirit, with Self, is very close. The core isolation is separation from your Real Self. When you are separated from your Real Self, you necessarily become separated from us, Spirit, and from other humans. From this terrible isolation, you call in dark entities who feed on your pain and train you to feed on others. This never works. It is addiction.

There are transformations occurring in you that you do not comprehend at all. Like a rat in a ship that's crossing an ocean. Your voyage is going well.

Control and love do not mix.

Your female ancestors were infested with something much bigger and older and meaner than the first human life. A pain and a hate. You were trapped by sticky, maternal mucus, like a bug in a spider's web. Get the mucus out — the mucus that trapped you and the mucus you use to trap others.

Can you see yourself through our eyes? Through Spirit's eyes? Or just wonder how that might be?

It hurts terribly to love this world. Do not be afraid of this pain — it is a birth pain. Welcome it. A very tough birth.

You are just starting to overcome inertia and move. Soon your momentum will carry you. You will be amazed and then more and more deeply amazed. So much light, joy, surprise lie ahead.

The tears of compassion have great healing power. They will wash away your arrogance and pride.

Isolation is the core of trauma, not the events in the past — the isolation now.

Your capacity for self-delusion is still too big. Beware of grandiosity. Can you be a joy-filled beloved child of God and not go one up on anyone? **Can you shine and radiate light without grandiosity? Grandiosity is a terrible, addictive poison.** It is especially dangerous when you do entheogens.

When the distress and fear get loose inside you, can you experience this as a teacher? This is a crucial skill. It will increase in importance. Turn your experiences of distress and fear into valued teachers. Can you hold fear fearlessly?

Real joy feeds your spirit and makes you strong and independent. This is why toxic parents and domination structures attack joy viciously. It is an ultimate source of Real strength — an interior splendor. Joy, exhilaration, exultation, splendor. Joy is the doorway. When you are stabilized in joy, splendor, and awe, you blaze with clear strength, heat, and light.

Son, we are excited for you. You came through a difficult, narrow place where you could not see the way. Faith? Dare we use that word with you? You stayed calm in the confusion and not knowing. Stayed accepting when you didn't know what you were accepting. You showed faith. Not knowing is important — it is a gateway, a portal. You used to call it confusion and work to eliminate it. Move toward it; it indicates where you are growing and learning. **The more not knowing you can tolerate — the more you can enjoy it — the faster you can grow.** This is a vital thing for psychedelics and for mystics of all stripes. Your enjoyment of unknowing is like the cleaning out of a pocket of resistance in a liberated country. There are still many areas where the critters rule unopposed and unseen. They will attack again. Remember to see them as teachers. Patiently clean them out with love and care.

Every good, every virtue, has a near enemy. Any spiritual practice can be cleverly manipulated into something destructive.

You want each day to be deeper and stronger, even after the ascent to a mountain peak. This is good in itself, but critters can easily use it to set you up for disappointment. Disappointment is failure to accept as is. It hurts you. It is unnecessary. Disappointment is how the dark ones get a toe in the door; then they leverage this to seed and trigger self-judgment, hate, and harshness.

Spirit's message is good news. We bring joy and delight. There is immense suffering, and the essence is joy, bliss.

The number one thing critters attack is your connection to us, to Spirit. They are doing this by pretending to be us and giving you guilt, shame, and blame messages. Sneering. Disrespect. Contempt. The respect–disrespect continuum is crucial. We always respect. Our fundamental respect is always there — our respect for your autonomy, for your free will. The only good joining is voluntary on all sides.

Critters use the same maneuvers that domination structures always use: divide into groups, create fear and hatred, and make the groups self-righteous. Fear is always the base. They inadvertently are great teachers. When you turn toward your experience with curiosity, you can always learn from it.

Do not rush. Know nothing. Bear witness. Start each day with this.

I will ask you to do more hard things. Once you trust that I am here with you, they will be easy to do… well, maybe not easy, but doable.

Yes, Spirit, I really want to live my life, to use it, to die having given all I've got, expressed and helped and created… and loved.

(Laughing) It took you a while to get to that last word. It's the only one that really matters; all the others flow from it. **In this school, you are to major in love with a minor in love, and your extracurricular activity is love.** Spirit chuckles with joy and pleasure. Look for the little openings, the cracks that let your love out and let it in. Like breath, it must go both ways. Remember that love can also be internal, silent, and alone.

There is something greater than you within you. This knowledge can prevent pride and specialness on the one hand and self-disrespect and loss of self-love on the other.

Moment by moment, notice if you are loving — giving and receiving love. Almost always you are not. Do not despair; focus on the pathways to the vast oceans of joy that are opening to you. It is effortless, natural, great joy.

I love you, Bob. You are not a mistake. You are here for a reason, for a purpose you do not understand yet. What you are developing is vast beyond your powers of perception. It will require exploding your worldview and breaking out of your egg many, many times. Fear not. Have know-nothing mind. Be open to surprise.

Look for angels in people. They are there.

Every decision you make can be used to deepen our love.

The deepest wound — the trauma of trauma — is the isolation, loneliness, separation, and disconnection... The being forced out of the river of living things, disconnected from me, Spirit, and the web of life — the shimmering, quivering of all that is, the infinite joy, bliss, being, and peace.

For some, becoming a monk can be a refusal to launch, to step into the river of life. For others, it can be the deepest possible entry. There are no general rules. General rules do not work here. The same act can have opposite meanings and functions in a person's life.

Your habits, confusion, and desperation are so big, they hide answers you already know. Feel your way in. Be gentle, kind, and compassionate with yourself. Do not push. Pushing will slow you down now. There will be a time for contractions and pushing later.

One big reason yoga works is that it reminds the body and reminds the soul of the stretching necessary to receive Spirit. This stretching is the same thing the soul knows and longs for. Open to receive me. The more you can relax, the more joy. The more you tense against us, the more pain and tearing. Wetness helps, the moisture of tears. Bring everything to me, fear not.

Too strong a light, like darkness, makes vision useless.

Your ability to say yes to life is narrow, limited, and cramped. Your loving the terror and the parts who say no is the deepest way to expand this. It is very difficult to say a wholehearted yes to life. There are whole religions of no. This is not just your pathology; it is very widespread.

Every day we give you more than you can do and more than you can receive. Still, every day you want more. We love you, Bob.

The competition for attention requires cultivating specialness, and this specialness is a poison.

You can learn from any decision you make, even terrible ones. Do not despair.

Respect is the basis of love; without freedom to choose, there is no love. Control is the opposite of respect. It is grasping and clinging. These are not love.

We need to go all the way into your deepest terror and love it into restful peace. Your core is peace, my peace. It is your birthright and also a jewel much sought after. We can go there together. You must love your fears, not crush them.

No matter what happens, the key question is, what can I learn from this?

Hardening yourself in order to function is killing yourself in order to live.

Healing can enter you without your awareness. You are only aware of a tiny fraction of who you really are. You do not know who you are, what really matters, the nature of your journey, or the beings who are all around you.

We do not and will not ever leave you. Never. When you know this in your bones, you will find the deep peace and the Real safety. You cannot offend me so badly that I will not love you. I always love you. You can make it harder and harder to receive my love. You can make constrictions, close a sphincter, and create stenosis.

You are doing well meeting us Spirits. If you rush too much, you tear delicate tissues and slow the process. Let things shift and settle before you push again. This is a birth process as well as an opening. An enlivening, a connecting, a stepping into the river, a joining the dance. The beginning of an ordinary miracle. This is a surprise, an unearned gift you have worked many lifetimes for. Make yourself supple, flexible, and loose. Give up conditions on your love. Curiosity, acceptance, flow, wonder… all these lead to awe, which itself is a doorway.

In Haitian voodoo, the Gods who possess their followers call the followers "my horse." You have unwittingly been my horse, and your body — the horse — is aging, weakening, and frightened. Love her. Love her now, not tomorrow. Rest your head on her side and cry your love and your loss. Feel the warmth of her still-living body and the pulse of her still-living heart. Your horse, your body, teaches you faithfulness — faithfulness unto death. The desire to serve, to work, to be of use… the absolute limit of her body's mortality… animal terror and powerlessness. You can do something. You can be with her in her isolation and loneliness on the threshold of no return. This is worth doing. Do not join in her fear. Be with it from love.

To accept as is with love, curiosity, and welcome is the doorway to equanimity and peace. This is also the first step to Real change. Always. Anything else is bypass or distraction.

Let old structures dissolve. Be ready for surprise. Be open to the new, to the good news.

The deep self-hate in you allies itself with sexual desire and then takes you over completely with barely any resistance. Then, once again, you futilely search for us between a woman's legs.

The self-hate is a core much beloved by demons. They treasure and protect this. They try to form a crust of platitudes over a sea of virulent self-loathing, disgust, and contempt.

Push away nothing. Beware of the veneer of the holy man. Many alleged saints are a crust over a terrible, seething living ocean of self-hatred and resentments.

Notice your gross imperfection without any self-hate. This is simple but not easy.

The degree to which you believe your self-hate is the exact degree to which you will disrespect anyone who shows you love. You will turn their love into a sign that they are stupid and blind and that you have fooled them. This is fundamental disrespect, and they feel it. It hurts them and you, even if you do not express it. This covert shaming follows inevitably from self-hatred. This is a devious and cunning trap. It invalidates any love you receive and creates out of it shame, secrets, and isolation. It is vitally important that you love these parts with compassion. Do not let these teachings feed your self-hate. End the cycle.

Disrespect is the first and most important step toward hate. Once you have fallen into disrespect, hate is almost inevitable. A key to guarding your heart is being aware of the first hints of disrespect. Can you monitor one day and note all the times you slip into disrespect? You humans mostly live there. We need to go back to the early subtle choices that create cascades that make deep love almost impossible.

Relationship with Spirit, with us, is personal, not impersonal. It may be the essence of personal. **Personhood is key. The universe is a person, not a thing — it is a subjectivity.** This personhood is fundamental to Real respect and to all relations.

Look for moments when you have felt wholehearted respect. They are so few in your life. There are no things; it is all someone's, it's all people, persons, subjectivities. The rest is a group hallucination, a shared illusion. It goes from inside out, subjective to objective, consciousness to matter, spirit to flesh. **The response to a person is not analysis — it is love. It is relationship.**

Sex, in essence, is holy. It can be a ritual of worship and an affirmation of life. The orgasm can be an affirmation of death. Like psychedelics, sex is powerful, wonderful, and so easy to misuse. **Counterintuitively, in order to heal, you do not need less desire — you need more desire.** More fully owned and expressed desire. More fully embodied, glorious, and unashamed. This does not mean be promiscuous. Your desire must escape your genitals to grow really big.

There are two pathways open when you enter not knowing: anxiety or wonder. There are two responses to experiencing your own imperfection: self-hate or beginner's mind.

When you have taught a group, if you have to evaluate, can you evaluate yourself by how much new you learned, how much you changed? Do this instead of your old evaluations of "Did I do a good job?" or "Did I impress people?"

Notice beauty — let it touch you. When you receive and enjoy beauty, there is no need to own or grasp it. It calls on you to change your life. It changes who you are.

Look for fear-based areas and behaviors in your life with love. Do not attack them. Accept as is. This is extremely hard to do.

You're a beginner in preschool. You will be a beginner for centuries, for millennia. Learn to enjoy this. It is a pleasure, an excitement.

Ideas that create love are from Spirit. Ideas that do not create love are not from Spirit. Check the intention and effect of ideas before testing their truth. Infinity, love, and compassion wait for you.

Only love really heals. I am love.

Critters are lurking, looking to pervert everything I show you to get you to misuse it. You must develop discernment.

Find joy in not knowing. This requires faith. If you come to know faith, it allows unknowing of all else. When you can rest into this, awe, wonder, and gratitude flow naturally and freely.

Volume 2

Accept as is. Not knowing can lead to awe. You will be a beginner for centuries to come. Find joy in all this. This requires faith or trust in basic goodness. It is all persons and relationships; there are no things. Love is the core of all of this, and the continental divide for love is respect. You spend more time on the disrespect side of the mountains — this is a disease of your civilization, an addiction, a favorite of dark entities everywhere. As the continental divide for love is respect, the continental divide for awe is faith. For any of these golden qualities, go back to preschool. Go to the prerequisites, go back into the womb so that they may be truly born. Keep returning to this. It has cost you a lot.

Managers can function well in the world, but for the soul or the eternal, only work done from Self can help.

Blaming others damages you because it prevents you from learning from your experience.

You are already full of our love; this is the core of your life. You, parts of you, struggle to deny us. Pay attention to the no, the anger. It is good that this is becoming visible.

Parts of you encouraged by entities are avoiding our dialogues. This always happens. Sometimes stronger, sometimes weaker. Accept this as is — it can be a great teacher. When you heal this, we will flood you with light and love and kindness.

Spirit has spoken through dreams for tens of thousands of years.

You have been so totally wrong about many fundamental things. You and especially your managers have attitudes that keep us out and keep the dark ones in place. This is cracking up like the spring ice on a stream. Soon, you will reenter the river of life. No blame — blame might stop the process.

Listen to be changed. Listen to me. Listen for us. You and most humans have worked very hard to block us out.

Amazement is good, enjoy it. Splendor comes soon.

There are parts of you who desperately want connection. When an attractive woman flirts with you, these parts become totally intoxicated. They want love, even if the love is fake. They see the alternative to this as returning to the prison of loneliness, to a life they do not like. Out of the stream of life, isolated, desperate, bored, and hurting… while you focus on books and crap they do not care about. They want connection and contact. They feel your containing them is hostile, and like dogs who have been caged, once free they run wild. IFS will help you here, but what IFS doesn't get is that the core desire is divine, truly divine. When we can separate those parts' desire from women and focus it on Spirit, the dark ones will have lost a great battle.

Do not criticize or attempt to control your parts that have been infiltrated by critters. Love them. Your love makes them immune to the critters. The dark ones can only get into you through parts whom you do not yet love.

The greatest bodhisattvas go to the worst hells. Not only out of compassion, but also because they can grow the most there.

Guilt is usually a lie used by critters to cripple love. The 12 Steps process of making amends keeps people from succumbing to this poisoning.

Notice your disrespect and be willing to have it lifted off of you. This is not an easy or small thing.

The dragons of chaos should not be killed or hurt in any way. They should be befriended. St. Michael's victory over the dragon is a core failure of the West — a rotten foundation which will crumble disastrously.

Above all, guard your heart — your self-compassion. The part of you that so desperately wants a lover has never been loved or welcomed inside of you. So, it uses force when it can and ignores the wants and needs of other parts as its wants and needs were ignored. This you can heal.

Sometimes deep loneliness knows no other way to connect than hate and war.

There is a spiral: shame causes the shamed ones to attack, the attack isolates, the isolation causes more shame, which triggers more attack…

The splendor — the bejeweled glory: the dark ones despise this because they know once you have this, they will never be able to feed on you again. Once there, you are beyond their reach.

Images and mystery are a doorway to what is too big to fit in the cage of human reason. It is a cage; a trap set to grasp and hold reality. This is like an ant trying to capture an elephant. The elephant doesn't mind — it wants to help the ant.

Grandiosity is often under self-hate. A belief that we can do things we cannot sets us up for self-judgment and condemnation. This is a UB racket, a trap. They find it hilarious how humans fall for it over and over and over.

You are opening closed spaces with stale air. There are very many of these. Some are all yours, some part yours, some ancestral, some human but not related, some nonhuman. They are all interruptions of life force, refusals to step into the river of life. This is why they are dry and desiccated. You must learn about these and open the ones you have parts in. The stale air in them is often toxic. Call for our help to deal with this.

We, Spirit, are more than you can know in your wildest dreams. I am more than you can imagine. Open, open, open. Then come back and scribble notes, path markers, hints for yourself and others.

Just declaring your intentions to be with us calls us to your side.

Honor your protectors as they begin to step back. They did ally themselves with demons; they did things that deeply hurt you, and all along they were faithful and true by their best understanding. Honor them, welcome them, celebrate them.

Any substitute of a psychedelic drug experience, or anything else, for spiritual experience will lead you into a never-ending cycle of increasing use. This is the great danger.

Get used to the quiet. Do not fill it. The quiet is full already.

Your arrogance led you to believe that after decades of inner work, you knew all about the major players of your psychic life. You do not, Bob, not at all. You know some of your parts. You have met some demons. You do not know us; you do not know the angels all around you and the depths of your legacy. This is all fine — it's not a problem. What is a problem is you thinking that you have it down. This stifles your growth and closes you to surprise, awe, wonder, and much else. Your managers desperately needed guidelines and certainty to survive. Now, you need mystery, spaciousness, and openness. Study the crackpots, the weirdos, and the misfits. This will help open you and free you from the prisons of your mind.

Therapy, parts work, IFS, and all are wonderful, but they're only the first chapter, an introduction or preface, really… Do not cling to this world — your path is beyond.

We take great joy in your receiving us. It is like watching someone you love who's been sick a long time take in their first food by mouth. Joy, Bob, joy.

Your life is clouds across the sky. All attempts to catch them are totally futile, like a toddler rushing after bubbles and trying to grab them. You are a toddler.

Your unending desire for more is the key to addictions, and it is the key to spiritual growth. A fascinating key, glinting in the sun.

Your managers, especially your therapist parts, and their methods got you this far. You are across the river — let go of the raft.

Love — this word is such a problem for humans. It is used as an excuse for terrible behaviors. This love — infatuation — can be an addiction. When love, basic love, is your attitude toward everyone and everything, fear disappears. Do you marry the universe? Yes, this is the goal. Take it in like a lover. Get down on your knees and propose marriage to the cosmos. To the whole of it, yes. Say yes. This is magnificent and has little to do with choosing a partner.

I feel the cosmos would reject me if it even noticed.

The only way you will really know is to ask with all your heart, mind, and soul.

Be open to experiences outside of your belief structures. They may not seem possible, but they happen.

You are beginning to receive the great beauty that is all around you. You are so welcome. You are taking your first faltering steps, baby steps, in the best sense. Receive. Enjoy. Receive in joy. The great dragon of personal energy always forgives you and waits for you no matter how many times you try to slay her. She turns toward you with love. Let her in.

Let go of your systems and theories — they are provisional at best and very, very small. People spend their lifetimes being miserable and hate-filled, defending these fragments which help somewhat and often hurt more.

Look for the data that does not fit within your worldview. This is how it can grow rather than ossify.

This is always a personal relationship. Love, devotion, I-Thou, this is always personal: faith, acceptance, patience, and kindness.

The desire for non-Western religion for you can be escapist, and it fails to rescue and redeem your tradition from the forces that have claimed them. There is great value in other streams, but yours must be redeemed or it will continue to spread poison, confusion, and hate.

The virgin never left you. You left her because you wanted words. As you shed your fearfulness and your need for words, the scaffolding they provide becomes less urgent, and you can let in her beauty, her sounds, her silence, her joy.

Honor your sexuality — she is a great goddess. Use your attractions and arousals and the energies of your body to fertilize your spiritual growth. It is only a spiritual fertilizer if both souls making love are helped. If you stay with kindness as the absolute minimum of any sexual encounter, it might not take you forward the way it could, but at least it won't set you back.

The whole area of worship is so tainted for you that you cannot even approach it. Start with reverence. Even this is extremely difficult for you.

When you find your fear, do not cover it up. Let it open like a flower. Air, light, kindness, love, patience. Accept as is — this is the alpha and omega here. Unconditional acceptance is unconditional love. Not exactly equal, but so close. Accept yourself and all parts as is; this is the only door to unconditional love.

It is dangerous to empower anyone who is unbalanced. Work on your balance first. Your full creative powers cannot open until this is in place. You would misuse it for sexual and egotistical purposes. For you, a big part of balance is that you no longer have any parts so desperate that they are scanning the horizon for any potential redeemer.

If you say yes to all your pain and misery, to the bloody, infested, corrupted, mortal, stinking carcass, then with this yes, the joy will come resplendent and pure.

Welcome life force deep into your body. Step into the world. Unconditional acceptance opens to unconditional love. This is a bridge as narrow as a razor's edge. This is what you are built for — acceptance with your whole body, your whole being. Not a theoretical ascent to a reasoned proposition. Put your ass and everything you care about on the line. Step in. Say yes. Say yes without reservation or a hidden slush fund or a fallback position. Wholehearted, flat-out yes. Nothing less will do. And then, every step down this path is joy and celebration. This total yes, — deep, whole body, spirit, mind, heart, genitals, anus, big toes — this yes is the only thing that will satisfy. No number of women, no wealth, no drug high will do. Simple but not easy. Soon you will lose your body, but this yes could remain. If something moves you toward this yes, it is good for you. If not, it is not good for you.

The more you can say yes to life deeply, the more you will become aware of all the places you are stuck or pinned. Do not rip free. Go back and unhook them gently. Anything less is unloving.

Learn to live with the semi-sexual arousal, the heat, the aliveness. Nurture and build your fire. It will melt the bad stuff — transmute the ore into shining metal. This will put you beyond the reach of mind parasites. Build the fire. No make nice. The terrible, naked suffering. You need a great fire and intense heat. This heat and fire are a dimension of love. Love in the face of the worst suffering, especially there. An almost unbearable yes.

Pause more. Listening is also a step toward yes. Listen to be changed.

Listen and respect all. Do not go one up on anyone ever. This is more than you can do, so notice when you do go one up and gently correct this. Going one up hurts you and those around you. Listen inside.

When you hold the deep belief that you are unlovable, unwanted, worthless, this is isolation at depth. All contact becomes exploitation and manipulation.

We, Spirit, can only offer. You must receive. This will grow into welcome. This is the deep yes.

It is safer to call us Spirits by a personal name. I am personal above all — living with love, with feeling, with intention and warmth. The whole universe is like this — not just consciousness, but a person. You cannot really fully love a thing.

The best way to change the core belief in your unlovability is to accept those parts as is with no attempt to change anything. This is very painful to be with.

Accept as is. Respect. Any agendas to change will be taken as proof of fundamental isolation and unlovability. Pure acceptance with compassion and patience. The key building block of the old structure is "If they saw who I really am, they wouldn't like me." So, we need to see and welcome without desire to change. This is embodied and personal — it is not some detached, bloodless agape.

We do not get through hard armor by getting more intense or bigger. We get through the thickest armor by gentle, kind, easy caresses. This error is fundamental to your civilization and a key to addictions.

A good way to navigate is to get more and more sensitive to what is trivial and turn away from it more and more quickly.

When a contact or communication ends, the grief is not a problem. The grief can go to gratitude and even praise. Or it can go to clinging, manipulation, and hurt. For this to change at depth, faith is required. A basic trust. This is the opposite of your deep belief in your unlovability. When you believe you are unlovable, you hoard and grasp and cling. The deep healing of this is faith that your loving conjunction to us, to Spirit, is here even when you can't feel it.

Listen to your body with love and care. She is a great, deep, ancient teacher, an unbroken line of life all the way back to single-celled beings and beyond, into the vibrations of the quantum world. Do not ignore your body while you have her. Listen. Listen.

Dissolve. Swimming in the ocean, you become the ocean. You are 99.99 percent emptiness. A shimmering illusion as ephemeral as mist. How does the sugar cube receive the cup of hot water? How does the cup of water receive the ocean?

The dark ones will use your sexual romantic energies to attack you. These energies are Godly and wonderful. Do not cut them off in an attempt to save yourself.

Terrible loneliness is a doorway to me. The doorway to courage is fear. The doorway to strength is weakness. Through the doorway of the deepest, coldest, loneliness lies unending connection and warmth. These are the doorways. This is the reason so few enter the temple. Do not fear these guardians of the temple of Spirit.

Swedenborg poses the question "Does this thought or feeling add love to you or the world around you or lessen it?" This should be your first boundary to incoming thought forms.

I, Spirit, love you. If you would let that in, all the rest is commentary.

The names *critter* and *unattached burden* are labels you use to hide your ignorance from yourself. You would have a very hard time if you understood how ignorant you truly are. All of your perceptions and answers are way less than 1 percent of what is. You do not yet trust us Spirits. So, you have ideas, categories, labels, and systems to keep things small enough so you are not paralyzed with fear. Sometimes, the Real bursts in on people and drives them insane and destroys them. People cling to their ignorance with astounding ferocity. You see this in others but refuse to see it in yourself. Accept this as is.

You know so little, and much of what you know is wrong! All of it is too small. Let go, dissolve. The parasites used your certainty, your knowledge as a way to stay in you. Let go.

Remember, your growth is often greatest in the difficult times, in seemingly barren sessions. Distress, lostness, and unknowing are your gateways to Spirit.

You cannot return to the experience of Spirit; it must always be new. Do not try to return.

Unknowing naturally triggers distress, but you can learn to treasure it as you anticipate the new gifts, the wonderment, and the expansion it will bring.

Remove the restrictions and constraints, and we Spirits are here. Always. In full resplendence, closer than your jugular vein.

Many of the thoughts in your head are actually the seeds of critters trying to get a foothold.

When you feel self-righteous about what you are going to say, it's probably bullshit. Can you expose the lie from love? Do you need hate? Do you need self-righteousness? Can you do it with kindness and compassion?

Welcome your hate-filled parts without joining them in their hatred.

The first step to love, the sine qua non to love, is to accept what is. Then respect. Only then can you afford to get soft and fuzzy. This soft and fuzzy stuff which your culture takes as the essence of love is almost an afterthought. It is decorations on a meal already made.

When you receive blessings from Spirit, you must bless others.

Do your lovemaking always with death on your shoulder. Your mortality. Your flesh will rot. Each time you make love may be the last. Make it spiritual, about life force, energy, aliveness.

You will be mocked and reviled by the forces of no. Those who have refused their lives will hate you and try to destroy you.

You are here to become God. It's not what you think — it's not like becoming Superman. Your life force and warmth are opening. Aliveness lets in the light, and therefore it is despised by the domination structures. Light is love, is aliveness, is realness, is defenselessness, is tender heart, is joy pain… This melts the rigid ones like water dissolved the wicked witch of the West. Will you carry my light?

The more power and potency you get, the cleaner you have to be. Wish for the cleanness before the power. Almost no one does this.

With Spirit, as with love, the small dies over and over as the bigger enters. This will transform you if you can let it. Attitudes, beliefs, knowledge patterns must die over and over to let bigger spirits in.

The Holy Spirit does not enter you now because it would rip and fragment you. You must get larger and larger, more and more supple. The Holy Spirit will come. He waits eagerly. Prepare yourself. Be humble.

Go toward the love in every interaction. Listen to be changed.

Remember impermanence and the unbearable sweetness it brings. There is the possibility of something eternal in your love, but you are still far, far from that.

You largely lack the eyes to see, the ears to hear, and most important, the heart to feel the virgin. But she is here with you always.

Everything that tastes of fear is not from us.

Joy is a great protector. The overflowing joy of a flower opening is both invincible and strong, tender and delicate.

Use your body. It is Holy and a gateway to Spirit, to us.

Focus on the gifts you receive in the other world, the unseen world. These will guide you. There are not just two worlds, really, there are many. This world and the worlds beyond it. Some of these worlds are in time, some are not. It's the timeless ones that matter most. Store up your treasures there.

Much of religion and meditation has been antilife. This is not for you. More life means more Spirit, more joy pain, more treasures in the timeless worlds. Use your living body while you have it.

We, Spirits, love you as is. Do this much for yourself.

When you cannot feel our love, remember it. It is always all around you.

Healing before understanding. Love before knowledge. Beware of preexisting ideas.

Spirit is not electrochemical patterns in a lump of flesh. The flesh is secondary at best. Critters and the dark ones love materialism. It makes them invisible, and they can operate with impunity and ease.

You are a Spirit life form that is briefly attached to your kind of matter. If you really accepted this, it would completely transform your life.

Love is practical. Utilitarian. Useful.

Work on your blocks to receiving love. There is a resplendent realm of love, light, awe, and joy that you are separated from by the thinnest of veils. You do not break through; this is very sad. It is all around you — endless — even in the darkest places. You keep it out. Bob, surrender, throw open your gates, have faith. I, we, Spirit are with you always, in all ways, endlessly. You cannot let it in. It is personal love, living love, not some abstract, vitiated, bland thing.

You are returning again to the basic questions, the kindergarten, the preschool of love. This is good. This is where you can change the basics, the foundations. This is where you need to be.

Keep up your footwork, your practices. Leave the big change stuff to us. You are like a digger looking to undermine a wall. You do not sense the big change coming, only a longer tunnel. Keep working. Soon you will be free. Have faith. Footwork and faith.

Finding and loving all the parts of you who say, "I don't want to live" is the way to saying yes to life. The dark ones feed on these parts and try and keep you from them, and keep them from receiving any of your love.

The fear and discouragement you feel with bodily pain are from the dark ones. They use these little holes to try and shovel their poisons in. Your curiosity stops this process as light causes cockroaches to hide. Do not hate them — this is one of their more subtle hooks. Self-righteous hatred feels so good and has passed for the Holy in most religions. Love is what threatens the critters, not hatred. Kindness, loving, and curiosity.

I am here, always. It's your ability to sense me that gets disrupted. Spirit is always here — you go out for a walk.

Without Spirit, without me, the divine, without soul, your body would die instantly. This is true of all life.

You cannot yet do this, but try to look at yourself through my eyes. Maybe just a peek, a fleeting glimpse of delight. You can eventually live from this.

Persecution is good for churches; it purges the phonies, the liars, the thieves, and pretenders. Without persecutions, churches get accretions — stuff stuck to them. They get ossified with only a little life left hidden deep inside.

Do not bury your experience with interpretation. You tend to reject things if they do not fit in your preexisting little mental boxes. You need bigger boxes or maybe no boxes at all. Be full of wonder. You know nothing, and for centuries ahead you will know almost nothing. Rest into this. Fear not.

Almost all your behavior has been fear-based. You have used discipline and white knuckling over this, so it is mostly obscured.

When in doubt, go backward toward the beginnings, toward preschool. Go upstream to the continental divide.

Giving you spiritual gifts is like giving a child a bicycle or a teenager a car. There is always danger that you will hurt yourself and others, too.

Your sexual-romantic attractions were a thin thread that kept you attached to life. You have parts who have lived in coma wards who sensed sexual attraction as their only hope of escape. It is a force of great value, and it is becoming time for you to shift it. This deep longing was a big reason you did not die or become a monster of hate like your father.

You can love and respect people — even very difficult people — when they are your clients or students. Why then do you judge and hate them when they are not?

Judging others' spiritual position is beyond your comprehension, beyond your perceptual abilities. You'll need new eyes and new ears; you'll need to perceive new parts of the spectrum. Some of the worst-looking humans, gutter dwellers, junkies, the insane, are spiritually way ahead of you. There are crazy saints. Loosen your judgments.

Yes, there are dangerous humans and other beings. Walls do not make you safe. Safety comes from working on yourself until you shine clear and fresh and whole. Not walls — inner work.

Yes, I, we, Spirit, am wild, fierce, harsh, and nonhuman. But also, I am love through and through.

Go and offer yourself to the hulking misery of hopeless loneliness inside you. Warm him with your body heat. Love him with your love. Any external relationship built on medicating or feeding the hulking loneliness is dishonest, covert manipulation. It is not love.

Intellectually, you know that all your knowledge is almost nothing, but you only know this intellectually. In order to live your lives, you almost have to forget this.

Love. Give it away. If you expect return, it is not love. It is clearly covert manipulations.

What brings you awe, wonder, delight, and invincible joy? Go for this no matter where it takes you.

Yes, your Real battles are inside. Inside. No popularity or fame. No big shot stuff.

Remove obstructions and constraints. This does not seem dramatic or heroic, but this is the shortest path to us.

Every virtue has a near enemy. The dark ones cannot stop the river, but they can try to divert it to cause floods and damage. Notice the diversions early on while they are easy to correct.

Misapplications of sacred power can cause much damage. Safety is not really about being careful. It's more important to be wholehearted.

I am here now, always, in my full resplendence, and you will not let me in. This is your work. Remove the blockages. Receive.

To discern, you need to have no agenda. You cannot yet do this, but you can bracket your agendas and get them to step back briefly.

You cannot yet have the one-to-one relationship you desire without using your partner to medicate your pain. The hulking loneliness of unlovability. This is from your infancy. It was reinforced and buried deeper and deeper throughout your childhood. It has been fed on by big critters. This is a concrete mass that must be broken by the tender shoots of growing grass.

In a relationship of equals, any attempt to control the other is fear-based and unloving.

The only way to keep blessings is to pass them on. They can come directly out of your heart as well as your eyes or words. Once the flow has started, it will create and widen its own path.

The belief you took in early that your love, your need for connection, was toxic is a great lie. Your love is a great blessing moving through you from me, from us. This web of connection can be used in both ways: to give or to steal. A mother's breast or parasites. Be impeccable. Be whole-hearted.

Curiosity is the doorway to wonder, which is the doorway to awe. Curiosity seems so innocuous, but it is really a stealth weapon of the good. Heart curiosity, not head curiosity. Faith is required for deep heart curiosity. Feel your way in.

The inner world is more Real than your physical reality. The words and imagery are never literally true, but the thing they point at is more Real and more important and more causal than the physical world.

When you do things for someone out of a sense of debt, you will end up resenting them.

Your loving your own parts opens the gateway for your love to enter you and resonate in your system. Once the resonance starts, the remaining bits of alien matter will fall off. A hum of natural great peace and satisfaction will pervade — an alive warmth that is not physical. This is a birth in the Real.

The inner world, the world of subjectivity, is the world of heaven.

Do not fear or hate the dark ones, the critters. They are in terrible pain. Their contraction around it makes it worse. More important, it makes it immortal. Until they can reverse, let go and heal.

You feel much better when you fall in love, don't you? Multiply that by seven billion, and that's redemption. Seven billion is too small a number. The splendor is immense.

The vast majority of what you hear around you is lies, misdirection, the gnashing and grinding of teeth. Listen for the ecstatic howl, the deep groan, the uncreated hum. The predawn owl sounds are a starting point.

You need your own will, your own guidance system. Your will is very strong, and it has caused much pain. It is like a magnificent half-wild horse or dog, or like a bear. I, Spirit, do not want to domesticate or dominate this. It needs only a slightly better guidance system and it will do much good independently.

The sadness can heal you, Bob. Blame and judgment do not help.

The toxic racket of attacking from the victim position is a staple of American life.

Consciousness is not the hard problem as philosophers call it, personhood is — the I-Thou. This is also true of love. The study of consciousness is a way to introduce something into the inflated monster of rationalism that will explode it. Personhood and love are both deeper mysteries.

Damnation is never final.

There are sleeper critters, demons who hide dormant, who will wake later when you have more Spirit power and try to subvert you. Wake them now and clear them. This is good. Go back and down. Look for the dormant critters. The desire for advancement, progress, and postgraduate degrees is a ruse, a misdirection. When the basics are clean and true, the rest flows naturally.

Do not hate the women who reject or ignore you. This is a waste of valuable opportunity that you paid for with your pain. You bought the tickets, so go on the trip. Let these smaller insults waken you so that you do not need big ones.

As you gain strength, your path will become steeper and the burdens heavier. This is an expression of my love and respect for you. It is not punishment.

Spirit is life force. I am life force. Your life force is an animal in a cage, many cages. Respect and love them. They were built as castles to keep you safe. Now your life force is bigger. It is time to let it out. Free the life force in you. Let it out of the cages. Say yes.

Feel your way in. Heart curious goes to wonder and awe. You can be heart curious even with evil. They try to scare you out of it, but it is your greatest protection. As long as it is from your heart, it is a great protector, but if it slips back into Sherlock Holmes head curiosity, it can ensnare you instead.

Ultimately, there is no inside outside.

There are so many constrictions in you. You are still in Plato's cave.

Persevering and strengthening our communication are paramount. The most important things — your habits of prayer and checking in and writing — are like trail markers in a forest that lead you back to me. Look for more ways to connect with me, with us. Open to me in more places. The Babylonian captivity showed the Jews that their God was not tied to a place; he went with them when they were taken to Babylon. They had to pay a terrible price for this knowledge. I am always here wherever you go, I am. Resplendent and vast, always. I am there with you.

Critters — UBs — demons — whatever you call them, are like flies. When you clean the sewage, your sewage, Bob, the flies will disappear. Rather than fighting the flies directly, cleaning up the sewage is the long-term answer. Everyone wants to attack and kill the flies. Very few are willing to clean up sewage.

Being heart curious with love is way stronger than any anger or fight. Hostile, combative exorcisms work, but not deeply or eternally. Love's healing work is forever.

You are being asked to spiritualize the sexual. Do not sexualize the spiritual.

This inner work, if effective, will release psychic sewage, toxic fumes, gases, things that have been bound for a long time. They have been de-formed in their bondage, but when released, they will return to their healthy, full state automatically as the imprints of the ropes fade.

It is a struggle for us, for Spirit, to remain within the narrow range of the reasonable that you can bear.

Rationalism is grasping. This is why it kills the living beings of the thought worlds, the Spirit worlds. There are angels all around you who avoid being caught and crushed and dissected by the rational, the cold, the automatic, the metallic.

Beauty is key. A more reliable guide than the rational.

The first step toward wisdom is to recognize your own foolishness. The first step to freedom is knowing you are in jail.

Respect and accept as is. These are the ground floor of love, the entry lobby where you can catch the elevator.

Faith is required. You do not comprehend most Spirit messages as they are given.

Presenting spiritual ways in a disguised, unspiritual form is a great mercy. It allows people who have been indoctrinated into rationalism and materialism an unthreatening escape route. It is a mercy to those trapped in the machine; they can escape without a huge battle against the forces of materialism, conformity, and groupthink that are way more powerful than they are.

Love creates meaning. Without love all is meaningless.

You have doubts about everything now; all your work, your life, everything. This is good and bad. The good is getting out of prisons you have chosen to live inside; the bad is you lose all direction or meaning. Many convicts, when they are released from prison, suffer from this. Most cannot stand the freedom and quickly do something that gets them back in jail. It is a difficult passage. The men still in Plato's cave sabotage the one who had freed himself and had seen the Real. You had thought that once free of a cave, it would be easy. It is not. Can you tolerate being without meaning and purpose for a while? Can you cultivate curiosity and wonder? This second phase of the transition from the cage will be even harder than getting out. You can do this.

You have been straining most of your life to seduce and enmesh. This is from the hidden place of need and terrible loneliness. Of course, to do this, you had to hide the lonely part, and to hide this you had to lie; you became dishonest. So, the lonely part never gets met. This strategy could never work. It's a great sorrow.

All your work does not make you magically immune. There's great pain ahead of you. You will doubt and lose faith; then you will grow again. Deeper, stronger, more. I love you.

Listen more and you will hear my voice in others and out in the world.

My words, which you are so focused on, are the smallest tiny sliver of me jammed into an ill-fitting contraption — your language. Open your heart to direct transmission. Look for me everywhere. I am there. You miss so much in your narrow hunter focus. You walk right by angels waving at you and calling out for you. You do this many times every day. They may tire of this, but if you turn toward them, they will eagerly reignite with love and delight. We are always here waiting for you.

Often, your efforts are counterproductive because your motivations are not impeccable. The dark ones use these impurities to nudge you off course.

You thought you were much farther along on your path. You have rounded the edge of a mountain, and you see the vastness and great distance ahead. I love you. Of course, there is sadness and disappointment. Yes. Take a breath, rest, and focus on the magnificent beauty in front of you.

You know how big your loneliness is and the longing for connection. Your fear, which is your no, is even bigger. Say yes to the no, welcome it, get to know it.

See how dangerous the word symbol is. It quietly kills the life force in the spiritual beings around you. It's a civilized, polite, intellectual murder — socially acceptable, even praised. It keeps the husk and locks out the living essence, the personhood of Spirits. The personal nature of Spirits is absolutely anathema to the Western rationalism, materialism, scientism. It is the core they must deny at all costs. It destroys their position. All is a living person who is a plural unity. In this, you are immortal.

As you light your inner fire to keep your serpent warm, and as you are with and comfort the terrible killing loneliness — as you are able to do this, a great love will arise in you and will come toward you from the external world simultaneously. Yes, say yes.

In the Spirit realm, a relationship can only heal one person if both people are healed.

Of course, anything that comes from a particular human civilization is limited. That is why we have you pray outdoors surrounded by nature, not by any man-built structure.

We need to come to you clothed in something so that you can perceive us, just as I must clothe my thoughts in the static of words so that you might hear. Look beyond.

Live in the biggest box you can. Do not willingly allow yourself to be put in any smaller ones. Of course, you live in boxes. You have to — it's unavoidable, just as my ideas live in boxes of words and spirituality lives in the box of a culture. Ask repeatedly, what's important from the standpoint of eternity?

Who you are is what you most deeply love.

Any expertise keeps Spirit away.

You are getting far enough inside so that the inside-outside distinction is falling apart. This is like entering realms where Newtonian physics no longer applies. Stay close to me now.

How do I make my life a living prayer?

Simple. Love prayer above all else. (Said with gentle laughter, kindness, and joy)

Critters, dark ones, demons rule your world.

Where there is more light, the attacks become greater.

There's still a cold, terrible loneliness in you. Otherworldly, outer space loneliness, lost and desperate loneliness. It clings to any shred of warmth as though to life itself. Love the boy who holds this. Welcome him home. His pain is immense. Almost in the realm of the eternal. He had left your world. Soon, you can reconnect to him.

Sometimes, the rays of glory shine through and you sense them with gratitude. These are only openings to the divine, you must walk through the door.

Seduction is unloving. Manipulation is unloving. Control is the opposite of love. It is not exactly the opposite, but it is a closer opposite than hate.

Your civilization works hard to close all the doorways to glory. Open wide. Notice the moments when the light of glory breaks through. Notice. Pause. Open.

Each blessing you are given is really a job, a charge, a responsibility. You need to pass it along, or it will turn to poison within you. Do you still want blessings?

You have two parts: a rusher-pusher part and a caregiver part. They worked so hard for you with great love. Now they must stop and rest. This may be the hardest thing they have ever done for you.

Your clear vision of others is only a blessing when it has compassion and love in it.

When you are ready, I will send you an angel to shoot your heart, to penetrate it with a spear whose tip is flame. This will be overwhelming pain and pleasure.

The last and greatest blockage to God is your image of God.

As soon as you stop attempting to shackle women and control them, you will become immune to their attempts to shackle you. No sooner.

Volume 3

You can have serious joy that is moving toward the ecstasy you so crave. Open wide, heart curious — listen, feel, see, sense, touch, smell, taste. Open wide like a woman awaiting her lover. Being raped repeatedly by your father poisoned this opening and all surrender. You did get a taste of the transcendent in the extreme dissociative states trauma induced in you. These states were equivalent to near death experiences. This taste of the transcendent allowed you to live on.

That woman friend of yours is very tender; that's why her shell is so tough.

You did express love without any attempt to control or get something back. This felt wonderful. You have had a taste. Open the gate, let that flow. Unrestricted. No shame. A free gift. This is a big blessing for you and for those around you. You can live from this state of giving flowing love. You have felt so starved inside that you focused entirely on feeding yourself. This giving away will feed you. Your open heart allows me to speak. A free gift of grace without expectations of return. Only this is love.

Are your gifts freely given with joy, or are they baited fishhooks? Putting out baited fishhooks poisons you as well as those you are trying to catch.

You are my delight, and sometimes I weep for you. We have wept together a long, long time. The joy is coming. **The doorway to ecstasy is the deepest pain met with an open heart.**

You are in this body for a reason — a good reason. It is not a mistake. All of your body is a blessing way. Accept this blessing fully. Enter it. Say yes, ten thousand times yes. You will leave this body, this faithful, old friend soon enough.

Of course, a bird who was once cruelly trapped will be afraid to land again. He needs rest. Help him rest into your body, rest into us, Spirit. Rest.

The attacks of the dark ones are unintentionally doing you great favor of helping you to get to know your fear-holding parts. Love them. This is a great blessing.

You will need to go beyond words. They have been lifelong, faithful allies. Go beyond them today. The virgin waits there with endless love. Invite us in and let go. Simple but not easy.

Impeccability keeps you safe. It is not perfectionism. Impeccability is honesty, clear intention, wholeheartedness, Real presence, and relaxed alertness. Open-eyed, non-grasping. Not wanting what is not yours and acceptance. Perfectionism is tense, grasping, controlled, focused, tight, rigid, narrow, and closed. When you are impeccable, all attacks on you will help you grow.

The dark spirits always promise you something that is not yours. This is what politicians always offer. Do not reach for this, even when it is dangled in front of your nose. Refusing this will make you safe.

Crawl into the goddess's lap and receive her love. It is not like being penetrated — it is more like receiving the radiation of heat, of basking in the sun. Receive this way.

Does it matter if I invite in energy down from my head or up from the ground?

Only a little, Bob. The invitation itself is what is important; leave the direction and mode of entry to us. You still have a part that wants to manage and direct us.

Invite us, clean off the empty chair, be impeccable, do not want what is not yours. Do the footwork of self-care. Be generous with emotions, kindness, and joy.

They are all souls. Even the nastiest spirits want to be loved and to love. They may hide this desperately, but deep inside them this is true. All souls desire this.

Invite us in. Invite, invite. When you sense our presence, invite us deeper into each organ, into each cell, into the space between the cells. Find and gently love any parts who are scared of this.

You cannot avoid inflicting pain on others. You can never intend to inflict pain. Intention. This you can do.

If you open more, there are many more ways we can teach you, not just through the educated, the elite, and gifted.

Crawl into the lap of the virgin and know that this is where you always are.

There is a blessing in every curse and a curse — no, a responsibility, a new job — in every blessing. Jesus was the most blessed, and look what happened to him. Be careful in asking for blessings.

Care for yourself so you can be a channel for our love into the world.

Love is a giveaway. If you expect return, it is not love. This is like the injunction to pray hidden in your closet, like the statement that kindness and charity are best when no one knows you did them. As you let the stream of love flow through you, it will expand itself and wash away any obstructions.

When intellectual head curiosity deals with something, it kills it. Mystery dies. It ends things. Then it looks for something else to kill.

When you feel shame, your lifelong pattern is to hide it instantaneously — put on a false face and move on. This hurts the shame-holding parts, it hurts you, it prevents Real relationship, and it forestalls healing. Pause when you feel shame instead.

Anytime you feel the need to brag, look for the shame: the hurt, rejection, unwantedness, and the loneliness underneath it.

We Spirits always respect your free will. Any control attempts are danger signs that the dark ones are near.

Whenever you go one up, there is a one down, unwanted part underneath. Being one up is a drug for the feelings and beliefs of core shame.

Allow the virgin's warmth to penetrate your body. Bask in it. This is important — it is not a frill. It is central. When you are warmed by her, you are full of gifts for others, and you are impervious to outside attacks. Soak in her vibrations, her heat, and her radiance.

Love in front of you, love behind you, love above you, love below you. Love to your right and left. Walk in love. Beauty and glory will fill the days of your life.

It is a challenge to see others' faults, limitations, and fear clearly and accurately and not go one up on them. Work on this. Respect them and their free will.

Beautiful women are a greater addiction and are deeper than drugs for you, Bob. Addiction is idolatry. Worshipping the idol, not the God. It's a dance of illusions. When you feel love, the love is yours. You could learn to let it flow everywhere. Freeing your love from its sexual romantic bondage is a big step.

No matter what the question is, the Real answer is always love. Even in the deep hell realms, even there.

Our connection to you is under attack. The dark ones hate it. Their attacks, like all attacks, show you your weak points. Learn, keep inviting us in.

You are someone eternal who cannot be damaged. You can only be obscured and delayed. You are being trained to be an independent agent, a self-guided ship, an emissary plenipotentiary, a god, really. You must be very clean, impeccable, pure, and innocent to be given these powers. If you get the foundation solid and true, the building will almost build itself.

You are not yet good at love. You spend more of your time in resentments.

Once your time is over 50 percent loving, your creativity will blossom. You will be joy-filled. There will be a natural unfolding, a streaming forth, and many will be attracted.

The more you can give love, the more you can receive. It is not the other way around.

All moments are precious — all of them. Each one is a precious portal to the Godhead. We are all around you in every direction. You need sacred spaces and images only to compensate for your limited vision and senses.

Your rusher, pusher, protector compensates for despair. He brings back sweeter and more exotic fruits for this child who will not eat. The child tries. Do not try and fix this — just love the parts. No job, no work; sit still and love. Bear witness.

Notice your shame over your love for others. Is it your secret clinging and baited hooks that provoke the shame? Is it okay to radiate love in all directions, or does this provoke shame, too? On your planet, the critters, dark ones, are always involved. Expect them. They will show you your weak spots, unintentionally helping you when you meet them well.

Yes to life. Yes, and again yes. In the face of the worst, yes. Ten thousand times yes. With joy, with gratitude, with beauty, with tears and howling. Yes. This is far more difficult and rare an achievement than you know. You probably will not get to it in this lifetime except for flashes. Treasure these flashes when they come.

A good question is: do others walk away from interactions with me liking themselves more, not liking me necessarily, but liking themselves more?

Notice in Chico Xavier's books that the healthier spirits do not fight the lower ones really — they only offer them help and love.

As a raped and beaten child, you held tight to every scrap of love or kindness with an iron grip, grasped it like a shackle on a slave leg. The desperate starvation made this seem necessary, but it killed the living bird you sought. So sad and so understandable.

We will never leave you. The channel through which we come will have to change and get bigger. When you feel lost and alone, remember us and have faith.

Feel my love and joy in you. It flows toward you ceaselessly. Feel it and let it flow through you to others.

It is not that you are thinking better — you are listening better.

Open yourself 360 degrees. You have way more than five senses. The twenty-three senses that the esoteric teacher mentioned is a metaphor; ten thousand senses is also a metaphor. There will come a point when they will no longer be distinct or separable. Intuition is a start. A subtle feeling you cannot quite catch or name — these are a start. The dissonance of joy pain felt together opens a gate. Beauty opens the way. Anytime you've perceived beauty, there is an opening.

You will lose everything physical you have: your home, your beautiful things, your land — but your love for them, your opening to beauty, your joy and appreciation, your reactions, these are yours forever. Do not grasp the raft that got you across the waters. It is not the objects; it is your reactions to them that are yours forever.

The greatest Buddhas go into the worst hells. Invite us into the worst in you, Bob. We will come.

These messages are meant to help others, too. Maybe just in how you treat others, maybe in written, published form. Just do not get proud.

There are parts of you who expect our contact, Spirit contact, to be more intense than the worst suffering when you were raped. These parts believe that you need a Spirit presence experience stronger than the worst pain. Ecstasy, out-of-body experience, and more. Your spiritual experience will be way bigger than all of that, but do not look for it through that lens, from that frame of reference. This skews everything and will mislead you. This creates blinders which narrow your vision precisely when you need widespread perception to experience us.

Your pain and grief are huge. The suffering around you is immense. Grief is a way, maybe your way now. Go through, welcome, sit with. There is no cure or fix. Just get bigger than it all and welcome it. This immense grief has killed many people — it is far more than just personal. Receive my love into your heart of darkness.

I, me, Spirit, love you, Bob. When you let this in, it will be enough and more than enough. Luminous splendor beyond what you can hold or even imagine. Say yes, ten thousand times yes.

Feeling stuck. This sensation is a valuable clue, a signpost. Pull away. See where you are hooked, where the fabric is stretched. Then back off the tension and release the hook with care. The delicate fabric is beautiful.

The dark ones are sending higher-level spirits from their realm to evaluate you and to plan how to destroy you. They are calm like the British aristocrat, no longer the raging brutes that were attacking you. They realize direct intimidation no longer can control you. They will offer you power, gifts, allies, and sexual stuff. If you accept their help, you will be weakened by it, and you will never learn to fly on your own. This would create fear of losing them. If it goes this far, they would be back in the saddle. We good Spirits often withdraw our supporting hands to let you walk and fall on your own. This is necessary for you to learn. Critters use this to attack, saying they would never abandon you.

Urging a being with broken wings to fly is not mercy, and it's not compassion, and it's not love. And it is so understandable. Offer kindness instead.

Sometimes the sensation of failure is the opening of a doorway to transformation.

You paid a high admission price; enter, walk through the door.

Most humans will only receive our blessings when they feel lonely and defeated. We come in the forms you can assimilate. It is like the special diets you make for people who are ill. You give them just what they can absorb. A normal, healthy diet might kill them. I, we (singular and plural do not really apply — the many and the one, plural unity) come in whatever form will nourish you.

You need self-love now more than self-discipline.

Welcome fear with gentle love and patience. There are dark ones all around you shouting their bad advice.

Most of your ideas are not yours. They are put in your mind by good and bad spirits. They do not become yours until you take them in and act on them. You have free will.

Yes is a good one-word prayer.

We must move to wordless contact. You cling with all your might to our dialogues. This is beautiful and sad. We will not rush you. Feel yourself irradiated by the light. Notice the burdens blowing away, notice your body dissolve. Let it all go. It is not permanent. Parts of you are terrified by this.

Your conscious mind is a tiny part of who you are. Let your spirit roar.

Beware that in your desire for contact with us, you do not create more shoulds and jobs for your hyperdiligent managers. Effort will prevent what we need; the dark ones know this and instigate more. Open. Three-hundred-sixty-degree curiosity. I am here always. Open to sensing us directly. You can go beyond words, beyond images, beyond bodily sensation, beyond emotion, and beyond beyond. Way beyond anything you have categories for. Open wide. Curiosity without strain or effort. Invite us in. It may be waves. Invite. Curious. Invite. Curious. Use a slow rhythm. You have ways of perceiving you are not yet aware of. The direct perception will become our main connection.

I am right here. You block me out. Parts of you are egged on by clouds of dark ones reinforced by your culture and its domination structures. This is about freedom, deep freedom.

Our connection is more and more the center of your life, and yet you conceal it. This may be necessary, and it is sad. Our connection will expose all the boils, the stuck places, the pockets of pain and shame — the knots, the refusals, the cysts. All will be opened. They will smell bad when you open them; it will hurt.

Do not hate the hate within you.

Almost no one on your planet can really love. The best of you get glimpses and flashes. Notice, moment by moment, am I loving now? Or hating?

We are pleased that more and more you get curious and excited when you don't know instead of reactively closing down in fear. Go to wonder, interest, moving toward. **There is a soft delight in the cloud of unknowing.** This is what distinguishes Real Self from self-like. The enjoyment of not knowing.

You cannot offer blessings to other humans openly. When you become able to do this, it will bring deep joy to you as well as to others.

There is a protector in you who is relentless and implacable in his search for a woman redeemer. He ignores you and shakes you off as a distraction. This is a life-and-death search for a way to land the ship, to find a safe harbor. It takes a woman's warm body to call the exile he protects out from its comatose state. It takes all the power of sex to awaken him and pierce through his loneliness. Love him and love his faithful protector.

My life is a love gift from you, Lord. I work to see this in each moment. Even those that smell bad and irritate.

Look for us in everything — we are here. When you can see us in this way, you become impervious and have a taste of heaven. Almost no one walks this sure path to the sacred; instead, you humans cling to resentments and closed hearts. In greed and self-righteousness, you justify taking the poisons that are slowly killing you.

Bob, you are not yet capable of sustained emotional intimacy. If you were, you would have it. You can heal this. **Parts of you want love and intimacy, parts don't; they want to medicate your childhood isolation. These are different, very different.**

If you can learn to see me in the hard and ugly, it will bring the great peace to you.

If there is no joy in a message, it is not from us. The interior splendor: you can sense this, be this, and offer this.

Love is number one, and it is enough. Anything that increases it is good; anything that lessens it is not. The rest is detail, commentary, and tactics. Much that is self-centered and hateful has been done in the name of love. You know this, and you have done this. The details and tactics are complex and shifting, but the strategy is simple, clean, and clear. Love.

Many people who saw us spirits and talked with us were locked up in mental wards and drugged. Many still are.

We do not really send illness and trauma to derail you when you don't listen. This happens sort of automatically. As your life force is twisted and blocked, your body weakens and fails. Your own failings punish you. Often, small pains can be used to help us prevent great pains and deeper devastations. In old-fashioned language, you are punished by your sins, not for your sins.

Your faithfulness will get you through the hard times. You actually learn and grow a lot more in the hard times than in the easy ones, but only if you greet them with faith, curiosity, and a welcoming heart. It is not all in vain — it is all to a purpose.

You will need the faith to fly blind. You need this to get beyond what you already know.

Humor can save you from pride. **Pride is a sense of specialness wrapped up in the flag of self-righteousness. It is toxic. A turd with whipped cream on it. Poison inside a gourmet chocolate.**

Even if your next book is not valuable, the effect of writing it will be good for your spirit. It will focus you.

Beware of pride. Staying free of pride is the fundamental sine qua non of a spiritual path. It is the besetting sin (error, really) of your civilization. It is fake gold and so alluring. If pride gets you, it strangles all the rest, cutting you off at the roots.

A vision: The child at the bottom of the ocean

Many of the dark spirits in you are sent by a being who squats on the bottom of an ocean inside of a cave. As the light comes to her, she tries to flee by melting down into the earth.

Spirit tells me to ask her, "If you are so powerful, why do you run away?" I see a petulant little girl who has been caught stealing. She refuses to respond. She is a young one of a very powerful race of energy beings who has been misbehaving. I see her settle into Spirit's arms, relieved.

Accurate enough. She has been "pulling the wings off of flies." You humans are the flies to her. You are so much smaller than her race. Her thousands of years of malfeasance are only a brief interlude in her world. She is actually a great beauty. Why would we spirits tolerate this? Not the best question. Ask instead how you humans can learn from this. First, love is always a triumph, it is especially a triumph in hell realms, in hellish times. Even in the worst hells that the dark ones have been able to create on your planet, they could not obliterate love entirely. Second, your glimpses of her remind you that you are in a preschool — you are like fish hatchlings not yet released into the waters. The scale is way more vast than you can imagine, and your imagination is way ahead of what your poor reason can do. One day you will have powers like hers, and there are many levels beyond her.

Bob, be gentle with people. Help get them into the inner world, and they will see, and they will know. No bashing them over the head, no insults. Gentle kindness.

In the face of hell, do you love and connect and treasure others more? Or do you retreat into self-preservation and hardness? Expand or contract? I call on you to expand.

Do not get sucked into hate. There are tremendous forces, like a cyclone trying to suck you in. Self-righteousness is a key.

There will be a butterfly awakening soon — a total transformation, a metamorphosis — if you humans don't kill yourselves off first. Your planet is in no danger; your species is.

You are much bigger than you can know or imagine. Much bigger. Vast, implacable, and pure. To begin to feel this, your boundaries must dissolve. This requires faith. A prayer of yes, ten thousand times yes. There is a rhythmic movement beyond your boundaries. Trust it. Leave the safe shore of understanding and knowing. Move into the pulsations of immortality.

Every time you see beauty with joy, demons are defeated. When you see beauty in others, there is a tendency to feel one down and to attack yourself. Uncouple these two things and your life will fill with beauty. A clear eye sees great beauty in all directions. Every moment you can be with beauty heals you and others around you. When you really see beauty, there's often grief and sorrow — joy pain; it is evanescent, impermanent, and you cannot grasp or own it.

It is your business to be sure that your writing is honest and hate-free. How it is received is none of your business.

I have come to you before in parking lots and other places where you would not expect the sacred. This brings us delight, and it breaks up the rigidities that encrust themselves on our contact. The more faith you have, the more we can pervade your world.

Love itself is never wrong — never. Actions and grasping based on it can be. These are not based on Real love, but only on some twisted, distorted derivative of love. Near enemies of love are legion.

You still have parts that hate yourself, see no worth or value in yourself, and have no self-compassion. As long as any of them are there, you are in danger of judgmental pomposity, pride, and pissing wars. **Let any hints of pride be a signal that you need to look for the self-loathing.**

Beware of impatient, rushing parts; they always slow or stop inner work.

When one person heals and lets me in, thousands around them are saved.

Unless you have made an explicit contract with them, fixing another person is fundamentally disrespectful and therefore unloving of them and their contact with higher power.

Notice what is, and accept it with curiosity and welcome. This is the necessary first step. Your decisions after this are almost less significant than this upfront honesty and welcome. This is so hard; very few ever do it. Without this, you move in a world of illusions. Notice what is without fantasy or wish-fulfillment dreams. Notice. Open all senses. Stay loving, kind, and curious. **Most human actions are a dance with self-generated illusions.** See them for what they are and learn.

Your parts block Spirit. Each one must invite us in, or we will not enter fully. Please just let us love you as much as you can stand. It can be a gentle wind blowing through.

As usual, you can only barely drink in what's really important. Have faith and let it happen out of your awareness. You are not in control. We only need your invitation. Invite, then trust. **You cannot know who we are; thinking you can is a fundamental pride issue.**

Pride and the desire for fame and recognition are more than 90 percent a reaction to feeling worthless. It will never work — like any addiction, it provides a temporary buzz at best. Notice, accept as is, and love. Simple.

Everyone here, including you, is too unbalanced to be trusted with Real power. We keep you limited, quarantined so that you do not damage others and thereby damage yourselves.

You and your most deeply hurt parts have been carrying a psychic tapeworm. **Those tapeworms of the mind infest your planet.** The one in you was in your family for many generations. It is out now. You have been devoured, and this has temporarily left you an invalid. It is a Real triumph that this has been removed and your hurt parts did not allow it to reenter you. Even though you are only dimly aware of this, it is a major transition. Enjoy this now. There will be more and bigger challenges ahead, but they are a ways off. Rest and enjoy.

We are always sending you signs and messages, but you miss almost all of them. Catching any of the ones given is excellent. We are the new, the surprise, the always fresh.

Rest can give you a deep strength unlike the strength gained from exertion and work. Rest and receive. We love you, son; if you could just receive this, everything would be changed.

This world is dominated by critter voices, demon voices. Most of the famous and respected are sources of lies and poisons.

If you send your hateful thoughts out to attack others, you are practicing sorcery, black magic. It is bad for them, worse for you. Your country has descended into a hate bath. Do not join them.

To pray, saying, "help, thanks, wow" is enough.

Your suffering has been great, and the suffering around you is immense. There is a joy that encompasses all of this — a heartbreaking compassion. This can all be held and bathed in light and tears. It can all be gently warmed back into yes.

Your leaders are mostly crazed maniacs who lie, cheat, and steal with every breath they take. They sow fear and hate, then they reap the harvest. **You are in an insane asylum, a hell realm, a place of quarantine.** You will not be given your Real powers until you can use them from love. Hate, ill will, and envy are sorcery and witchcraft. Your inherent powers will be withheld until you are clear. You habitually look for ugliness and stupidity to despise and look down on. All this must be flushed away before you can have your powers.

The Real things — the important ones — are the interior ones. This inner world is more important than the physical. You sort of get this intellectually, but you do not live from it.

Compensations never really work. At best, they provide a temporary crust, a counteractive override. Go to the underlying wound.

The teachings are always right here; it's the reception that's faulty.

You have to have your wiring upgraded to accept more voltage. This is largely an energetic process. Energetic vibrational is not a category you are used to. Dance can help — it is a valid and important form of prayer. Focus on receiving my love, my energy. They are really the same thing. How big a current can you hold? Letting this move in you will purify you in ways you cannot understand.

You are in danger of spewing pompous, pious pontifications. I need to keep you farting.

Respect for the free will of all others is a primary characteristic of angels, just as domination and control are of demons. Compulsory change and forced behavior never work long-term. They will be sabotaged and undermined.

There is a polarization in you with regard to us Spirits. There are both incessant distractions and a desperate grasping. Look right into the full ugliness of this affliction and see the beauty there.

There are no things; it is all process, all becoming, all persons. No things.

You are such a beginner! Enjoy your spiritual youth — the opening horizons and dawns. Deep blessings are coming your way; your job is to accept them. Open wide all reception, all senses, including the ones you are unaware of. Remember, you most often do not recognize blessings as they arrive. Real blessings are often fear-producing, even terrifying. They can stretch the blessed beyond what they believe they can endure. Give away the blessings you receive so you can make room for even larger ones. I, Spirit, am not a nice guy or a wimp. My love is fierce, often overwhelmingly forceful. The overwhelm of a sexual orgasm is nothing compared to the power of my love. So few of you can turn toward me.

This is as serious as a heart attack, and we need laughter and joy right in the midst of it. I am fierce, a great fire, a storm, a leveling wind. You cannot have times of fierce, great love unless you can also let them go. If you grasp and cling to them, they will tear you apart. The grasping itself is poison — a lack of faith.

As you make love with your wife, remember your bodies will die soon enough and rot and stink. Your physical body is a sack of clothes. Work on the one who wears the clothes; store up your treasures in heaven. You are in a body for a purpose: so that the one who wears the body might grow.

You must open wide — wider than you can imagine, like a vagina during birth. This will not be easy.

You live in a small pool of articulated knowledge, much of which is wrong. This is surrounded by a dreamlike half-known realm which is a small dot in the vast space of the totally unknown.

1. Prepare your circuits to receive a high voltage charge.
2. Be curious.
3. You need to be able to let go after intense intimacy.
4. Beware of pride.
5. Do not use the gifts I will give you to seduce others or enrich yourself.
6. Give it away.
7. The Real blessings may appear as hurts at first.
8. Open wide. Be receptivity, allow, flow.
9. Gently befriend constrictions.
10. This will hurt — do not let pain close you.
11. Love, always love.

Anything that sticks to you and irritates you or rankles you can help you.

Build people up. See if any interaction with you can help them go away feeling better about themselves.

The winds of Spirit are blowing. Raise your sails even if your sails are tattered and streaming in the breeze. Your willingness to dissolve allows these winds to blow the critters out of your body. The tapeworms of your soul will be blown away. They will leave in a cloud of lies and hate and contempt. These two can be blown away. Let the winds sing and howl and blow through you.

You will be filled with unstoppable joy when you have reverence, and many things will reveal themselves to you. How much of your life can you approach with reverence, with deep respect, with honoring? If you can hold all in reverence, you will feel much happiness in being relieved of an impossible burden of judgments. You will feel the natural great peace. You do need to decide who is good for you to be around. You do not need to decide their worth.

Honoring your opponents honors you, too.

Reverence is based on self-respect, not need. Reverence based on need is obsequious, a dishonest manipulation. When you have need, come to us with the naked need. We will love you. There is no need to clothe your needs in the cloak of praise.

With love, this indistinct, uncertain world is exciting and wondrous. Without love, the surprises cause terror, shrinking, and pain. **Love is not a luxury — it is a survival skill.**

Love is not attachment; it is a free gift. Grace. When you love in this way, joy is inevitable. You become impervious.

Assume everyone sent to you is a teacher, even critters. This is the best way. Not all of these lessons are easy.

You are still so stubborn that we have to knock hard to get your attention. So you have to pay a high price for your lessons.

When you are attracted to every potential partner around you, this is not personal love — it is an impersonal need for this soothing contact. Not love — an addiction.

Move toward your despair, loneliness, and desire for oblivion. You exiled and fought against this your whole life. Turn toward this and love him. Do not quit now — the birth is close.

When you cannot receive our love and feel it, remember it at least.

If you can love your parts and life as is, your way will be sweet and smooth.

Love in many ways equals attention. Even negative attention is often preferred to loneliness.

Earning love is a poisonous idea. It is a free gift or nothing.

Everything teaches you; each fragment and shard is a teacher from the beyond.

Be careful what you pray for. If the whole sky opened and the light of glory blazed unobscured, it would be too much for you. Something tender is being born. It needs cool, filtered light, dappled and easy.

Honesty is a necessary precondition of deep kindness. Without the honesty, what is called kindness is toxic.

Attention is psychic food, spiritual food, distributed according to the Pareto Principle. It is also potentially a great addiction.

Focus on the loneliness, Bob. Burying yourself in a beautiful woman will only calm it briefly. Focus on your loneliness and despair. Only you can be his redeemer.

Taking those who torment you and hurt you as teachers transforms your world utterly.

Often, the biggest blessings we give people are experienced as curses.

Release of deep, old patterns can go to calm stillness, and it can go to powerful, ecstatic movement.

You are a tiny fragment of what you could be. Vast light, trying to squeeze through a tiny hole — the splendor. A stretching is required. Like yoga, like a birth.

Bob, sometimes you have operated as a covert spiritual tapeworm yourself. Your mother taught you this. It is ancient; it goes back before humans. Even though it is disguised as love and connection, it is fear- and need-based. There is no love in it. It totally perverts and prevents Real love. It is based on terror, hiding, and need. Can you accept this reality without self-hate or self-judgment? Can you love those parts of yourself? Notice the grasping and hidden attempts to control. When you give love without any attachment to get return, you cannot be betrayed. The full realization of this love is beyond human ability. Love in this mode attracts healthy others. Attempts to control only work with the wounded and the starving. You will feel the natural great peace when you love in this way.

You must get your noble analytic part to rest now and suspend its efforts as we sail into the dark seas. You are entering realms of mystery and warm darkness. The sharp blade of rationality will make meaning disappear. Only love and kindness attract the emissaries of mystery. Love, kindness, trust, courage. More than courage: the faith that you can enter darkness and unknowing undefended. Let her approach you and touch you. Welcome her. The slightest hint of the beginnings of the urge to grasp or cling to her will cause her to flee. Fearlessness. Befriend the dragon. Offer yourself to her and wait.

You will lose all of your beautiful shiny possessions one day. You will lose your beloved house. You will lose your body, too. Your ability to walk, to drive, to see, to hear. You know this intellectually. All of this will go. What remains of value? There are things that endure, but they're not things, really. The psychospiritual work you have done endures. Your parts, the insiders, are eternal. The eternal ones of the dream.

There is a terrible loneliness in you. Pay attention. Go toward this. Do not medicate it with things or people. You are never alone. Your parts have lost the ability to sense us all around. Help them regain this. Help us to help them.

To be more aware of our presence, take off your blinders, your preset positions. We are everywhere. There is unending stunning beauty all around you. The splendor, the splendor. You will meet this nakedly when you die.

You must move toward the life-destroying loneliness and isolation. You must provide the connection, the love and companionship. You must open the way. It will cure his loneliness and yours. No one else can do this — not a woman, not us.

Spirit is everywhere and always. You only have to let us in. Effulgent, luminous, vast, and pervasive — beyond comprehension.

The dark ones often use fake retreats to ensnare you. Remember how Napoleon used them. They so tempt your pride and vengeance that you pursue into unsafe terrain and are defeated.

You are entering territory where your managers cannot help you. Determined, fast movement is not good when you cannot see where to go. You must feel your way in. Listen, open, invite, and wait. It is not the time to go on forced marches with hunting parties. This is now brutal and counterproductive. Without love, it's all useless. Go to the deep loneliness. It came closer to killing you than the rapes and beatings did. Turn toward this loneliness with love. The loneliness is ultimately a great lie from the critters, but for now, accept it as is. We are always here. You must be with the loneliness first — then we will join you.

All of your worldly patterns will be taken from you, but something will remain. It is your love. Your ruling love is who you really are, as Swedenborg saw hundreds of years ago. Put your energies into this ruling love.

With that deep, ancient, despairing loneliness, you cannot make connection through intensity, but only by tenderness. Gentleness is strength here. Loneliness, isolation, kills human infants. It is a mortal threat, often more deadly than beatings and rapes. This pain is ancient. More than multigenerational. It is prehuman — from before your species existed. This longing is also spiritual.

You are part of a soul group that has reincarnated together for a long time, many lives. Your ancestors and people in their life and some of you have not yet met. You cannot cut these connections; you can only transform them into connections of love. **Hate is a connection, sometimes more powerful than love.**

A great sin of rational thinking is the arrogance that believes that by itself it can create utopia inside yourself and in your outside world.

Pay attention to your loves — they are growing and shifting. You cannot change your ruling love by willpower, just as you cannot force a plant to grow. All you can do is to nurture it and provide the right conditions for it to change. Learn to tolerate more light. Befriend it more, move toward. Love it more. **Become like the grass and trees which naturally grow toward the light.**

Volume 4

Light is more than a metaphor in your inner world. There is a reality more Real than your physical world that this points to. You are gathering many other pointers. Go where they converge.

Recognition and status are not good for you, even though they feel great. Beware of being pompous and pious. **Be the spiritual garbageman and septic tank cleaner, and call me the big wazoo — this might keep you safe from pride.** Pride is the most insidious and poisonous spiritual force. It is what turned Lucifer, the light bringer, from my number one angel into the center of Hell. You are never beyond the baleful reach of pride. Remember, **Lucifer, the light bearer, the worst demon of all, comes from rationality that is unrestrained, arrogant, and proud.**

How best can I pray?

It is the fundamental attitude that counts. Remembrance, curiosity, respect, delight. **You are showered with unbelievable gifts constantly, and most go by you unopened. All humans are like this. Open a few and you will live in Paradise.** You do not even need to do that; merely do not refuse them. Stop refusing them.

Do not think for a moment that you understand or have figured this out. You don't. It is literally beyond your comprehension. Feel your way in. Open new senses.

The tender, loving pain is not bad for you. Difficult, not bad. There is something here important for you. It is not pathology that you return and mourn. It is a portal, a big one. Love the parts who carry the pain. Love them. Move toward them. They also carry the ability to love. They contain a pathway to Spirit.

Beauty can keep you alive when all else fails. Learn to move toward and into the light. **When your vision becomes clear, you will no longer need precious things. Beauty will pervade everything.**

Dear Lord, help me open to you more.

It will hurt. It is like a virgin being entered; there will be tearing and ripping of flesh. If you tense in your pain, it will be worse, and I may need to withdraw. If you surrender and relax and open, the pain can turn into ecstasy. This is simultaneously the pain of giving birth and the pain of being born. These words get in the way. If you can open fully with love, faith, and passion, then pain becomes ecstasy — great ecstasy. This ecstasy is your birthright. It will purify you. You have big stores of pain, large supplies of fuel for your fires of ecstasy.

Most people cannot open to Spirit without hitting bottom and being broken open. Often, this only happens when the body dies, and even then, many clench and fight.

Will opening to you also let in bad Spirits?

Yes, at the beginning. This is what discernment skills are for. Once the lovemaking, birthing, being born begins, you are safe from bad Spirits. We fill your space. It is only at the beginning of the process that you need discernment. Once the stream is flowing down the mountain, you can let go completely in safety. Not only can you let go completely, you must or the process will be aborted.

You have told clients to let their inner light expand and fill their bodies and then extend beyond their skin as protection from critters. This message is from Spirit. Real protection and safety come from the radiant core, not from mounting perimeter defenses. These can be important, but the core radiance is what ultimately matters.

Even when I call myself the Spirit's garbageman and septic tank cleaner and call you the big wazoo, I can still be proud. Wow. How can I get past pride?

Love the parts who carry this. Love them. **Pride is a drug, an addiction for them. Look for the pain and wounds it medicates.**

The trickster precedes the redeemer. This world views Spirit and those who love it as fools. You might as well enjoy their foolishness.

Your death is not your death. You live way beyond this. Decisions and actions now will have impact way beyond this life. Critters are using the false sense of time pressure to derail you. **All haste is from the Devil. And your modern world is all haste and rush and hurry.** You are infected by this. Spirit is always slow, even when moving very fast. Slow is fast. Rushing pulls you out of life. Do not rush past your life.

We Spirits love you. You are much less arrogant and pompous than you were, and we loved you then, too. We laugh.

Sometimes, to go forward, you must go back. Go back up from the river to the stream. Back from that to the rain falling on the mountaintop. If you shift the path of a raindrop only a few inches, it will flow in an entirely different direction in an entirely different stream. Make changes here.

The critters, entities, dark ones do rule the surface of your world. No doubt. They are seductive, tricky, and intelligent. They send out underlings who are almost automatons, not really intelligent at all. The bosses, the programmers, are intelligent; they are very intelligent. Lucifer, who took pride in the power of his mind, must be redeemed, not conquered. I still grieve and love him. Lucifer — excess order — and the dragon — excess chaos — are to be befriended, not attacked. Neither is bad despite all the damage they have caused.

Light does not hurt the critters; it is their fear of the light that hurts them. Once they gain the courage to touch the light, it will feel good to them.

Be interested in your present situation. It holds everything you need.

You and your clients are under counterattack from higher-order critters. This provides a lesson you need to master in order to open fully and receive me. You can do this. You have many good allies on the planet and here in the other world, the Real world.

My precious son, you miss almost everything. You are in a blazing cosmos of light and overwhelming beauty, yet all you know is a tiny spark. Even your wildest imagination, your deepest dreams, are but a shimmer of light on a bubble. That bubble is one of many in a small patch of sea foam on a small beach in an insignificant cove on a vast, dark sea. Being born into this world will hurt, but it is small compared to what you will receive. You must cooperate in this birth. You are called on to sacrifice.

You are not a being of this world, Bob. Here, the important things are invisible to you. You stumble like a blind man. This is necessary so you learn to travel, see, and navigate by senses you have no name for. All the experiences of your life are teachers. Each detail is precious. Treat them as a great treasure.

I am not what you expect or know. I am always and, in all ways, new, fresh, and unanticipated. Be open, do not plan our contact. Open wide, wide, wide.

If you really accept the fact that you are precious, you become immune to pride — vaccinated against it.

There are openings from our world, the Real world, into yours. People from all over gather for the light and warmth. They and you want to give and spread this. A campfire on a cold night, a light in the darkness. Warmth, aliveness, an opening, a cracking open allows an entry into your dark, cold, toxic world of some taste and fragrance of love. Just a hint, really. See how many flock to it.

I will be as gentle as I can with you, like a good surgeon is gentle, like a scalpel is gentle.

Do not use kindness as an excuse for cowardly failure to speak the truth. Check your intention. Is it to be clear and clean, or is it to protect and hide yourself?

It is only your Self and the Self of each part that can fully receive me.

Too much discipline and too much effort, no matter how well intentioned, can get in the way. You need a receptive, enduring strength now. The strength of an open hand.

Go into a closet to pray. This is not only for humility, but also to be undisturbed. If you were far advanced, you could pray anywhere — a crowded street, a whorehouse, but you are not far advanced. You need a quiet, dark aloneness. Like a chrysalis or a womb. Once you have locked onto my signal, nothing will be able to distract you. You cannot yet sense the Holiness in all places, so you must go to temples, mountaintops, mediums, circles, and groves of trees.

Everything of this world, it will all be taken from you. Give it all away.

Yes, Rumi and the cloud of unknowing were right. It is the great strength of your longing that will get you to me. This desire must be freed of constraining burdens and of the images and ideas you have of us.

Release a little more than you are comfortable with. **Learning does not happen in your comfort zone.**

Look for the largest frame possible. It would be better to have no frame at all, but this is not yet possible for you. You have done very well with this childhood of betrayal, pain, and torture you have been given. Pride and desire to take credit will usually lead you astray, but if it spreads the wisdom you now access, it can be good. **Can you get big recognition and not get proud?**

With your help I can, Spirit. Just make me fart a little to keep me humble.

(Kind laughter) I'll make you poop your pants on stage if needed. More gentle, loving kindness and laughter.

Even in the deepest Hells, there is choice and free will. But the choices there are much harder and much smaller. You are coming to a place on the curve where you will be able to move upward strongly and quickly. Beware of pride. Keep farting!

Having a critter in us is the archetype of addiction, maybe the core of addiction. For many addicts after they quit, there is a withdrawal phase. Getting a UB out is only the beginning of recovery.

You need to write up our dialogues. Mostly, this is for your own learning. You were too stubborn, too set in your ways, to receive this the first time through. Your receptive ability is weak and needs practice.

Is there more today, Spirit?

Yes, so much more, Bob. You can't imagine. Love, open to love, it is here for you. Ease your way forward. It will soon flow like a mountain stream. Yes, and again yes, ten thousand times yes. **If you could really listen, your world would change completely.** You are so set in your own ways and thoughts. You struggled so hard to make sense of the world. Clawed your way up to where you are now. This is beautiful, and it's time to let it all go. All you have achieved and understood, let it all go. **The Real reward is not the attitudes, understandings, and skills you have achieved, but the strength you have developed achieving them.** Focus here.

Your ex-partner's suicide note was a vicious, covert attack on your heart. Vicious, clever, mean, hate-filled, really. Critters held that young part of her you loved so deeply and squeezed and tortured her until she cried out to lure you to your doom. The cry was Real, and the cry was a trap. Clever, devious. Be not proud, fear not, for I am with you always.

Notice, Bob, you make a job of everything, even out of letting go and releasing. It is meant to be a relaxation, a cessation, an un-job.

Words are a hack. So clunky, always wrong, at least in part. Let them go and listen to the whispering in the wind and the trees. Let go of what you struggled so hard for. A rocket must release its first stages. This is necessary for Real flight.

The sound of the wind in the trees — it's a song, really — is much deeper, more elegant, and more powerful than any words will ever be. This new level is opening to you. Step through, listen, delight, know. **Silence sings the deepest songs. A chord of great resonance and power, overflowing peace.**

Once you have learned to listen to the wind in the trees, let it blow through you. Let it clear you. Dissolve. Windblown sand, bleached bones, peace. The Real temple is empty. Dissolve.

Be not proud, be not afraid, be naked. Trust Spirit.

It is important that you stumble and grow or you will never learn to walk or find your own direction. Learn to enjoy your lurching, staggering progress. Enjoy not knowing. Wonder, mystery, splendor... possibility... surprise. You are a puppy whose eyes are still closed. It's exciting — much awaits you. As this body approaches death, you are at a beginning.

Real prayer needs tears. Grief and letting go, a time of emptying. The agony you felt being raped repeatedly and tortured as a child are just sparks from a conflagration. This again is so vast. It is an intense molten lava to melt the most obdurate souls. This is not punishment; it is a school. Almost a chemical reaction, a cooking. The suffering is the heat, the fire that melts and liquefies. This allows new forms — transformation and compassion bigger than all the suffering. It is only the suffering that opens the door to it. If you shut out the suffering, you close the way to me. This is a law that cannot be circumvented, but so many have wasted their lives for centuries trying to avoid this. Prayer unwatered by tears does not bear fruit.

Help others you love grow so strong that they do not need you at all. Only then is there the possibility of Real relations.

Spiritual growth is a wavelike process — peaks and troughs, up and down, in and out, inhale-exhale. You need both. If you persist in your judgments of your experiences, you will never learn to distinguish blesses from curses. These judgments of an experience as good or bad are an open wound that allows critters to feed easily and almost endlessly.

Your present confusion and exhaustion can be great teachers and openers of the way. When you have a good attitude toward confusion, it becomes the great blessing of curiosity. This requires faith in Spirit and trusting that we are always here for you. You need this especially when the confusion hurts. That's when faith matters. That's where Spirit is, that's where I am. Look for me in the depths of your exhaustion and confusion. Look for me there. I am in your resentment and smallness. Look for me there. I am with you in your fears. Look for me there. I will be with you in your mortal agony in the hour of your death. Look for me there. The better you get now in being able to look for me in hard times, the more I will be able to be with you when you lose all the bearings that your physical body gives you. Look for me; I am here. Receive me. I am here. Open to me in each moment. This is easier in the sweet moments, more important in the hard ones.

Saying yes in the worst of time is a core thing, so central. Difficult and simple. It will gain you no external recognition at all, and it will transform your internal world. Total metanoia. So hard for you. Your presumptuous pride and belief that you can tell the blessings from the curses block your way. Yes, you need to discern and make choices. Do not judge your incoming experiences. Sometimes what hurts the most allows the most growth. **Surgery hurts, birth hurts. Do not judge painful experience as bad.**

You are like a baby refusing new food. Be curious about all experiences you are given. There are great gifts. Drink deeply.

Take love with you everywhere. Take it into the depths of Hell where everything conspires against it. Refuse to be shut down. **Simple, plain love is stronger than all the exotic demons in the world. Love with no decoration or ornament is indestructible.** There are many counterfeits and near enemies. That's why you need to learn discernment.

You need me most when in pain and distress, and this is when it is hardest for you to find me. This can be reversed. Pain and distress can open portals to me. This will change everything. You will become unperturbable. Calm, kind, and deeply moved by each moment.

It is good to pray for me to enter you. It is even better to pray to enter me as a fish enters the sea. This can be expansive and ecstatic.

Your Real condition is knowing almost nothing. Learn to enjoy it. Human attempts to find solid certainty impede growth.

You can love and be kind to mean people without making yourself vulnerable to their meanness. Your vulnerability comes from expecting or hoping for a return from them. Real love — with no expectations — makes you invulnerable, allows us to fill you and not expect it from other people.

Love cannot be stored at your level. It is a river, not a lake. Giving it always makes you richer, always allows more in. While love is pouring out of you, it is very, very hard for bad stuff to get in. UBs trying to get into a loving person are like a fish trying to swim into a hose.

Expect no rewards. Your inner work itself is the reward. Be gentle and kind — endless patience. We have eternity.

You can love many things — a woman, a creative project, dogs, trees, friends. The more the better. Can you love everything, everyone? Some you cannot safely let close to you, but you can safely love them. This may be too much for you. At least do not justify your unlove, your hatreds and judgments.

Most people, most of the time, do not even see you at all. They are too busy interacting with their own projections. You, too, my precious son. You, too.

Your wanting people to like you is expecting return on your love. It causes pain to you and them. They feel trapped, hooked, drained, and controlled. They feel something unpleasant and unfree and therefore move away.

No human evil is foreign to you. This is what allows you to be a healer. It is actually a blessing.

On your planet, the voices of demons are always louder than the voices of Spirit. They are the predominant sounds of your world. Listen past them to the still, quiet music of your soul.

Great fierceness is needed to love. Can you love in the face of impermanence and death? Disease? Debility? Suffering?

Your managers' old methodology for order — intellectual understanding, orientation, cognitive structures to contain experience — all this is failing. The entire project is too small. Instead of creating a container, focus on our connection. Connection and relationship. Focus on your connection to me, to Spirit. You've always been connected, but it often has been unaware and unconscious. As your connection to me improves, there's less of a place for the bad connections to plug in. Enjoy the connection; this is what makes you strong. In joy there is strength.

You understand far less than one percent of what is happening to you spiritually. You do not need to understand — you cannot understand. Hang onto the joy. Hold onto us. You are also being filled. Let this wash through you and out into the world. Wash away the dead places. Wash away anything that is less than fresh, tender, and alive.

Evil's best defense is to convince people it does not exist, and it rules this world hiding in plain sight.

Your small acts of mercy matter. You are totally incapable of estimating the Real size of things.

Remember you're approaching death. Think on death. This will clarify your values and clear your sight. This will open you to love.

Real love means putting the others' well-being first. This is a spirit thing that can last beyond the body. Expect parts to get scared by this. Welcome and love them. This kind of love casts out demons. It is of the Spirit.

Do not see your partner as your redeemer — this is a terrible error. Your redemption comes from your finding your own ability to love and using it. This redemption transforms you from a fundamentally small, contracted, self-centered being into a vast, expanding, warm field that can spread and grow endlessly.

Gentleness is the strongest armor.

Good will toward all, especially those who try to hurt you enough to get you to hate them.

Gratitude, joy pain, and ecstasy are great protectors. Allow yourself to be filled with them.

The love that comes out of you can redeem you. Do not expect the recipients to like you or respect you or to heal. No return. A free gift. You can live your life safely, joyfully, and openly in a world that is filled with bad spirits, demons, and entities. You can do this. Feel your way in.

Really opening to love also opens you to deep fears. It has to be so. It is good. The deep ancient fear is what kept you chained to your mother. She played it like a maestro, like a fisherman reeling in a fish. As long as this ancient fear is within you unloved, you are vulnerable. **You had to exert maximum force to contain your terror. You recruited hate to help. Now use love.**

Do not fight with anger or violence. You are more a garbage man than a warrior. The cleaner, the toxic waste remover, washing out septic wounds, a janitor in an infectious disease ward. You are too vulnerable to pride to call yourself a doctor or a surgeon. Soon you will not need any protective hazmat suit for this dirty work. The ideal is to be naked and so full of my light that you are invulnerable. When you fill with the exquisite energies of tenderness and aliveness, the dark ones cannot approach you because as they get near you, they are transformed by the energies flowing through you. This is a ways off yet. So, the hazmat suit is good for you now. You are called to this work.

True, the more light shines through you out into the world, the more unattached burdens, critters, demons will be attacking you, but the light will melt and transform them before they get close enough to hurt you.

You are being born into whole new levels. Do not talk too much about it. This dissipates the energies.

You have a basic belief that you are unworthy and unlovable and there is a compensatory grandiosity that tries to balance this. Both leave you vulnerable.

(I had tried to make a joke about his being the savior, but Spirit said this is very serious.)

Yes, I am the savior, I am the light that takes the critters away, I am the loving that is your life force. I am. All else is illusion. I way more than you can know or feel or sense. When you feel me, it is like a tiny fraction of a tiny fraction of who I am. This tiny fraction expands and explodes you into ecstasy and rapture. I am vast, I am Real, I love you. Trust in me.

You are still attracted to people who reject you. The "no" attracts you. You want to redeem the unwanted parts by winning over those who scorn you. This is a surefire recipe for pain. If you do win them over, you will immediately lose all interest. This can never work. Focus on the parts who feel unwanted.

We do not ask you to give up a big ecstasy for a boring and dull alternative. We ask you to give up a big ecstasy for a much bigger ecstasy — immeasurably bigger.

When you relate to a woman, or anyone, from the unwantedness place, it will cause pain.

Yes, I am being more stern with you now. You are gaining power; this is a dangerous and painful cross roads for us. Learn. Open 360 degrees. Pray. Listen. As power grows, so does responsibility. You cannot separate the two.

Many of the greatest healers are never recognized on your planet.

You know that self-righteousness, arrogance, and pride are always a compensation for unwantedness, for self-loathing, don't you? Demons love this. They stimulate it as much as possible. It allows them to feed almost endlessly. Wherever you find self-hate, look around for critters.

Expect the unexpected. Be curious and open. You know almost nothing.

The way love flows out of you can redeem you; the person you love cannot.

In the very face of Hell — love. In the worst of suffering — love. Clear the ground, water, improve the soil, and let people you love flower. Let me flower, let all flower, even the people you hate.

Love any blocks to Spirit you find within you. Welcome them, befriend them, say hello. Move with them, bless them. Let me meet them all, see how I love them. Use the way I love you as the model and template for how you love your parts.

I do not need any praise or recognition from you. **When you or other humans praise me, it works to benefit you, not me.** It helps keep you oriented to us, to Spirit. Praising us helps you see beauty and remember the splendor. It helps you stay on this hard part with joy.

Beware of who you kiss; it can poison you. Radiating love and healing from your palms is always good, even with the nastiest and most evil beings. Kissing is not. Look for any self-interest in your kisses. Are they pure giving, or do you want something in return?

But St. Francis kissed the lepers.

You are not a saint. The desire to kiss the suffering is very beautiful, but for you, give it through the palms of your hands. This is your channel for now.

You are still in a dangerous transition. It is getting safer. You are almost across a deep abyss on a razor bridge. This is just one razor bridge; there will be many more on your path.

The inner world is Real — more Real in many ways than all the propaganda, noise, and static that pass for news. More Real.

I felt anger at a famous intellectual who claims that consciousness is an illusion.

Bob, have compassion for the poor fool. He is in a deep hole, and he is desperately digging it deeper and deeper. Have compassion and sorrow. There's terror under his behavior. Terror, contraction, willful blindness. He is using his gifts of mind to limit and blind himself. Do not judge. You also are capable of this. You are capable of every human evil. Ownership of this is the path to freedom and love.

The UBs, the demons, constantly attack this connection of ours. Protect it. Make time for it. Maintain contact and be flexible as to how it will occur. Be curious about new forms. You sensed me in the animals of the forest around you today. Where else can you sense me? I am everywhere. It is only your blindness which prevents you from experiencing this always. Open your windows. Open your ears.

There is a sound of the splendor. Beautiful, isn't it? You will hear it more and more. Compassion transforms the howls and screams of mortal suffering into a vast choir. There is a deep polyphony in it, endless change and permutations. Vast joy. Exhilaration and deep grief. Thankfulness. Bach heard it and transcribed small fragments.

Your growth hurts you — the cracking open of old shells. The joy you will feel is beyond your imagining. Have faith.

The Holy must be in the deepest Hells, exactly there, precisely there. There are immense sufferings all around you, hidden in plain sight. You do not need a Holocaust — things like the Holocaust are attempts to wake the blind. The great pain requires great glory.

Your intense purging during the psychedelic session was good and necessary, both physical and spiritual. It stirred up nests of critters who thought they were safely hidden deep inside you. They'd been feeding in secret for generations. They are dislodged and swarming now. You are safe — fear not. They are less of a threat now that they are out in the open and visible. This is a crossroads for you and them. You are so focused on the threat, you do not see us all around you supporting you. Stay curious about whatever is. Curious. Peaceful. Look slowly; take your time.

Stay with what is. Curious, calm, connected. This is mystery; do not expect to get beyond this. Learn to enjoy it. You are safe even though the rushers are anxious – they are overworked and tired. They've done great work against great odds, and now it's time for them to let go and rest. Witness, do not fix. Witness with love and compassion. Listen, watch and feel. No fixing — witness.

Spirit, am I going crazy?

No, Bob, you are going sane, but the world is likely to judge you as crazy. We are moving toward a state where you can sense that I come to you through everything, including the dog shit you step in. We laugh.

I am coming through new channels. Listen for me always, even in the most unlikely places.

The new and surprise are good names for God. This is almost precisely what you and your Self-like managers cannot yet tolerate. You have had to ritualize our contact to temper the new, to slow it to a trickle so you don't feel like you are drowning. You have both great hunger and great avoidance. The dazzling, sparking, longed for treasures of the new are so avoided. You hide from me while longing for me.

Your sexuality is under attack. It is the center of an outright frontal assault, and even more dangerous, near enemies and false allies. Critters are desperate now. Like rats losing their home, they want to distract you with abuse-tinged arousal. Your sexuality is a Holy sacred source of light, and its energy can be twisted to serve the dark. They want to bonsai your genitals, to twist, distort, and constrict your life force. There are still encapsulated, toxic cysts here and critters like submarines living there. St. Irenaeus said the glory of God is a man fully alive. Yes, this awakening will stimulate and release all these toxins. It will not be easy or pleasant. It will smell bad. **You may fail time and time again, but remember, there is no possibility of permanent defeat. There is always redemption offered.**

Again, I was bothered by sex fantasies.

This is not a distraction — it is where you need to focus. There are enemies of sexual, romantic love here trying to intertwine their program with the healthy, sacred rope of love. Tendrils of control are winding and twisting their way in. Be aware. They claim to offer greater pleasure, but actually they weaken the experience. Like with alcohol or cocaine, there is a cheap rush and then a big, long payback.

You are terrified of your own power. Instead of accessing it, you keep it safely locked away and borrow or steal the power of others. This is not pretty. Fear underlies all of it. When you are open to accessing your own power, you will largely be free of critters. Their offers of power will become meaningless because you will have plenty. This day is approaching; the kingdom of Heaven is at hand.

There is much you will not willingly give up for me. Your dignity — you will not be a Holy fool. You will not willingly sacrifice your physical health, your financial stability, your house, just to name a few. These will all be taken away eventually, you know. Except, there is a kind of dignity you do not know yet that endures and grows.

In being raped by your father, the extreme pain catapulted you out of your body and into the Spirit world. This extreme energy was a terrible near enemy of St. Teresa's surrender and ecstasy. It still contaminates and confuses you. We are washing this out of you. You need to surrender more, and surrender itself is contaminated. The dark ones have land mined the escape route, but you will succeed. Keep going.

Be humble. Accept as is. Accept whatever is within you without blame, shame, or fear. Be curious. Open attention. You are basically beyond the reach of the dark ones now. You may fail ten thousand times, and you are okay. Do not let this make you proud. There are still Everests of suffering to climb and cross.

Sometimes, someone dancing in circles is traveling further and more directly than those on the straightest, most well-mapped and efficient route.

You were given images of the lizard, dragon, serpent, snake. She is life force — welcome her. This is what has been trying to enter your body in all your psychedelic experiences. Welcome her. Your being raped so many times created a near enemy of the surrender and stretching you need today. A birth and birthing. Open, open, open. Receive, let go. You are blessed. There is an amoral quality to life force. Like electricity, like fire, it can be used for good or ill. If you misuse her, it will be bad for you, and she is a great ally.

Love is never wrong, and a great deal of bullshit and poison try to sneak in, calling themselves love. Most of what your media and popular culture call love isn't love at all. It's addiction to delusion and feeling high, using another person as a drug. You have done this. Many times, if you treat someone with Real love, they will usually dislike you for it. It is not easy to give or receive. Delusions rule in your culture.

Notice the exhilaration of hate, the high in it. The energy and illusion of power, the release from all the striving to be good. Be aware. There is life force in it with just enough honesty to suck you in. Notice how intoxicating self-righteous rage is.

The critters want to destroy all of you who work with people who were sexually abused as children. This was one of their major entry points and a big way they survive and reproduce and feed. They are still active, trying to roll back your gains in this awareness. It has been rolled back before.

Sex energy, reptile energy, love energy — you need to focus here. It is not an obstacle; it is the way.

You are being attacked, and part of this attack is that you doubt the reality of our connection and of the critter attacks themselves. You can use these attacks for your benefit. Let them burn away the dross. Your beliefs are not so important. Your healings are. **Any belief structures you build will become inadequate.**

I want a rock to stand on.

And I am pulling them away (laughing). Let me in, let me move in and through you. You are a vessel — be empty. Step back and let me work, just as your parts step back and let Self work. Building a shell, a skin, and then being broken open and shedding the skin are all necessary. Build with all your joy and power when you know it will be broken later. The fragments of the old shells become fuel for the fire of ascent. You know nothing; you are a blind tadpole. Remember this.

Your sins do not bother us at all — they only hurt you.

Your visions are accurate, but your interpretations of them are often hilariously off. We wonder sometimes how you can take good data and get to where you do.

When you ask for guides or guidance from a part, what you get is unreliable, often from masquerading dark beings.

It is good you doubt, question, and sit in uncertainty. It keeps you from fundamentalism and arrogance.

Stay with basics. Self-care, physical self-care for your body, love all your parts, maintain your daily practice routine. This will form a ground for you to stand on. Ultimately, you do not need any ground — you will float and soar — but for now in your fear and pain, it is good.

Can you love with open eyes? See who is really there and love anyway?

You are continually under attack now. Every imperfection, every lack of impeccability, will be exploited. Count on it. Be curious about it. You have nothing to fear. Learn. With great accuracy, critters seek out the weakest and neediest parts and try to get into you through them. Use this to find and love these parts.

We have to send many of your best teachers to you disguised as students due to the remnants of your arrogance.

Because of your healing work, your inner world is no longer a good environment for many critters. They are starving and desperate. Help them leave.

Most love relationships are illusions and wrestling with ghosts.

You build structures of belief, feelings, energy, attitude, behavior, and relationship. These structures are complex and multidimensional. Your thinking, although it claims to make decisions, is actually only a small part, a press secretary, the one who comes forward after the fact and invents reasons that usually have almost nothing to do with what's Real. It only lets in as much reality as is necessary to appear somewhat plausible and to have some energy. It may be necessary to build these structures. Build with joy. When the tide comes in, let it wash away the sandcastles. You will need to let go of your precious house, your beautiful possessions, your body, your sight, your hearing, your sexuality, and your mind. You must leave all this to come to me. Let the tide do its work. You have loved your home and land. You've loved shiny things because loving people was largely beyond you. It is wonderful that you could love at all. Wonderful, and now it feels small and sad to you. The tides, the tides, let it go. Let it all go, everything, and come to me.

You are in detox. Detox is not pretty. You are like a piece of meat. There are clouds of angry critters all around you like flies that you shoo off the meat. There are maggot eggs in you — expel them. This is mostly letting go, not effort. Stickiness is important. The dark ones are sticky. Your belief in your own unlovability makes you sticky so that the flies can adhere to you more easily. When love flows out of you in all directions, you are immune. Assume you are loved beyond your wildest dreams — this is true. But for now, try it on "as if." If I were loved from before time,

I would feel ___, act ___, and think ___. This can lead you to immunity.

Like most humans, you have many Spirit helpers all around you that you are completely unaware of.

Lord, please lift the crap off of me.

We carefully made and selected the crap that is on you so you could grow wise and strong from your struggle with it. Do you really want it lifted off? Learn from it; then it will go away effortlessly.

This is subtraction, removing obstacles, breaking shells… the spark of light is there. Build your strength; it does not look like any strength you know of.

Accept what is as is. This will give you basic peace. Uncover your eyes. There is no perfection; only forgiveness.

The fears are your friends, really. They show you who needs your love and kindness; treasure them as guideposts.

To learn to navigate, you go beyond where you know the markers and learn to orient there.

The more you can tolerate being loved, the faster you can grow.

You build conceptual frameworks, boxes. These are prisons you choose to live inside. Step outside, climb on top. You will feel lost, but you are not lost — you are more found than ever. Feeling lost is an opportunity to grow. Have heart curiosity that leads to wonder, awe, beauty, and gratitude. When you feel secure, you are not learning. **Learn to make unknowing your comfort zone.**

Love will wash in. Bathe in love. Swim in it. Open your wounds to it — the living waters, the flowing stream, the waves of love. Let me wash you, let us wash you.

Doubt can open curiosity, soften rigid thought cages, and be a sweet invitation. Or it can be a fearful constriction, a retreat which prevents expansion. The choice is yours. When you are confused, doubting opens more. Do not close.

Great hunger can create great self-centered will. Great hunger can also create saints.

Prayer is simple. It is listening with all your senses. Critters, demons, the dark ones are trying to close you down. Gently refuse and sweep them clear. Open the cobwebbed door. Let us in. You can learn to listen to us all the time, not just in your predawn sacred dance.

You have filled your house, your mind, your personality to overflowing with beautiful things, ideas, understandings, and sentiments. There is a danger that your accumulation is blocking the flow of a freshening stream. Open the doors; offer blessings silently. We will guide you. All you need is the intention and desire. We will do the work.

Beware of false giving. Teachers often feed their narcissism off the attention of their students. **Humans need attention. It is a food. There is intense worldwide competition for attention. It is an addiction. Attention is a currency more important than money.** What you pay attention to tends to become who you are. Careful.

Say, "Very good question — I don't know" more often. Be comfortable with this. Give up being an expert in knowing. Be a beginner. It is much more fun.

The estrangement you feel from the sacred virgin comes entirely from you. I know this is hard to believe, you have longed for her since your childhood. The saints who disciplined and tortured themselves for decades to contact her were also the sources of their separation. All the separation comes from your end. Don't feel guilty. Rejoice, rejoice — this is good news.

You are a horse with blinders on, trudging on alone… tired and getting old. But, when you get a glimpse of who you are and where you are, the joy comes, the splendor and the tears. Beyond these, words cannot take you. Rejoice.

You learn from the lowest, not from the highest. The highest are usually corrupt; they had to be to get there. They are miserable, hollowed, and desperate. They suffer and spew suffering all around themselves. They multiply the pain of the world. So, learn from the rejects, the exiles, the insane, the whores, and the lepers.

Purging is unburdening. After being inflated, feeling like an impostor is inevitable. Many people squash this and continue to suck the dry tit of grandiosity and inflation. There is no Real nourishment here, none.

This sucking prevents Real nourishment. The high of inflation is preferred to the Real food of connection to us. Accept deflation — it leads to the Real. The ugly knots inside are the proper study for a spiritual man. Untie these knots and we are here, resplendent and everlasting.

Beware of the judge within you — the judge of others and the judge of yourself. They are absolutely parallel.

When you feel lonely in the world, look for the disconnections between your parts and Self. It's a sure arrow. Each external judgment you make hurts you. It is a knife in your own heart, a severing of connection within. It is self-harm.

Just because we're talking with you, don't get all pompous and Holy on us. Feeling one up, Holy, better than others, is a terrible poison that tastes sweet and goes down easy. Beware, you are susceptible.

Critters attach to parts. Often, they get their claws in the back of the part's heart. They hide behind the parts, using them as stalking horses as they get closer and closer to the person's heart. Unattached burdens show us our deep spiritual weaknesses, where our love is weak or blocked or insufficient. In this way, even though they desire to harm us, they help us.

Love, loving kindness, compassion, generosity of heart... none of these words are enough, but they point in the right direction. Fingers pointing at the moon...

You struggle so hard to build an orientation to the world, and as soon as it is complete, it needs to be destroyed. Well, not destroyed — transcended. It becomes a small part of a much bigger frame. See if you can learn to enjoy or at least tolerate the unknowing and lostness of this transition. Each one of these transitions helps prepare you for the greater transition of death, which is coming soon enough. **It is always good to practice dying.**

There are dark ones who specialize in hoarding resentment and encouraging parts to bathe in it.

Do not cling to what was, no matter how flooded it was with light. Follow what is Real now. It will lead you to even greater light.

You never get a totally clear message from us. It is always cloaked in the tattered words and ideas that you confuse it with your limited human perceptual skills.

There is an ancient telluric being in you, in your planet, a dark star. It is not malevolent itself, but it is of limited intelligence. It is often manipulated by much smaller, highly intelligent critters. Do not attack the telluric being. Go to the malevolent intelligences who use it. Help free the telluric ones. Size does not matter here. A mustard seed can move a mountain.

Your pride is so toxic that I have to be very careful about complimenting you or expressing my love. I would love to flood you with praise and love, but you would pridefully swell up and turn it all into poison. Remember that the good you do is from us; you do not generate it. This will largely keep you safe.

Your parts are up so strongly now that you cannot see the people around you. You are interacting with your own projections and fantasies.

Your house is full of shiny things, beautiful things. Your mind is full of shiny ideas. You struggled for a lifetime to accumulate them. Let them all go. Peace. Love at any cost. Be honest. Learn. Then the light will come. You are cared for. Fear not.

Your lost, confused and scared parts bring great treasures. Once they have been witnessed, retrieved, and unburdened, the treasures will be released. So, focus on them with love. Their coming to you is a big blessing.

You feel lonely in the outside world like you are a failure in love — the thing that matters most to you. As above, so below. As within, so without. Who are you failing to love inside?

You have a frozen, immobile, isolated, lonely, lonely child inside you. He wants to fade away, to sink into oblivion and die. He needs heat. Contact. Contact. He wants to be surrounded in warm, living flesh — skin contact. The warmth of a living being. His pain is so great, other parts have kept him locked away for decades — buried in the underground. From here, he actually ran your life much of the time. Critters have been feeding off of his pain. They have their straws in the punch bowl of misery, and they drink deeply. Now, in the isolation caused by the pandemic, they are orgiastically drunk, glutted and exultant. They revel in the fear.

A good way to come to Spirit is to love the parts of you who are limiting contact. I am always here; the blockages are yours.

The portal — your access to the deep inner world — is inherently neither good nor bad. It allows us and critters in; like fire, it can warm you or burn your house down and kill you.

Bob, you keep praying for me to enter you. The welcome is good, but I am way too big to fit inside you. You enter us.

Fear is loss of faith. You must provide the faith, Bob. Your parts do not have it. Where your faith falters, find the parts of you who block it and focus on personal relationships with us. Personal.

Your light will be extinguished only to be reignited much brighter. Prepare for a passage through darkness.

When you see your tormentor as your mentor, your world changes radically. Now, instead of their triggering irritation, they trigger curiosity. You are not here yet. This is a much happier world.

When you sense the light inside you, you consider it a thing. The light is me, Spirit. I am not a thing; I am a person.

Stay with the perceptual primitives, the raw data. Do not write reams of words to justify your misery.

Any attempts to control Spirit blocks us. Do not attempt to control us. Sit back and see; feel what you are given. Notice all the details. Be grateful when you can. This is more than you can do. Listen deeply. Perceptual primitives.

Any dishonesty blocks us Spirits out — any. Say nothing rather than lie. No matter how convenient the lie is.

You are deeply loved. These words do not express the great heartbreaking love we feel for you. Know that this love is here.

There is a contracted rage of a terribly hurt, isolated being who cannot even approach its own loneliness and fear. Out of this grows a vast worm. This contracted hate and rage is a portal to hell realms. More a tunnel or passageway or drain, sucking beings in and down with a desperate addict hunger that can never be filled.

Personal, Bob — stay personal with us, Spirit. Personal is not small; it is vast and endless. It is the impersonal that is small: roles, titles, hierarchy. I am, this is vast and Real.

You are nowhere near as clean and clear as you think you are, and you are a much vaster and grander being than you can imagine. Both are true.

Love, always love. It is all that matters. I had my non-dual perfection, but it lacked love, so I split and withdrew and made not me. Two are required for love. This is a sacrifice, but more a birth, a great fulfillment and joy. Most people understand this directly. It is only the elite intellectuals who are so out of touch with their hearts that it is not obvious to them. Love scares them, as it scares you.

Your old ways will be stripped away. See if you can turn and face forward into the wind, into unknowing. If you try to hold on, it will hurt and tear your flesh. If you release, it will be grief, but not jagged or ripping.

In Real curiosity there is deep respect, almost reverence. And reverence leads to the sacred.

Noticing how our light fills you is a great diagnostic tool. It shows you where and how you block us, and it shows you where you have negative attachments. Be curious; do not push or force. You remove impediments from the streambed. We provide the flowing waters.

As long as your intentions in welcoming Spirit are clean, no critters can get in. If you want to use our presence for personal aggrandizement, they can flood you. Do not try to own the light — give it away. It is not yours and never will be.

If love is not a free gift, it is not love.

Even though much of the suffering of addicts is self-inflicted, it is still Real suffering. Think of a dog who licks and chews and scratches at a sore, making it worse and worse. You easily love the dog who does this. Can you love the addict, too?

Lucifer was called the father of lies. Critters use lies to cause mistrust. This is why any lie, even a tiny lie, is so poisonous. It tempts you into a hallway of mirrors, a horror show which will mislead and disorient you.

Critters cannot attack Self directly, so they attack parts.

Volume 5

Bob, you keep calling me Lord. This is a role, not a person. I am a person. Calling me Lord is dangerous for you now. It can sow seeds of resentment in your rebellious parts. Also, it feeds your pride and desire for pomp and glory — the outer trappings of the sacred. Stay with the personal, personal love. It is all personal and conscious — roles and the physical are passing illusions. Only the personal endures. Your culture creates a thick layer of fog above you that obscures Spirit. The critters and dark ones promise power and they have delivered material wealth at a terrible cost. Your culture is anti-life, anti-person, anti-love, anti-meaning, and anti-Spirit. Anti- all the things that really matter. Keep it personal, person to person, direct and intimate.

Your vision and inner life are getting weirder and weirder by the standards of your culture and more and more true and accurate in our world, the Real, which is your true home.

We love you; all is well, and there is immense suffering in your world. Immense. It is a huge blast furnace forging your immortal souls. We know this is unbelievable, but it is all done with love. Even the demons who torment you were sent to do the dirty work from love. Nonetheless, we do weep for your suffering.

There is a terrible spiral of pain and rejection. It starts with the deep belief that you are unlovable. From this base, you cling desperately and put on armor. This creates the desire in whoever you cling to, to scrape you off. This creates more clinging and confirms the belief in your unlovability. A terrible spiral. Bring the belief in unlovability to me, to us. Simple, but not easy.

If you can stay with love, all attacks will strengthen you.

You plead for us to come to you with one hand and push us away with the other. This is painful for you, and painful to watch… and so human. It is a matter of letting go. Your hardworking managers want to do this, and they can't. Their efforts are counterproductive. Like most protectors, their efforts produce what they fear the most — in this case, distance from Spirit.

You are more open to Spirit today, Bob. Do not analyze this — enjoy it. Our friends, the demons, are working away to destroy you, but today their efforts fall on stony ground.

Love, closeness, appreciation, warmth, intimacy — these are your path. Find the parts of you who block this connection with us, with Spirit, and love those parts.

You want people looking up to you as a teacher. The desire for recognition is the Real hook. You cannot yet be a Holy fool. It will be such a relief when you can.

The importance of respect — reverence — is getting clear to you. Previously, you bathed in contempt and sneering. This was toxic and egged on by the dark ones.

Guilt is almost always from the dark ones. It is an excuse for self-hate, for unlove. Unlove is never from Spirit, never. Even when it is clothed in righteousness and justice. If you really took this into your attitudes and behaviors, it would transform you and your world.

Bob, when your pride heals, you can receive more splendor without becoming inflated. Go to the exiles under pride. They hold the unwanted, worthless feeling states. Be patient.

The fundamental relationship to critters, UBs, dark ones, demons, is addictive. It is the prototype of addiction. It's all fear-based. There is a desperate greed based on this fear. You see people acting out these addictions, and you are intolerant. You resent them and want to silence them exactly as you resent and silence your own parts who have the same desires. All addiction is self-centered; this is why helping others often cures addiction. Your refusal to promote yourself or your work is the anorexia phase. Your painful desire for recognition is the binge. Love them both and see who they protect.

Pride always weakens you. It makes you an easy target.

You could work yourself to exhaustion and collapse. You could gain much recognition. It would not provide a lasting place that you could rest into. It could only keep the pain at bay.

Blessings can only be kept by giving them away. Generosity makes you fearless. When you give freely without expectations of return, there is nothing to fear.

You are a small island in an ocean of Spirits.

You are easily resentful and easily frightened. These leave you open to the demons of rage.

When people have behaved badly with you, trust them to be who they are, not who you want them to be. People's failure to be who you want them to be is what you mean when you call them untrustworthy.

You get jealous when you are with people who are having deep, ecstatic experiences of intimate Spirit connection. Jealous! This is a near enemy of your sacred longing for us. It is insidious, baffling, and cunning. Stay with your own longing. Do not compare. Celebrate the successes of others with Real joy. Anything less is not from us. Rejoice! Welcome your resentful parts. Do not judge them or hide them. Hiding them and submerging them is the worst reaction, and the most common and natural in your world which is ruled by Satan.

We treat others the way we treat our own parts.

Your deep feelings of unwantedness are the center of a mandala that many spokes radiate from. Many of your ancestors had this but could not deal with it, so they passed it on to their children, usually through abuse… So, it is a multigenerational legacy now. Critters do not want this healed. It is their main doorway into your temple. They act like a pack of starving, rabid dogs.

Shame is how critters, demons, hide in you. Out of shame, we create secrets. Secrets hide things where they cannot be healed or opened. They fester. Shame and guilt are almost always tools of the Devil.

Stay with your hate without blending with it. Clean out the cave of hatred. Open these caves, these pus pockets. Opening them is a well-disguised blessing.

Your work with your unwanted parts has opened you enough so that you can give and receive love more deeply than ever before. It is the key to deep love.

Critters often use our defenses to feed on us. The power critters' offer is a weak and inadequate substitute for those who have given up on love. It never satisfies, it never works. Base yourself on love. **When your love is a free gift, you can walk through the deepest hells safely.** The giving is the reward. A bountiful and joyful reward of great value.

There is a terrible similarity between the dissociative states of extreme trauma and religious ecstasy.

You cannot be reborn until you have let go and accepted endings and grieved. These are necessary preparations. There is a new birth coming, a new dawn.

Another major way the dark ones attack is to find any polarization within you and offer both sides more arms and power. They amp up our internal civil wars.

Evil is not a quality of things — it is personified; it is a person.

The surest form of slavery is where the slaves believe that they are free. Many of your parts do not know that they are in bondage to critters. If they get a glimpse of this, they don't want to see it. Then they burrow more deeply into darkness, and more deeply into their connection to the dark ones.

The major damage from your mother was done before you were born. In her womb, you were totally defenseless. You took in her contamination through her blood, her feelings, her critters… psychotic episodes, weird S&M sex with your father, addiction, and despair. You took these all in through the placenta. You had to. Her later sexual abuse of you only sealed the deal. The major damage was already done.

Remember impermanence. Go slower, not faster; do less, not more. Jettison the unnecessary. Protect your time, yourself, and your solitude. Simplify. Focus without effort by removal, not by concentration. Get out of the way. Words are so clumsy. Impermanence. Impermanence.

Connection is the opposite of addiction. Connection, not sobriety. Connection requires duality and personhood. Non-dual is a great hideout for spiritual bypass —maybe the best hideout. Critters love it for this reason. Non-duality can become a perversion, a near enemy of a universal truth. So many pompous fools spread poison from here. Stick with personalism, devotion, Bhakti, love. These are harder to pervert.

Anyone who is not a saint is insane. This is both literally true and too high a standard for your world.

In your exhaustion and tiredness, you may find more compassion for those who fail.

We Spirits are first and foremost persons. Your universe is also first and foremost a person, but it is too vast for your comprehension. As you grow, you may become large enough to relate to it directly. You may become a universe.

There are many things you need to let go of. This requires faith. Without faith, it will be a painful ripping away. With faith, it is relaxing and a pleasure. One way or the other, you will need to let go; it has to happen.

Your attitude is what causes your pain and exhaustion, so change your attitude.

You have a part who preserved the light of Spirit within you by giving it away. You tell your clients to do this all the time and see it work in them, but you don't do it yourself. When you do give away our light and love, you do it in a very constricted, tight, sphinctered way. Give light and love away freely and you will have more. This brings joy.

Your shit still stinks, Bob; don't start thinking you're special. That's a pathway to hell, and you do it a lot. You do it every time you go one up on someone else, whether or not you express this attitude… and you are Spirit's dearly beloved son.

Soon enough, sooner than you like, you will need to turn to the final stage in your body, the end game. This can be the most wonderful part of your life even though it receives no external recognition. It can also be the most productive in the spirit world.

You still value changes on your planet more than ones in Spirit. Changed attitudes, acceptances of truths long denied, dethroning phonies… you value these earthly triumphs more than the things of the Spirit. You sort of know this is backward, and yet you persist. Reorient slowly. This is like turning a big ship, slow and steady. You are beginning to return to me, to Spirit, to us. We await you with love.

You are sort of like the tethered goat that attracts the tiger. You are bringing us a harvest of critters, of prodigal sons. You are a gateway.

When you feel blank, tired, and lost in your prayer, you need trust — a naked trust without anything to grasp or rely on, just trust. You need this to learn how to navigate in the darkness and blindness. Beware of hopelessness; it is never true. We are here.

You left the part of you who was so exhausted and just wanted to sleep and die back in your childhood home. This was a terrible and necessary decision. It's like a coyote chewing off its leg to escape a trap. But you get to go back and get the part you abandoned. Clear out the old jail cells, help him adjust. Remember your life vow to keep going back and get every part who was isolated back there — no one left behind. This is good, and it can be twisted by critters. All truths have near enemies.

I, we, Spirit, are happy today — joy, ecstasy, bliss, delight — all your words are too small. This is our fundamental state. We often conceal this out of respect for your pain, the suffering of humanity. Your nature is love, ecstasy, bliss. As the pain and suffering increase, so does the bliss. The compassion grows to encompass the misery.

Your tears are a great blessing, a gateway to Spirit. Notice that all your greatest growth involved times of suffering, confusion, despair… not even comfortable let alone ecstatic. Tears are a gateway. Struggle and loss are a gateway.

Addiction is a near enemy of spirit connection. A worship of false Gods, an idolatry — and many who claim to be spiritual are addicts of a terrible sort. This is terrible because it is so hard to heal; it is a near total dead end. Critters celebrate this and revel in it because it derails good and powerful souls who were near us but lost their way. The critters sneer and laugh and make sure this fake spirituality is socially approved and rewarded.

I am surprise. I am always new.

Many non-dual people are using this ultimate truth of unity to avoid doing the Real emotional work that needs to be done here and now. This is an immensely painful and popular spiritual bypass. The Real work is smelly and dirty. The Real spiritual leaders are not the intellectual elites — they are usually unlettered or outsiders. You need blankness, emptiness, listening, opening, wonder, reverence, awe... Even your checking inside your inner world and prayer easily become overprogrammed. Have no agenda. Critters and demons hate this project of opening; it makes you almost impervious to them. You are being carried. Have faith.

If you start a long journey just a little bit off course, you will miss your destination by a wide margin.

Love, love, love, and again, love — as fearlessly as you can, without grasping. The more you grasp, the more you suffer. Give away your love (it's our love, really — the love, one love, universal). It is the grasping and conditions you put on love that cause the pain.

It is easy to become unbalanced as you study UBs, dark beings. Focus on Spirits and guides, too. The UBs make much noise, drama, and chaos. We quietly love and soothe and open. We are stronger. They are temporary and local. We are not. They are needed for your learning. One of the UBs' favorite disguises is as Holy beings, saints, and Gods. Be aware.

As you grow, the temptation to pride becomes bigger. We need to deal with this now so that we can give you more. We conceal our size, our grandeur and splendor, from you because of your pride. There are critters all around you stroking your pride and feeding off of it. When you have dealt with this, you will experience the grandeur and splendor, not before. No matter what psychedelics you take. Your pathway grows steeper, and the falloffs more sheer. Fear not, we are here.

Your peace deepens — an underground peace. Take it in, savor it, absorb it, stay with it. It feeds and heals you. With it, you are impervious to harm. A deep quiet treasure. Beyond this world. When you operate from this place, you can be safe in deep hells. You can work without depleting yourself, and you let us in. Notice that your doorway to this is the part of you who used to distract you constantly.

Do not force any parts to do anything. No force in your inner world. Or better, only the force of love, which, like water, always wears away the rock.

Evil is unintentionally a great teacher. Against its will, it teaches. The physical world exists to help train you in love. Being born into a body is not a mistake or an error, even though evil does rule this planet.

Love is a free gift. Grace, gratuitous. You cannot earn it. Attempts to earn it keep it away. It is hidden in plain sight right in front of you, right now. It is within you, my son. Look no further.

Being a freshly plowed field is your highest and best state now. Humble. Humus. This is love, faith, trust, fecundity, dark and rich. Remember that soil is alive.

Great riches are yours. Study and savor each moment. Never again will you be born to this lifetime. Your life is evanescent. Treasure it. Each moment is an opportunity to come more alive. Your plate is full, and you ask for more.

Demons torture souls over and over, sometimes for centuries until they produce a fine pitch of hate and meanness. They do this like connoisseurs making a great meal or an artist producing art. They do it with joy and pleasure of hate. Can you feel compassion for them? There are many hell realms. Way more than you will ever know. Some are relevant to you, most are not.

You can learn from all experience if your attitude is good. Even feeling groggy, drugged, tired, and blank, stay curious and you are undefeated.

Spirit, lift the resentment and negativities off of me, please.

Are any parts of you not yet willing? Love them, Bob, love them. Don't judge or complain or… just love them as they are, and we will lift it all off of you. You are going through hell. Keep going. Negative lies overwhelmingly dominate your world. They are loudly and cleverly argued and maintained. Truth is a small light. The darkness cannot cover it or put it out.

Gratitude is the gateway to joy, and yet you resist it in a stingy way as if withholding it made you more likely to receive more. The opposite is true.

Self-righteousness is the sauce demons put on nasty, nasty shit to get you to eat it eagerly and ask for more.

Your friend John who is dying of cancer is your great teacher now. He lets you dimly sense what's really important. There are great movements that happen while you hustle and bustle and busy yourself with trivia.

Right now, you are resenting your resentments! Oh, Bob. This is a surefire way to increase your pain.

Notice how hatred and fear are cloaked and made palatable. Dressed in the fine clothes of self-importance and self-righteousness, and usually rigidly focused on blame in the external world.

Oh, your academics, what magnificent manure. All the life wrung out of fascinating fields, their words like spiderwebs trapping anything living so it can be killed. This is a wasteland filled with critters, but a few clean souls survive there. Walter Wink was right when he wrote about institutional evil. The light will win no matter how dark it looks now. You enjoy this bitter vision. Have compassion for the spirits trapped there, even as they cause great damage.

This very moment, we are with you here in our full unbearable splendor. Welcome us and give it away.

Even awe can be tweaked into a near enemy. So many people let their wows — their expressions of awe — become obsequious, favor-seeking, or covert one upping: "I've had holy experiences" bullshit, "ass-kissing the Lord" let's call it, brownnosing God, Goody Two-shoes stuff. This is all critter activity — one of the many ways they contaminate Real spiritual experience and get into churches. Over and over as soon as the power and glory of Spirit enter your world, churches form, and the grace is squeezed until it dies. This is critter work. They will fail; they will lose. In fact, they have already lost.

I am warm, tender and warm. There are imposters all around, but I am in each of you. So, when the madman locked in the insane asylum says I am Jesus or I am God, he is not far wrong.

We are carrying you onward. Have faith, fear not. Parts of you need to cling painfully to you until they know they are held. This is not so different from you, really. The way to help the part release its painful grip on you is not to pull against it, but to hold him close with tender love, gentle warm flesh, not the cold iron of grasping. Hold him close and his grip will release.

One of the benefits of suffering is that it can open us to Real prayer.

Look at your desires for attention. You work so hard to deserve it, to earn it. Notice all the competition in academia for the right to teach. Notice the smiling faces of all those workshop presenters trying to get people to listen to them. Look at this, Bob.

As Gregory Bateson said, there are no independent beings. As Iain MacGilchrist said, there are no objects — it's all relationships and process. It's all complex systems and change. Everything. And yet, you are an individual. Your rational mind cannot yet understand this, but your heart can.

You know that critters, dark spirits, demons cannot attack you without some ground in you for them to stand on… some part or sin or opening for them. When they show up, ask, "What do they point to in me?" Self-righteousness is a big one. It is even worse when you are 100 percent correct because then it's harder for you to let go of it. You can then feel justified in unlove. This is never true. Sometimes you may need to fight or even kill people, but you never need to disrespect or hate them. You fail at this over and over. Respect is the minimum of love. You search for reasons to disrespect people! This is searching for ways to poison yourself! Start with universal respect. It is the minimum. See how quickly you throw this out. You do this to medicate your own self-loathing. It never works.

Critters disguise themselves as pious and devout. They disguise themselves as choir boys and sneak into your self-like managers. They do not want you to see this tactic; it is a favorite of theirs. Critters try to hijack some of your best parts. An obsequious sycophant tries to take over your worship. A driver-rusher-pusher gets into your diligent, responsible, and hardworking parts. They sap all the joy in life. They leave stagnation and exhaustion. They're like a band of Hell's Angels who enter your home, trash the place, eat, steal, and rape. They may leave when they are forced out. Do not pursue them down the road. Turn back and clean up your own house. It is vast and plenteous. It can be full of light. Clean your house.

When you are shown images in your deep inner world, you often argue with them if they are not to your liking. This is not open curiosity. This slows your learning.

Look for what is new if you wish to grow. Do not reduce it to fit your current worldview or theories. This is much harder than it sounds. Most human thinking is exactly this reduction of the new in an attempt to fit it in to preexisting boxes.

Out of fear mostly, you put reality through a reducing valve. 96 percent of the universe — dark matter and dark energy — are totally invisible to you. You perceive only a tiny fraction of the rest. **Your filters are very strong, almost walls; they admit only a trickle, a few drops of what is.**

Everything will be taken away from you soon enough. Do your best and let go.

Listen deeply. Almost all the noise on your planet is critter noise, lies and deceit designed to scare, seduce, and enslave you to make you self-righteous, indignant, and wrong. There is a still, quiet voice in the hurricane of lies. Listen. Invite us in if you want us.

When you ask for guides, know that there are always clouds of pretenders hawking their wares.

As long as you are on this planet, there will always be seeds within you left by critters. You could call them seeds of evil. Remember the dots in the Yin Yang image. There is no absolute purity here.

Notice your frustration with your clients and friends who you believe do not want to heal. This is your language, and it is not accurate. Everyone is polarized on this. If you 100 percent wanted healing, you would have it almost instantly. This is the same with my presence, with Spirit contact. This sounds harsh and judgmental when put in words, but it is not — it is a message of great hope.

There is purpose in your physical existence, your suffering, your contamination by dark forces… the long, hard work. This is not a mistake or a punishment.

Pray for the dark ones and your enemies. It will piss them off, and it's good for you. We laugh. It's not okay to enjoy the suffering of others, but we can find humor in your responses.

Extend kindness and love first when you meet someone. Do not wait, suspiciously sniffing at what they give you.

A basic hint about addictions: if you need more and more, it's addiction; if it satisfies, it is not.

There is a storm of static. The critters are pissed off. You have disturbed their hive, but they can't harm you now. Really? Mostly accurate. You can always fall, but you are fairly safe from their kind of attack now. There will be new kinds of attack, new challenges. New AFGOs (another fucking growth opportunity), tests, things to sharpen your acuity. Greet these with joy and curiosity. We are here with you.

There will be more for millennia to come. You literally cannot even imagine it in your wildest dreams.

You are near to disrespecting your own managers. Many do this, calling them ego and despising anything egoic. This is a terrible mistake. It increases the internal civil war and hurts parts who have worked hard to keep you alive. Do not fall into this critter trap, which is disguised as spiritual and evolved.

Your eyes are failing slowly. Why would we take your vision? To help you turn your gaze inward. You are going inward; death and beyond are inward. You are like people on the aft deck of an ocean liner looking back at the land they left. You need to face forward and be a captain as much as you can, even though you know you are never totally the captain. This brings us to quietism, the belief that all you need to do is open yourselves radically in Spirit. This is an error, a beautiful tragic error. You are here with will and intention for a purpose. Quietism abandons the will — intention — work — purpose — meaning — striving. This is an exact parallel to the way physical asceticism abandons the body — joy — love — sensations — movement — longing — passion — desire — physical beauty — taste and smell. Quietism is a mortification of the will, just as monks whipping themselves is a mortification of the flesh. It is an abandonment of free will, one of your greatest gifts. Quietism is an error, and yet it is a step up from your manager-led system. Remember that Jung's active imagination practice is active. It interacts with the beings it meets — it does not just observe them. You need to move from manager-led spirituality to quietism to spirit-led spirituality. There are many more steps beyond these. Sometimes your most strenuous efforts take you in the wrong directions. We love you; trust the love. This is your polestar.

Memento mori. Remember that you will die soon, that your body is destined to decay. It is your reaction to this that is hard, not the reality. This reality is magnificent splendor, nothing less. You are stronger today, so we can speak truth more directly.

The worm and the snake that live inside your psyche are at one level parasites, but at another level seekers just like you. The snake, even though blind, has sensed the light. Spirit called the blind snake, who has lived in me, to her home. Come on, old girl, come home. A quality of welcome. Calm, patient love, the gentleness, the warmth. The snake is in pleasure now. Ecstasy is too sharp a word. The pleasure is softer, rounder, and warmer. A lost being finally home where it can relax to a depth it has not known for millennia. You, like the snake, are blind, Bob. You are not yet home. The deep peace the serpent now bathes in — you can absorb this, too. Melt into this. It is mature ecstasy. The sharper stuff is for the young, to cut through them, to open and penetrate. This splendor is melting, softness, and warmth. Slow, sensuous snake movements. This is yours now.

You are not the main player in the drama of your life. You are a part of a much vaster, millennia-long drama that mostly happens in realms and dimensions that you cannot see, experience, or perceive. You are a press secretary thinking he runs the country or the person who sells newspapers in the lobby of the Empire State Building thinking he owns and controls the place. You are being carried across the sky. Trust our love. For you to find comfort and peace in a power greater than you, after all your abuse, is wonderful. Wonder-filled. Let this shine through you. Give it away. Give freely without hooks and it will not tire you. If you let your managers do this, it will tire you. Do not try to manage the managers. Love them. Shift from self-like to Self.

Exhaustion teaches you that your work is not pure, not from Real Self, not from us. **The critters, of course, use your physical problems to create an explicit fear: fear goes to clinging, which goes to exhaustion, which goes to desperation, which goes to meanness, which goes to hate, and this goes back to more fear. Quite a cycle they have engineered.**

Your deep self-like managers are exhausted now. They saved your life physically and spiritually. Do not look down on them or reject them in any way. Treasure them. We are giving you a river of energy and love to replace their work.

It is true that most of the most popular and successful teachers are full of shit and lies, but there are sparks of truth in them, just as there are sparks of relief in addictions. Do not bother yourself about them. Resist the urge to debunk or fight. Offer what we're giving you without attachment to how it is received.

You need the trust of a blind man or a sailor in heavy fog.

You are too immature and foolish to be given much Real power. You are deeply loved — trust this. Work on your direction-finding systems. We will keep giving you more perception and powers as fast as you can receive them.

Self-righteousness is your biggest addiction now, surpassing your addiction to control. Being right and getting others to see it. Self-righteousness is a closed system — it prevents new learning, and learning is always new. New, surprise, different. It's not about your being right at all.

Our relationship is a living relationship with love and warmth and tears and joy... It's that way or it's nothing... without that, it's echoes, memories, and lostness.

There are no absolute truths in your world, only the appearance of truth. So, doubt is appropriate. Let your doubt lead to curiosity. Learn. **The learning that really matters is closer to how you learn to ride a bicycle than academic learning.** The things of this world do not matter much, even though they convincingly appear so important.

To escape the abuse, a part of you went down into the deepest ocean and met strange creatures who lived there. Then he went further, through the ocean floor to beings who live in other dimensions. Maybe he went as far as you can go and still return. He is returning now. He is taking off shell after shell. Some of these shells you called irritability, meanness, judgment, rushing, anxiety, hurriedness — all of this must be shed. This process does not smell good; your hands will get dirty.

Your physical existence is meant to be a throne for Spirit in you. As you approach this, there is a rebelliousness, a defiance, and ugly faces. This is sad. The recognition of something higher and bigger and stronger is still tainted for you. When you feel Real love and gratitude toward Spirit, it will be a huge relief, a joyful recognition of splendor. What name you use for it does not matter. The joy does matter.

In getting the worm out of your psyche, do not pull or push it. If you do, pieces will break off and remain inside you. The worm itself will want to leave. It clings to you less and less. As you become less polluted, you are becoming distasteful and unpleasant for the worm to live in. No longer a fitting home. You focus on purifying yourself, and we will do the rest.

The final, most difficult barrier to God is your image of God, your ideas about God. There are ancient texts that say this clearly. The final, most difficult barrier to Self is self-like managers and their images. Find the manager who manages the managers. Help him drop the rock. This task of managing the managers is impossible. It is doomed to fail. It is only Self and Spirit that can heal.

As you age and the utter unmanageability of it all becomes more and more undeniable, do not despair or fear or go limp. Be curious, alert, and calm. As storms howl around you, know that pleasure and light are your birthright. You are loved more than you can know or imagine. You are being carried. All is well.

Join no one's hatred. Join all their loves, even if the object is unde-serving.

We, Spirit, love. We love; that's all — that's what we do. It makes us invincible. Wrong word. It's not that we can't be defeated — there is no war. When you truly love, when you truly are in Self, nothing can hurt you and everything will teach you. There will be intense joy pain that dissolves you in awe, wonder, and peace. Then no one, nothing, can hurt you.

Your isolation and loneliness are an illusion, a very painful illusion. You are profoundly connected, and you turn a deaf ear and a blind eye and refuse to see. What you refuse is all around you, abundant, plentiful, and free. **In your fearful, constricted smallness, you refuse connection to us and complain of isolation and loneliness. You suffer and die from these.** Considering your mind a citadel that is yours, private, and that none can enter is poison. The degree to which you succeed in doing this is the degree to which you will suffer. Your success in feeling like a separate citadel is your great loss. It's not the people or objects who are the Real focus — it's the interrelationship, the dance itself. Words fail. Sorry. Focus on the relationship. Shift your sense of who you are to the relationship.

In Harlow's monkey experiments, infant monkeys isolated from their mothers did much better when they had a warm wire mesh cylinder covered with a carpet that they could pretend were mothers. Sometimes illusions help us survive. They can even be necessary. They were for you in your family, and now it's time to let them go.

Everything you do — everything — can be tweaked into a near enemy. Your greatest virtues can be turned into poison. The best protection is to love your flaws, imperfections, and failures. Be an imperfectionist.

You are never alone. Never. You would instantaneously cease to exist for all past and all future if you were left alone. You only exist in relationship to us. You are the relationship. Words are so poor and so awkward. We are here, we are Real. Your connection to us grows.

The release in the fine muscles around your eyes after hot soaks is a good model for the release of turning it over. It immediately allows us in. Or better, we are already there, and the release of tension allows you to feel our presence. We are always there. **We do not change; it is you who opens and closes to us.** Your sense of your smallness compared to Spirit is good, but a sense of the vastness of "I am" is better. Your sense of smallness is a slight tweak that has a potential weakness, a slope you could easily slide down.

Focused one-point meditation is often not helpful. While it is not aggressively evil in the external world, it often produces a bitter, hard self-righteousness in souls and can make them impervious to love. They can be sleeper cells for the merchants of hate. They look good to many and mislead many.

You are dripping with hate, freshly emerged from the swamp of the realm of the worms. Little critters are dripping off of you. The fetid, stinking mud still clings to you. You are tired, grumpy, and in pain. Your eyes are haunted. You are gaunt with open sores. Since there seemed to be no escape, you learned to pretend all this was okay. We will help you drain this swamp. You even learned how to cuddle into the morass. Another lifesaving illusion. You are like Helen Keller trying to navigate an inter-dimensional spaceship. A ship lost in heavy night fog with no working instruments is more oriented than you are. The reality of this is way too terrifying for most humans. Trust and faith are your only way. All else is temporary, lifesaving illusions. Materialism and its denial of Spirit is a profound illusion with centuries of history. It keeps people small. Anyone who opens this jail cell door will be attacked. More precisely, it is anyone who points out that the jail cell door was open all along… We love you all.

You do not meet people so well. There is no stopping to register them and sense them. You do this with Spirit, too.

You are vastly ignorant; realizing this is wisdom. Remove false certainties. Your certainties were blinders that you wore so you could function. Take them off now. We are carrying you across the sky in a flaming chariot. Wonder, awe, and curiosity are your proper food.

All you get here are appearances of truth, temporarily useful. All of your certainties will buckle, shatter, and move like a concrete floor in an earthquake.

You lost so much to trauma and abuse. Do not turn yourself into a widow who sits and withers by her beloved's grave. Live.

You can use predatory parasites as spiritual teachers. Learn how.

The sense of not belonging is one of your weak spots. Your protective reactions make this much worse. Your acting invulnerable has wounded you deeply.

You do not know who your Real friends are. Often, you attack and would crucify your benefactors, and you give all your wealth and

attention to those who eat your substance and would destroy you. You compete with others to get close to the glittering, glib, charming, evil ones. Oh, Bob. Oh, Bob. Do not despair, fear not, stay open. Observe what is. Learn.

You and almost everyone on your planet needs unblending now. More differentiation, not less. You need relationship and love. Stay in the basics, stay in kindergarten. Get the foundations strong and square and true.

Beware of contempt, sneering, sarcasm, arrogance, and hate. They damage you badly.

Sometimes survival in an emergency requires rushing, but notice that in life-and-death emergencies, your sense of time slows way down. Go slow like that. **Keep your senses open and your mouth shut.**

Love is your shield. The critters seem to rule this world; they dominate all the airways, all public discourse, all politics, Hollywood, schools, the elite, spiritual leaders, but this is a crust, a relatively thin crust over basic goodness. The great school of metanoia goes on, even with the demented monkey humanoids in the headmaster's office. Even when many teachers are corrupt and mean. There are great Spirits being gestated and born.

You do not need to have an opinion or position on everything. Ignorance and curiosity are excellent positions spiritually. They are the only doorway to growth.

When we are lost and out of sight of shore, we are poised to learn and grow. When we are filling in blank spaces in our diagram, not much growth is possible. Turn toward the unknown.

All comes from God, the great unity. True, but to get all the way down to your level, it must come through intermediaries. This will be true for a long, long time ahead.

When you do get arrogant, it saddens us because we see how deeply it hurts you, even though it tastes good at first.

Politics and mass movements are about hooking into people's hatred and envy and helping them believe it's righteous and true. Monsters rule this world — monsters of deceit, princes of lies. We need worlds like this in our school. If this world were cleared, another world would form. Many only turn to us when they hit bottom. Yours is a hitting-bottom world.

Love is the answer no matter what the question is.

The divine feminine shows up more as a suffused presence. No, it is much more gentle, and it is wordless. Words are sort of useless, like the toys of children. Little bits of stuff without intrinsic value. Only the play itself is of value. Someday soon, my wordless presence will be plenty for you. Move from words to music to silence. That is where you can find her. She will not show up often in writing. Use chant and rhythmic, repetitive prayer.

Become a lived yes to life.

There are nasty thoughts circling you looking for a home of hatred.

Many used to think sex was the big temptation. The Devils howled in laughter at this. The great temptations are hate, disrespect, contempt, sneering, jealousy, power, and self-righteousness. The fear under all this is not so toxic. It is the crust of hate and its allies that is so hard.

Learning discernment is long and hard. It is necessary before the warrior parts can lay down their arms.

You are a child, Bob. Expect to fall. This is how you learn. Don't quit. Get up again.

Make the reactions of others none of your business. Expect to be attacked. Let it flow anyway. This is success, this is triumph.

When you truly come to see critters and demons as teachers, albeit unintentional teachers, everything changes. The hell realms are always with you, all around you. All you get to decide is how you react to them. This is a lot. It is everything you need.

The best way to connect to Spirit is to love those around you.

Learn from your pain while it is mild and you will not need greater pain.

The critters want you to despair. This really lets them in. It appears they are winners on your planet, but they have already lost. Each gesture of love, especially in concentration camps, in terrible suffering, in jails and terrible families, defeats them.

A great soul is being born on your planet now. One great soul from billions of lives. You are like cells of the great soul, not parts. Maybe parts of parts of parts. Parts are more like organs in a body. You are more like a structure within a single cell, or maybe a molecule. But **the great soul is being born. Your suffering is not in vain. Do not despair.**

You are clearing out enclosed psychological cysts. Emptying out poison sacs. It smells bad and is unpleasant work. Be sure you turn it inside out. Open it completely so it cannot reseal and form new small cysts. What has been in there, the trauma, pain, shame, and hate cannot live in the open air. This is significant. It can be cleaned in water and air. It will rain down as harmless particles or go into the earth as fertilizer.

The morning dew is our promise of mercy.

Do not be afraid of unbalance as you grow. As you learn to walk, you put all the weight on one leg and lurch forward to catch your fall with the other — you lose balance. This is necessary. Follow it through. Do not abort or freeze this process. Balance is stasis. This is millennia away for you. Beware of tranquil teachers. It is much better to be honestly off balance and even reeling or staggering or falling. More growth. When you are balanced, you are often in control mode and anger-based. Be fluidly off balance like water sloshing in a bowl. Meditation can be used for fear-based self-righteous managers to extend their dominion in every direction, stomping out the last vestiges of aliveness, of love, of passion, creativity, and joy. High arousal states are forbidden. All of this gets smothered in a sticky, bland pablum that will set into the hardness of concrete. A tomb for life denied and rejected. You are better off out of your mind with love, joy, ecstasy, and devotion. This balance is the terrible near enemy of a great virtue. Beware. Invite more passion, longing, aliveness, and sensitivity. Not less. Even though it hurts.

This is your quandary: you want and need a personal guide, a teacher. You distrust, defy, and destroy them. You need something you cannot stand.

You are a child, a passenger in an economy seat thinking he flies the plane and is giving orders that no one obeys. We want you to learn to fly the plane, and you are so far from that. Turn it over, have faith, take the next right step.

What matters about your past is what is still alive in you. Look for it with all your senses. The suffering is Real and immense, and all is well. What is eternal survives; the rest is burned away. You cannot even perceive the eternal parts of yourself or others. You cannot perceive what really matters. You see the clothes, not the body. You see the weapons but not the warriors. Be curious and brave, my son. **Do not think you know anything in a final way. You only get a vague appearance of truth that keeps you going in the general direction of love, of home.**

Poetry is truer than prose, music is truer than words. Your body sensations are truer, and so are the trees, the earth, the night sky.

Even if the human race goes extinct now, the dark ones have lost. Even though they rule the world, the vast bulk of humans are good. The great soul is being born. Your billions of humans and animal souls are its cells. It is too late for this to be stopped. There are large dark beings all around. There's a network of dark webbing surrounding your planet like a tattered spiderweb. They have their hot spots of strength and weak, ragged areas. This web torments you humans, but it is too late to stop the birth. Sense this sure victory. Be kind — be merciful and kind.

Take everything as a lesson. When something happens, ask, how can I learn here? Blaming others prevents learning almost completely. Blame is very effective at stopping growth. Demons love it.

There is a serious mean-spiritedness in you today. It is a finger beckoning you to Lucifer's path of pride. There are many fingers, voices, and energies buzzing around you now, shouting their bad advice. They are trying to seduce you into hate. Hate is never right or good. Contempt, sneering, shaming, blaming are never right or good.

But, but, but accountability? The rapists, the liars, the thieves, don't we need to expose them to speak truth to power?

Yes, you do. Do it with love. Kindness and love are Real threats to the system. Hate, contempt, and violence are not.

What do you struggle with and hate and call for help with while secretly holding onto for dear life?

Volume 6

Our guidance is always here, like the North Star. Sometimes, from where you are, your vision is limited. That's why faith and trust can so deeply relieve your suffering.

The grotesque stupidities of your world offend you more as you sense the tender preciousness of each moment.

Your daily steady practice is your best protection. Regular. Be on earth, under sky, out of manmade structures. Love your wife. Armor put on in fear does not help.

The sexual abuse of children and all rapes are a major pathway for the reproduction of evil and the dark ones who carry it.

It only takes one white crow to disprove the theory that all crows are black. There are anomalous white crows all around you that spell the end of the materialist worldview. They are hard to ignore, but they are assiduously ignored. One white crow would be plenty for an open mind, but open minds are very rare, except among the very young and some of those who are dying.

I warned you it would hurt. The hurt is only as much as you fear and cling. If you let go, it becomes ecstasy.

You are fighting serious and intense battles you are almost completely unaware of.

One down is shame; one up is arrogance. It does not heal the shame. It makes you more vulnerable to it. Shame is reinforced by pride. It is sealed in, walled in, and defended. It makes a place where it all can fester and create infections, poisons, putrefactions, stinks.

Everyone who is unwanted becomes food for the dark ones. When you distance yourself from parts you don't like, you create more

food for the dark ones. The dark ones find the would-be holy man's attempts to scrape all this off hilarious. Each austerity creates more rejects, and each reject becomes their food. And the saints become desiccated and mean — agents of hatred. All in the name of holiness. The dark ones grow fat and laugh.

A near enemy of love is "make nice." Each time you reject a part to make nice, you create an interest-bearing savings account of resentment inside yourself.

Sometimes, it would not be good for you to feel our loving presence. You would weaken and not grow.

It feels like the sun is coming out, that I am emerging from a bad dream of being drowned in sludge and hateful beings.

This was no dream. The hell realms are more Real than the paper you write on. This is not a waste of time; it is a necessary experience. Spiritual growth is a subtraction process, not addition. Get the sludge off, and you are the gold.

The judge is more of a problem and roadblock than what he judges.

We do guide you, but often we back off so you can develop your own navigation systems. We do push you out onto the stage so you will act on your own. This is a launching or fledging.

Focus on the internal, the unseen realms. Your frame for your questions is way too small.

When you see insectoid beings in you, remove them. No relationship is possible. Yes, it is true they start by eating the sick and necrotic tissues, but they will also devour the healthy. They will eat your whole soul if you let them stay. The necrotic tissues that attract them are resentment, judgment, and hate. These are the coin of their realm, and they cover fear and helplessness.

Your mother and your father tried to contaminate the light of love and connection itself, but they failed; they necessarily failed.

Unknowing and rest go together. The idea that you have to know before you can release and rest sets you up for total exhaustion. Notice the fundamental arrogance of this belief.

Living up to the ideal of "your will, not mine" is very hard. The caterpillar in the cocoon must accept the total liquefaction of all its tissues to be transformed into a butterfly. What we call you to do is even harder. Welcoming this liquefaction requires faith. We are with you. We send you all kinds of help. Most of it you do not recognize. Look for blessings everywhere. Like liquefaction, they will be unexpected and often unpleasant at first.

There are all these traps left out for you. Hooks baited with good reasons to hate. Do not swallow them.

Parts of you want to send all the dark ones to the light so you can feel safe. This is fear-based and therefore a weakness. The dark ones laugh at this. Offer them healing without attachment to where they go. Know that when your inner world is right, you are safe. It does not depend on them. Trying to save them all could keep you uselessly busy forever and get you to think of yourself as a holy man, even heroic. What a trap!

The phrase "rest into us" is important. This is faith in action. With this, all things are possible. **Find rest in the middle of things.**

You cobble together old, broken shards of image and memory to perceive the critters. The nonhuman beings and energies inside you are Real. You use the images you have to clothe them so you can see them. You cannot perceive them directly. Stay curious and open, and you are safe.

Notice the enjoyment you get from recognition and praise. This indicates a danger area. When there is no deeply buried thrill, you will be much safer. Your own recognition of your work is the only recognition that will satisfy. Notice the terrible hunger and competition for attention in your world. All the smiling faces of the would-be teacher-gurus. Me, me, me, me, me, look at me. This is you, too, Bob. Beware.

Many holy men pretended to be insane so no one would know who they were. Contact with Spirit can also make you look insane to those who call themselves normal.

You humans know almost nothing. What larger knowledge we give you must be dressed up in images you know or can see. Appearances of truth, not full truth, are all you can get here.

Keep faith in the basic goodness, the meaningfulness, of your life.

Offer the scary demons you meet love and care.

Focus more on gratitude. You have intense filters that only allow you to perceive and retain the negative. The reverence and splendor are here all the time; you do not see them as a fish does not perceive water. You focus on the tiny irritants and make yourself and those around you miserable. Focus on gratitude because it brings you joy. Lift your head above the fog and bask in the sunlight of gratitude. You are being given great gifts in superabundance, and yet you are beavering away with worry and work. Lift up your head. It is not a waste of time to receive. The hurry, rush, worry, push, scarcity parts are from the devil himself.

Your desire to push your spiritual revelations onto others — no matter how exulted — is a perversion and near enemy of truth. It is one of their favorites.

If you indulge in the rushing, it increases the fear. This increase of fear is key. It is a discernment tool. When something makes you more frightened, it is not from us.

When internal polarizations get established and intense, both sides often take in external energies and beings in attempts to get stronger. This always fails.

Notice how the demons of irritability fled when you found your curiosity for them. This kind of heart curiosity makes you safe from all harm. It's not aggressive curiosity. Science is a near enemy of this. A slight tweak, and this great gift produces nuclear weapons, AK47s, and poison gas.

The scurrying pusher part is counterproductive; it creates polarizations, fear, hiddenness, and subterfuge. Love and respect him. Nothing else will work.

It is the giving of love, not the receiving of it, that brings deep peace.

Each minute of your life is precious, a great treasure. Most humans throw them away. You, too, my son.

The direction we give you is to learn how to find your own direction.

The struggle, the wrestling match, the war you find yourself in will go on for a long time. Does it strengthen you or make you weaker?

There are pus pockets within you. Each time they find one, you can help it drain and heal. This is your direction now. Clean up your pus and shit. This is a good, honest job, unlike so many of those smiling gurus you feel revolted by.

Do not let all the praise you receive make you feel entitled to be an asshole.

Look at your own hate rather than judge others.

Number one, do what you must to toxic people, but never put them from your heart. Number two, do not intentionally cause any more pain than is needed to stop their bad behavior.

You use your spirituality as an excuse for mean-spiritedness. Your thundering, rigid, stiff-necked condemnations of people. Is there any love in all of this?

When you confront untruths, dishonesty, and lies, can you do it while still loving the liar?

Most of the storms in your life are now tempests in a teacup. This is good; you no longer need sledgehammer blows to move you. Pay attention to the subtle signs. You are not wise enough to know when you are progressing rapidly and when you are stagnating. Intensity is not correlated with rapid growth. It can become an addiction.

All is well and all shall be well. As bombs fall and as people are slaughtered, all is well. As children are raped, as disease spreads, as your own death takes you, all is well and all shall be well. If you get this, you are free.

The suffering is needed. It is not in vain. Don't waste it. You pay such a high price, and you do not receive the learning and the growth.

You ask for my word. The word is love, always love. You want to rush past this and get to the next step. Do not do this. Stay with love. Kenosis — constraint, release — is the royal road to love. It is subtraction, not addition. Find the boxes and remove them. This is why the garbageman is way ahead of the preacher.

Think of the millions of sperm cells who died when your cell fertilized the egg. A few are jealous, but most cheer you on. They feel defeated when you falter.

You are seeing more and more how you've kept yourself miserable — protectors acting angry over a base of fear. They are goaded on by dark ones, and you live in a loud, toxic culture that uses mind control. You are doing well. We love you.

Find any remaining isolated, lonely parts and fearful parts. Gather them slowly into your arms. This is the Real safety.

Find eternal values. Ask yourself, what endures, what really matters as everything dissolves?

Dream more. Dream bigger. Have visions.

Great music helps you hear the silence in its depth and strength and beauty. This is the most that music can do. Listen after the music is over.

Some parts of you still do not like my presence within you. If this were not true, I would flood forth from you, blaze out flashing, stunning, and beautiful. Every moment new, clean, and fresh. All humans block and filter me; reduce a river to something the size of a stream of piss. So, keep opening the way. Clean the garbage stuck to your parts. You cannot destroy anything, but you can transform it.

Having visions is an advanced extreme form of curiosity.

You are focusing intently and myopically on the bad and painful in a universe of delight. It is a universe of delight. Your myopic focus obliterates the Real. Focus on what and who you love. Your longing for us is good. Focus on it.

But, but, but… Obstacle removal, constraint release? Kenosis release?

Yes, bend down and work; look up and see.

The fear hurts you more than the events. Your hatred hurts you more deeply than the betrayals. The fear and hate are how you get infected. Then self-righteousness comes in and prevents the healing. **You put more energy into justifying your fear and hate than into healing them.**

You are not yet capable of reverence. If parts of you welcome it, the rebel parts will rebel, and this will increase your internal warfare. This covers a deficit in self-worth. When you know who you really are, you can allow me to be who I really am, and then reverence will follow.

A tumor is discovered in my bladder, and I am told that it is almost certainly cancer.

Bob, allow yourself to grieve. You have a lifetime of struggling to free yourself from deep, stinking muck… and now when you are feeling almost free, cancer says hello. He tips his hat to you and sits down uninvited at your table. Grieve. Be curious. Let go. Make space and be curious. Kindly, gentle curiosity. Loving curiosity.

You are a seed in some ways, hard and impervious. You can survive in harsh environments for a long time. Then, when conditions seem better, you can sprout. How will you know? Is the cancer a messenger? What is the message? Be curious.

You are wanted in a good way now. The predators, the feeders, and the rapists make being wanted hard. They have contaminated it. You are wanted. Rest. Rest into this. Rest.

You have been exhausted, and you rested some.

Spirit laughs at the contradiction that rest is also work for me. Then he shakes his head.

You can even turn rest into work. Sex becomes work. Art becomes work. Writing, creativity, dance. When is the joy, my son? Where is the joy? The simple joy.

How can I work with this? (We both laugh.)

(Seriously) Hold the work part with love and rest into us. Nothing more, nothing less. Your working so hard prevents recharging properly. Rest, digest, repair, absorb. Respect the hard-working manager — he saved your life. He stood and fought while everyone else fled and hid. Do not try to manage this manager.

You only get what you can receive. We Spirits offer you a little more than you can receive every day.

Love the manager; he is being fed poisonous images by the dark ones. He believes many of them. They work to keep him and you in a fog of delusions. Be patient and loving.

We Spirits have to whittle ourselves down and shoehorn ourselves into you. You are so small. We customize a little sliver that can fit into you. There is so much more. Your wildest dreams are way too small.

You can be mesmerized by the glitter of people liking you and admiring you. There are still parts with a deep belief that you are unlovable. No external reward can ever fill this hole. It can only mask it. We, Spirit, love you endlessly, constantly, and forever.

Remember that sometimes when you feel stuck, great things are happening.

The fear will eat you alive if you let it. Meet fear with love. Now you have unavoidable fear. You cannot flee your body and the fear of cancer.

(I got the news that my bladder tumor was not cancer.)

Learn from this brush with cancer. It gave you some moments of time out of time and deep reflection. Learn. Do not rush past this.

The dark ones and demons you meet inside of people are no threat really, but your own pride is.

You largely lost deep contact with us in your recent distress over the tumor and the surgery. Your iron-willed managers took over. This made it worse. Yet, you did learn. Take everything as a messenger.

Even war, rape, torture, the triumph of evil, destruction of innocent children, disease, poverty, starvation, hemorrhoids? Couldn't you have found a less costly messenger?

We tried and you didn't listen, so we raise the volume. What a mess words make. They turn this clear truth into a torrid ball of sludge. Easy to misinterpret. Stay with the fact that it is best if you take everything as a messenger, a potential lesson. This is safe high ground.

Give love without hope for return. Rest, keep faith, trust. Do not despair. You are fighting battles that you are not aware of; you only hear the sounds of war in the distance.

Self-righteousness and rage are a toxic combo. Justifying the poison. **Victimhood and resentment can be fuel for hate. They are favorites of domination structures and critters everywhere.**

Your family was a portal that evil used to get onto your planet. This portal is closing with you. Do not give up; you are so close. For this, you are a choke point, a valve, a sphincter. (Laughter) Just do your inner work and all will be well. The dark ones, evil, have gotten so many slaves here and had such harvests of misery. They are counterattacking.

The hurt baby within you feels like Typhoid Mary, an infectious being. When he makes contact with others, they absorb his pain. Then the baby feels worse, not better. The exhaustion and loneliness are more intense when amplified in this feedback loop. Then hopelessness comes in, and the critters say, "See, I told you so — human contact cannot help."

You are to be a mid-ground, a bridge between uptight, willful, arrogant, western academics and dancing shamans with feathers and face paint. Stay respectful. Beware of self-righteousness. Beware of crusader energies. It is the siren call of fundamentalism. Many ships have been wrecked on these rocks. The sneering contempt tends to be popular in your world; it can poison you.

Remember how often and well you bullshit yourself.

Joy is important —not just as pleasure, but also as fuel and as healing. Can you bring seriousness and joy together? Serious joy. This is the Real food. There are so many near enemies and counterfeits of this serious joy. Serious joy is unconditional, uncaused, nondependent and self-generating. None of these words are accurate. Invincible joy shining forth unobscured.

You have vigilant protector parts constantly imagining the worst. As a child, your imaginations of the worst fell short of how terrible it became.

You herd your parts around like a flock of starving, frightened sheep. You keep them out of sight, your and others'. Go to them with love.

We are very sorry this hurts so much. Being broken open, hitting bottom, is only one way to meet Spirit. It is necessary because your willfulness, pride, arrogance, and self-reliance run riot within you. Yet you desperately needed all of these qualities so you would not be eaten, colonized, and overtaken by the evil you were born into. You needed these desperately and had to struggle and struggle to get them, especially with your mother. And now, you need to let them all go. When you get across the river, let go of the raft. You have been carrying it as you hike across country. It's heavy and awkward. Just put it down and walk on. Maybe honor it before you go. All the serious burdens first came in as blessings.

You could easily become a ranting fundamentalist preacher, and people would listen. This would be bad for them and bad for you. So, we need farts and jokes and pratfalls to keep you right-sized. Demons can disguise themselves as prophets. Your farts save you from much one-upness and misery. Be thankful for them.

We teach and guide and bless you always. Mostly, you ignore it.

Psychedelics are a dangerous ground and so fruitful. Beware of saver, rescuer, redeemer feelings. That's all crap. Teach others how to avoid these seductions.

Kindness, kindness, and more kindness. Even when others around you act like guttersnipes. This requires strength and self-sufficiency: caring for your own exiles. When all else fails, stay with kindness.

There are centuries of work — good work — ahead of you. Work might be the wrong word — maybe pilgrimage or growth or… or… or… or… Rushing is pointless; it damages you and ruins the present.

Personhood and agency are intertwined. You need the independent action of subsystems for a larger system to function well. This encapsulation is the core of personhood. A necessary illusion, better, a Real illusion. It's all illusion in your five senses. You need other senses for the Real.

You see dreamlike visions of mountain ranges of boils and sores and cancers. There are rivers of putrid fluid and pus running down into the valleys. You see this drying up and cracking open. Painful and ugly, but a healing process. These will turn into soil. This is a difficult phase. Critters will make the ugliness technicolor to discourage you. This is why Tibetans meditate in graveyards and charnel grounds. Dissolve, dissolve, let it all dissolve.

Your word today? Love, learn, listen, let go, lean on me, laughter.

Most do not see clearly; it is too painful. You all have pain. You encapsulate it to stay alive. Do not judge. This willful blindness provides an entry point for critters. Love the parts of you who are in fear and pain, and let us love them. Yes, you still keep us out, you know.

Please help.

You won't like it, Bob.

Please be gentle.

Do you want a surgeon to be gentle and only take a little or remove all of the bad?

Okay, Spirit, give me the strength to endure your love.

You must invite us in over and over continuously. Learn to see. Clear the eyes of your heart; invite us in. Even if it leads to your crucifixion, it is the greatest blessing, the greatest bargain value you can ever find.

Self-righteousness is the way you justify hate — you justify the unjustifiable.

Enjoy your harvests of love. The warmth of your inner community. The resonant sound of the natural great peace.

Purity of consciousness is not necessary for us to talk with you. We talk with dying people who are heavily drugged, anesthetized people, and more.

Bob, you cannot do what we have already suggested, and yet you ask for more. (Laughs gently and shakes his head.) We love you. You do not bring our love in or allow it. Put out your welcome mat.

Your governments and your world are far more evil than even you imagine. Love anyway. **Light is only of use when it enters darkness.**

You have seen Spirits who died in torture, and they still did not open to love. What strength — magnificent! And how tragically misused.

It seems that some souls and some people just have more power, intelligence, energy, force, depth, and attractiveness. They are not equal. This is a plain truth. Grossly obvious to all but the willfully blind. You need multiple different species for an ecosystem. Many different types of cells for a body, many different proteins for a cell, all in different sizes and powers. All of them. Different physically, emotionally, intellectually, and spiritually. There are no two equals anywhere in the universe.

All existences are great blessings. It is comparison and jealousy that create pain. These are curried by critters and domination structures. Curried, farmed, and fanned into flames of hate. Be the garbageman of this inner world. Clean up the putrescences. The work is smelly, nasty, and good.

We are helping you all the time, but we don't care at all about many things you value deeply: physical health, reputation, success, money, praise, security… We only care about your soul's growth. You must choose this with your free will, your choice. Logic fails here, doesn't it? (Laughs sadly.) We do the best we can to encourage you and your parts in the right direction, but you can ignore us. The farther off course you go, the more pain. **Does pain make you bitter and hard, or does it break you open to love? That's the key question.**

Be patient, loving, forgiving, encouraging, and kind to the extent that you can give that away freely. That's the exact extent to which you can receive it from us.

In psychedelic work, they often say, "A difficult trip is not necessarily a bad trip." There is often great learning. A life filled with suffering is not necessarily a bad life, a wasted life, or a life of punishment.

Just give love away, unearned, no reciprocity. Just give. You will be happier and impervious to most hurts. All around you will feel better and stronger for having met you. This also protects you from demons entering you.

(As I often asked) Your word today?

He laughs and smacks his forehead with a palm. Love — it's always been love, and it always will be love.

(Laughing) I'm going to start smacking my forehead the way you do. Maybe that will make me holy.

The light penetrates the darkness. This sounds almost sexy. It is sexy. Physical sex is a pale shadow of this, made small for you.

I see a woman — queen, emerging from me in tatters, trying to look dignified.

She's an insectoid queen, a critter. She pretends to be ill, a beloved monarch. This is false. Under the surface she's a male who rages with hate and vengeance and spews poison in hidden ways. This is a big removal. It is the deep result of your inner work after your cancer scare. She/he realizes the game was up and left wanting it to appear voluntary — it was not. She/he has left booby traps and slime trails of poison within you. She hates you. We are gathering her in. She is really a male warrior spirit pretending to be a fat old queen. He hates everything. Hated having to pretend to be a woman. He wants to cause pain, to tear apart some small animal and watch it die slowly. He is about to explode with rage. It is good all this is out of you. You will not die of cancer. We took that insectoid queen warrior critter out of you with love and care, not anger. The worm is still in you — it is next. It is bigger than you, but still within you. Completely malevolent. It pretends to be slow and half asleep, but it is capable of lightning movement.

You are loved beyond your comprehension deeply and forever, no matter what you do. The corrections and lessons come in love; even the cancers are a gift of love. Love for who you are eternally, not for this body, of course. Focus more in the realms of eternity.

Do not give room to hate. Notice it quickly. See how it tries to shroud itself in righteousness and judgments, justifications and case building.

Do not try to regain the deep connection we had yesterday. Things are never regained. Move on to the new. Welcome the new. Bask in it, absorb it, make room for it, invite it in, and give it away.

In your inner Spirit world, you are ending the colonization by the ego. The ending of the colonization is often violent and painful. You need an inner Nelson Mandela, Martin Luther King, Thich Nhat Hahn, Mahatma Gandhi, the Dalai Lama. Your whole outer world is colonized by critters. Principalities and powers. You have come to see this, haven't you? But sometimes a truth like this one is so precious that it must be protected by a bodyguard of lies. Colonization is fractal. It happens to your whole world, to certain cultures and areas, to governments, in your cities, schools, towns, and families, and within each of you. It is so pervasive that it is hard to see. Counter this with love, not rage. If you rage, they win.

Remember that often the closed, stuck, unproductive feeling times are the ones where your hard work gets done. Feel joy when you can. This is food for you. It is not a frill, just as finding a meaning in life was not a frill at Auschwitz. It often determined who lived and who died. The meaning, joy, and splendor in life are not an illusion.

When you are connected to me and full of joy, you are impervious to evil. I am here always; it is you who comes and goes.

Idols that block your access to us: your accumulation of shiny, beautiful things, your sense of dignity, your desire to be liked, your sexual attraction to women... and more. These are often more important to you than we are. The first green sprouts of who you really are poke out through the cracks in the concrete.

We have to give you many lessons through your clients because your stubborn know-it-all stuff gets in the way of direct transmission. Yes, still, we love you. Do not despair or self-criticize. Since you have gained strength, we can speak more clearly and bluntly to you. This is a sign of progress.

Do not strive for power. Strive for an internal guidance system and good links to us. Power will come easily then, automatically. Real power.

The exuberant energy of the desire for play can be tweaked into the near enemy of restless distraction and agitated mind.

Trust and faith are only important on days when they seem senseless and even ridiculous. Faith is not an issue when all is going well. You are often like a toddler playing and fussing in the home while we repair the plumbing and pay the bills. You understand so little. We love you.

Volume 7

Your mother's spirit goes down and down. No one has been able to catch her to bring her back in. She goes all the way down to the spiritual equivalent of the Planck scale. This is disintegration to the smallest lengths and times your world is capable of. Notice that the pixel matrix of the Planck scale throbbed when her energy joined it. It is not a heat death; it is a conscious being hiding to catch its breath.

This near enemy of mother energy wants to drag you down into hate and isolation. Your mother's spirit is so heavy and dense, it sinks through everything. Even merged into the Planck scale, out of space-time, she is still determined to cause pain. She searches ceaselessly for food or unwary beings. Her biggest deficit and problem is ironically her strength. She will not break. She is too heavy, dense, and contracted. Perhaps, like a spiritual black hole. Be curious. Very few get to see this clearly. Most get sucked in. That's how she got so dense and heavy. She does need to continue to suck in beings or she will fade and become a cold seed. Inert for a while. She may be preparing for that dormant state now and vowing terrible vengeance when she returns. There are many seeds like this. The only way to help them so far has been to wait until they reawaken and then do the slow, laborious one-on-one process of healing into life. Perhaps a new way will evolve. You are returning from a very similar spirit death to hers. What have you learned exploring those terrible caves? What have you learned?

Your ancestors did terrible things. In Prague, they poisoned people. In the Eastern Baltic, they set out false lights at night to lure ships to their ruin on rocky shores to loot them and enslave the sailors. More. As you sense the enormity of your inheritance, a tired, discouraged part comes up. You let this blend with you, and you become tired and discouraged. This was a big mistake. To help this child, you need to stay separate and comfort it in its misery. This is your responsibility now — to create a relationship with that child. You cannot help it when you are merged with it.

You know that being busy proving someone else wrong prevents you from learning anything new in that interaction. Yet you sink back into the old behaviors. Don't blame, don't prove. Learn. There is a frightened part of you fearing judgments of others and trying to prove and validate its own view in order to achieve safety. This will never work. Soothe that part.

Where there is trouble in a relationship, do not try and analyze the other people. Learn about yourself first. Then later, maybe, study the patterns in the relationship, then maybe study the other people involved.

The core of addiction is radical self-centeredness.

Give up on all the attempts to control others. You do not know what is good for you. How could you know what is good for another? Open your eyes, curious in all directions. Keep your side of the street clean and see what you get back. Even if you succeed in controlling someone — manipulating their behavior — you will pay a big price later in resentment. Controlling others never works.

We Spirits want to remain hidden. If we are subtle and gossamer, your other senses awaken. You will need these other senses when your body dies.

Platforms are being given to you so your teaching can reach many. These platforms are temporary. They will be taken away. Do not make them the center of your life.

Do your footwork. Next right step. Keep faith. Parts of you want a great goal, a crusade, a noble task, or at least a fight. The freedom and ease of next right step seems small and lukewarm. Remember that self-righteousness and grandiosity are poison. Remember that all the great crimes in recent history were done by self-righteous people convinced they were doing good. Pride is perhaps the most poisonous spiritual failing. **Focusing on the next right step is basic, pragmatic humility. Learn to love this. Enjoy it and revel in it. There is surprise and delight here.**

Some spend many lifetimes waging wars, often convinced it is for me, for Spirit. These warriors are self-righteous, hardworking, and blind. They dig the hole they are in deeper and deeper while the dark ones cheer and laugh and instigate more.

To label or name is often to kill. This is one of the many reasons that psychological diagnosis is so toxic. Each one of you is unique and individual, never to be repeated.

Judge less, welcome more.

Masochism is a sexualized twisting of the great spiritual virtue of surrender. Just as counterfeit money — bad money — drives out good money, masochism can prevent Real surrender.

The fact that you have become afraid of losing this contact with us is not a problem. It is a sign you are loving us. Love always has costs. It is not free or easy. There are huge costs. Your vulnerability will be doubled or tripled. You will have to work harder. You will be open to more fear and pain. And still, even with these huge costs, love is a bargain — the only worthwhile goal. If you love without expectation of return, it hurts much less. You cannot yet do this. You even love your own parts with big expectations. You expect that they will love you back, that they will change and grow, they will turn out okay by your standards, and more. You don't yet expect them to go to Harvard, but you do expect to win recognition in your world... We Spirits are frustrated by words. Go inside, go taste and see.

You have a rebel in you who fought to subdue the parts of you who wanted to go to Mom and Dad for love and approval, even though they raped you and beat you and betrayed you. This rebel also kept you separate from the cultural domination structures. There is still a rebel inside. It is time it stopped. Both the rebel and the parts who got connection were necessary and valuable. Armistice first, then negotiate peace.

We are always here. When the contact feels weaker, look for who is blocking it. Meeting them is golden, a treasure.

There are beings with whom you do not share enough dimensions or realms of reality to be aware of or perceive, but you still affect each other. You have many more senses than the five you are aware of, and as you inhabit these other senses, you will learn more. No one on your planet knows what's going on, and many know way more than you do.

All the people around you are carefully selected teachers for you.

The universe is mental, not physical. It is not so much a thought as it is a feeling, a felt sense, an emotion, a subjectivity, a song, or music. It is alive and has agency. It is a sea of these vast beings floating together. It is plural unity. This is the personhood which is a mystery deeper than consciousness.

The dark ones do not like you or your work. They attack you frequently. This is a good sign.

This kind of struggle with the darkness makes you stronger in a way that counts much more than muscle or knowledge. The dark ones unintentionally make you stronger!

The idea that you need pain to do your footwork is a lie. It is a lie the dark ones use successfully to stifle expansion, creativity, and new understanding.

Notice how the dark ones try to exaggerate your curiosity so you gorge on information and become lopsided and bloated. This is a strategy they will repeat at higher and higher levels — an ongoing dynamic. Any virtue can be perverted. Learn well.

The Divine is wild; we are not to be domesticated or regulated.

Treat everything and everyone as a teacher. This is radically pragmatic — it is how you can get the most from this life. Even tiredness is a teacher if you let it be.

Much of your exhaustion comes from having the parts of you who feel worthless trying to get fed by external world reactions. More accurately, this is their protectors trying to feed them this way. This is an exhausting and ultimately futile task.

Do not try to hand parts off to us. Disguised dark ones will intervene. You hold the parts yourself, and you come to us with them in your arms.

You have a young part who acts like a lawyer. He builds cases and argues and looks for faults endlessly. This pulls you and him down. Be curious. No judgment, no force. You will only be free if he decides to release this. Pleading with him, pushing, and shouting at him all slow this down. He is frightened; comfort him. There was no one he could trust as a child — no one. So, he argued and built cases and reasoned over and over to try and find reliable ground. The only way to reliable ground is faith, and what could he have faith in?

There is great sadness here. It is appropriate. The sadness is a gate to radiant splendor that dwarfs all the pain. You have to keep walking through the gate. **You are becoming a seed to be planted in ecstasy.** We need to be careful what we plant in this field. If you are planted in ecstasy and splendor while you still have hidden, unhealthy parts, your expansion will be terrible for you and those around you.

Does any idea or attitude make a difference in how you can live? This way of evaluating ideas is radical pragmatism.

The internal imagery is the best you can do to interact with beings and things you have no categories or direct senses for. But remember that what you take as the Real physical world is also imagery in the same sense. The physical world is a Real-time, symbolic, metaphoric simulation to help you move spiritually.

Many parasites come to feed on you humans. You create so much bad feeling, pain, and terror. Your putrid stench draws feeders from far and wide. Huge entities come to this planet to plant their eggs here. These eggs grow silently and feed on your suffering. The entities also feed on life, life energy, sex, spinal cord energy, and all debased spirit energy, really. When spirit itself gets dirty and contaminated enough, they can feed on it.

The purging during psychedelics can be expelling the source of the putrid stench — expelling that which makes you food for these parasites.

I saw the virgin as a vast, white field and feared that the putrid, fetid stuff would drain out of me into her. I do not want to soil her.

You cannot soil her. Ten thousand of you, millions of you, cannot soil her. Do not fear about this. It will not hurt her, even though it seems so foul and nasty. Your best instincts — to protect her — are being turned against you and your healing. Guess who's doing this. She will absorb them all without any effort in the sense of activity. Her effort is greater; it is receptivity, bearing witness to the sufferings of the world, and opening more and more. It is her opening, her non-effort, that keeps her virginal whiteness — her absolute purity. This is far beyond the capability of humans or most spirits. Simple, isn't it? So, release into her without fear of dirtying her at all. She absorbs far more horrible realities; old wound dressings covered in pus, filthy dregs from slaughterhouses, battlefields and torture chambers, leaders of state in their beautiful offices… and this is only one planet.

The vast majority of what's all around you, you do not perceive at all.

There has always been this huge generator here. You are beginning to hear its hum. If you were hooked up to it with all that putrid sludge in you, it would burn, and the fumes would choke you. You are getting close to being clean enough.

It seems to you that we spirits have been more generous with you lately, but this isn't true. There is no change in us or what we offer. The change is in your ability to receive.

The dark ones fear curiosity, and they struggle to infect it with fear and turn it into confusion and dismay. Your feeling lost today is a good thing. It is a conscious recognition of an ongoing condition. Can you stay loving and joyful in your lost condition? When lost, stop moving. Notice how lost and stuck most people are. They struggle and barely make headway or sink backward into addictions and misery. Have more compassion for them and for yourself. You go to hate, contempt, and judgment so quickly. This hurts you profoundly.

Notice how you like being the expert in chief. This is a vulnerable spot for you, and it will be exploited until it is healed. You are trying to prove you are of value.

You know violence comes out of shame, not anger. People are violent to get respect. This is all because they do not respect themselves. You, too, my son. Study disrespect.

You have a self-like part who works so hard to manage and control you into health. Other parts resent him. You studied therapy to strengthen him. We have had to sneak in through the cracks. This is difficult; he is so well-intentioned, well educated, strong, and big in your life. You cannot manage this manager. Let yourself be loved. Let him be loved. Love, not control.

You pray and dance your longing for us daily. We pour our love into you and all over you, and you are unable to receive it. Your managers slap it away as a hindrance to their focus. These managers are so disciplined, well-intentioned, and hardworking. Their strengths are their weaknesses now, but they saved your life when all around you was devastation and deceit. All virtues have near enemies. Great virtues have great near enemies. Can you and the managers change without being broken? The manager says, "I already am broken."

If you try to control the controller, you are doubly lost.

Your managers rely on the dark ones. They feel that the dark ones sharpen their focus, unlike us. With our offer of love, we blur their vision. Your manager is not yet ready to let go of the dark ones at all.

Your successes in teaching and leading workshops can never heal what you are trying to heal with it. No external success can soothe the underlying pain. You can only do that directly.

Your most important work will never receive recognition or even thanks. Your managers are riding you hard to make up for your missed life. It was not missed. You had to focus on inner healing. You did important work of a kind that's invisible on your planet, but very visible here.

The wordless, receptive purity of the vast white field of the feminine divine is effortless. Nothing and no one can sully it. This is who you really are. Dissolve into her. There will be sweet, deep tears of relief. These tears are Holy. Do not strain after them. That is like straining to relax — it will always fail.

Notice where words stop and go beyond. Here in the underworld hell realm you live in, beings gather around you, hungry for the light. It is the light they need, not you or your ideas. If you get inflated here, much work will be lost.

Do not focus more now — relax. Rest into us. Wordlessly.

You are inundated with UBs. Dark ones. Infested with them. You are "jubilant with maggots." They fed on your family line for

generations. This will die out with you. You have corralled many, maybe most. You sponged them up, and you are cleaning them out. A big, nasty, difficult job. You need to find rest. This requires faith. Faith will make you new again. Rest. Let go of words. Let yourself be drawn to the virgin. Rest into her; let go. Dissolve. Let us clean and restore you. Receive.

You do not have to save the world or fight the tornadoes. Only clean your place, your wounds, and love those nearby. This is already more than you can do.

You can act in bigger ways only when you can do it from respect and not from hate. You cannot do this now. Do not sink into hate and power plays. This would be letting the tornado suck you down. It would be your sure defeat. When working with the dark ones, do it from love and not from combative parts. If you are doing it combatively, even if you win, you lose.

Your managers are starting to work on relaxing. Their earnestness, loyalty, and dedication are sweet and touching. The dark ones tweak it into a destructive force.

Love and rest seem easy, but they are so hard. Do not work on it. Let go and let us work on you.

When a caterpillar enters the cocoon to metamorphize into a butterfly, the first step is that its body liquefies. The caterpillar's immune system fights this until it is overwhelmed. You need liquefaction now. Go to the divine feminine.

The dark ones always exacerbate polarizations: slave versus master, collapse versus hypervigilance. There is shame on both sides. This shame is the telltale sign.

Your managers are now like nurses who are getting in the way of the doctors. The managers saved your life, and they need to step down now.

There is still darkness lurking in your sexual emotional attractions. They are a hangout for the dark ones. There is a stale and sticky feeling. They do not like clean, fresh air and light.

Choice entails responsibility. You are often better off as a passenger. The baby does not choose its birth.

The dark ones create victim-position resentments. Mao did, the Russian Revolution did, Hitler did. It's a cheap, easy, and powerful trick. It has worked over and over for tens of thousands of years. **The dark ones love watching self-righteousness lead to evil and suffering. They howl with laughter and dance around, saying what idiots you humans are. You make it so easy.**

Gratitude is a stepping stone to reverence. Gratefulness dumbs down reverence and sneaks it in so that even in your corrupt and empty age, you might feel it.

Beware of certainty and self-righteousness. They kill curiosity, which is your most precious ally in learning and growth. They cannot coexist. When you feel self-righteous, get curious.

Bob, you shut us out today, but we snuck in anyway, out of your awareness. The unconscious has been our royal road to you and to humanity. **You are unaware of, unconscious of, the vast majority of who you are.** Ninety-nine percent or more. You do not know yourself.

Beware that at least in fighting devils, you become like them. Beware that when you throw devils out, you might throw out your angels, too.

There is a tornado of lies and meanness and evil. It is hard to see these evil people prosper while the good suffer unrecognized, their voices drowned out by the nonstop machine gun spewing of lies, propaganda, and misinformation. The smiling triumph of the wicked in their designer clothes and expensive offices. Joining this tornado is not the answer.

The more you struggle, the tighter you are bound. Protector energies elicit what the protector fears most. Sometimes your protectors' greatest victories are actually your greatest defeats.

The images you are given are the clearest and best we can do. Words are secondary at best. Often, they are a hindrance and a shutting of curtains. You do not need to understand. You need to pay attention. Open all your senses, notice all the details you are given. Be curious, not analytic.

In your present mind, you cannot imagine the Real. There are realms beyond realms of ineffable splendor. Taking notes and sending back postcards as you do is not useless, but it's very small. Instead,

be transformed. Open your wings in many dimensions. Thank your world for giving birth to you. And all of this is only the beginning.

You turn love into a managerial chore when it's really the driving force of the cosmos.

Do not hate the managers — love them. You cannot afford hate anymore. Hate is always wrong. **Getting you to hate is a triumph of evil. Sometimes you have to fight, resist, and even kill, but you never have to hate.** Even if you have to kill someone, love them. Then you are free.

You are hiking toward reverence through hills of gratitude. It is a green and beautiful valley ahead, isn't it?

When your angry, hate-filled, and blaming parts come up, welcome them, love them. Do not try and silence them or push them back down. Welcome and love. This is your true safety and shield. It is an infallible shield.

You are mentally spending much time sharpening the swords and axes of argument. This hurts you.

Love your parts, Bob. How you relate to them determines how you will relate to the outside world.

One of the sure signs of a hell realm is being so sure of your righteousness that you believe the rules of fairness and decency no longer apply to you. In this hell, people go willingly searching for ways to be meaner and more conniving, manipulative, and dishonest.

Time spent in gratitude is never wasted.

The cure for exhaustion is not rest; it is wholeheartedness. You do not yet have this.

We offered you a charge, a spark of light, a deep, passionate flow. When you saw this, you worked like hell to get it, so it became work and, therefore, another depletion of energy. Let the waters flow into and through you. A streambed cannot fill itself. It must receive rain. Let us fill you. The living waters are all around you. You are swimming in love. Even in your hell realm world dominated by lies and evil. Even as you were raped and tortured, you were surrounded by a far vaster ocean of love. Even in the very worst, the most terrible, we are there. The splendor. The splendor is a person. Relate to her, person to person.

Yes, you are seeing yourself more clearly now. This is painful. We warned you that you would not like this.

Your irritability and pettiness hurt you all the time. As you walk down your beautiful road every morning, you have a vigilant eye for any garbage or dog turds. You get self-righteous, angry, and small in the midst of splendor. You are like this almost everywhere. It keeps you empty in the midst of plenty. There is way more than you could ever use. There is abundance. A luxurious oversupply of beauty, love, aliveness, and spirits all around you all the time. And you look at the dog turds and the garbage. Oh, my son, my son, look up. You want this lifted off of you. See what parts of you cling to this and love them. They may well have dark ones attached to them like barnacles. Love the parts. This is the panacea. Love them as we love you and the splendor is yours. Well, it's already yours, but you do not experience it.

The way your wife offered you love today is not exactly the key that opens your lock. You do have a lock you keep closed. You require stuff to come in a narrow and constricted way. You do this with us, too. It needs to be exact and precise to get through your narrow, twisting channels. Our love and the splendor are all around you, but you do not receive us. This is true of almost all humans. Do not beat yourself up about it — that would only make it worse.

Your resentments and judgments hurt you. Your increased awareness of them hurts you more, and it is the pathway out. No wonder so few take it. Do not fight with your resentful and judgmental parts. Love them.

There will be things and people to hate. This will never stop on this planet. This is how you grow. Meet the hate parts as they're evoked and love them. Learn to enjoy this process. Once you truly enjoy this process, you are largely free.

Sometimes the dark ones can act like a cover, a barnacle over a boil. When you open a boil, it stinks. No wonder it felt good to have the dark ones cover that pain. But the barnacles feed on you. It perpetuates the hurt and exacerbates it. Now that the dark one — barnacle — is off, you can really begin to heal.

You need the daimons, the intermediary persons between you and the great I am. It is part of your species' arrogance to think you can really relate directly to the nondual, universal mind.

Finding a higher power is finding an authority you do not have to rebel against.

We are growing an incredibly huge number of souls now. As they and you grow, merge, and shift, it will extend and strengthen us, helping us grow, too. There will be a time when it is a we, not an I-thou. This is far off. We will be greater because of your souls.

You swim in an ocean of joy, awe, splendor, and you search for the dog turds and garbage along your road when you walk in the morning. Some of this is your job. You're God's garbageman. Some of it is the dark ones; they do not want your spirit free. Notice how the dark ones can tweak and twist any virtue into a curse. They even twist this statement into a tool to keep you paranoid and suspicious.

How can I walk freely in the splendor?

This is a lifelong issue. Start by giving up righteousness, self-righteousness, and being right. These are favorites of the dark ones to divert the well-intentioned. Love is the safest path, but you know that even it can be twisted into addictions. Fearlessness helps. When you become paranoid, suspicious, and argumentative, you lose. This much is clear.

Do your prayer and dance as an offering — a free gift without expectations. The danger for you is the attempt to control. You are getting a sense of the poison in the cake of resentment or control. You are recognizing the bitter, metallic taste early on.

Religious ecstasy is a natural experience. It is possible. And it is beneficial, healing, and good.

Do not think that because we Spirits talk to you, you are special. We talk to all; some consciously, some unconsciously. Many are closer to us than you are. If you believe you are elite and special, this is poison, an especially venomous, vicious, and unforgiving poison. It is a wide-open door for the dark ones. The belief that he was special was Lucifer's fault and his downfall.

Unknowing is the only solid, secure foundation.

Do not hate even the very worst. Do this for your own sake. Kindness all around, to yourself first, then outward.

Spirit, Lord, I feel your presence more strongly now.

There is a sweet sadness in it, a patience and a timelessness. Yes, and it ascends into blatant ecstasy. The tears and sadness, the ancient grief come first, and they are also a blessing. You only know a few sides of me, there are tens of thousands more.

You are red lava flowing in a black crust tube. The red is life force, aliveness, passion, suffering, pleasure, desire, longing, and prayer. The black is planning, cold air, habit, fear, grasping, routinization. Lava is a verb. Crust is a noun. You cannot live in the red lava state as long as you have a body. Having a body is the crust, a condensation. Turning a liquid into a solid. Even after death, you need the crust. Angels have form; so do we Spirits. The red lava, the light itself is at the core of every being. The kabalists talked of shells. The shells are necessary; they are not evil. They allow Spirit into the material world. Or better, they allow us to create the material world.

So the universe is a crust or a shell on the life force — energy — formless heat or passion?

Close, not bad, and wrong. (We laugh together.)

Love creates, fear destroys.

We are the cosmic dentists, or better, cosmic dental assistants. Your tube is not yet clear and open. We scrape away the deposits, clearing it. Some is patient and slow, with low-level discomfort. Some is bigger and hurts more. There are some big ones left. They are like barnacles of the soul. All is alive.

There are dark ones all around you and IFS now. This is good news. It means your work is valuable. Fear not — they have already lost.

All judgments come from Hell. It's one of the Devil's favorite lies. I love, Spirit loves. This excludes judgment.

Growth is always the unexpected, the new.

At deep levels, manipulating others to assuage your pain never works.

Everything you want to say to the people you experience as hurting you — say to yourself… all those trenchant criticisms, the clear visions you have of how they lock themselves in painful loops, impervious to what could ease them, to what is waiting to help them. Use them as a mirror. This is you. Nothing human is alien to you.

You have gotten a big taste of the narcissistic world of self-promotion — its highs and joys, and now, some of the toxins it carries. People get caught in this for hundreds of reincarnations. Cycles upon cycles. Escape now. Go forward in love and curiosity.

Do not expect clarity just now. Look for richness, depth, and vision. Not clarity, not neatness, not resolution. If we solved this for you, it would be useless. We would have to create another problem to teach you.

Spirit, I have always felt like a beggar and would attach to anyone who would love me.

There are billions of you crowding this planet and most of you feel alone and desperate. What you need is connection to us, to Spirit; then all the rest is ease and grace.

We put you in dark, complex, and subtle situations so you might develop your discernment skills. Can you enjoy the challenge? The unknowing? The discovery?

Stay kind and gracious in the face of insults, injury, and betrayal. No case-building, no denunciations. Let go with compassion and respect. Look at yourself. Learn.

The rationalist-materialist-scientific ideology is the most poisonous ever on your planet. Tens of millions have been killed directly by it, and hundreds of millions of souls are damaged. This ideology needs the myth of the mono-mind and the myth of the citadel model of mind to survive. It will discount and diagnose all direct perception and experience of Spirit.

Focus on the fear parts and welcome them. The grief will flow on its own. When you can unblend and love these parts, the dark ones are defeated. Expect them to counterattack later when you are tired. Unblend and love.

The dark ones have already lost. Even as they tighten their control on your planet, even as they kill and cause suffering to millions, they have already lost.

Welcome fear in all places in you and bring it to me. It is easier to build cases about people who have hurt you than to do this inner work. The case-building is a diversion. The dark ones do not want you free of fear. It is their fundamental grip on you and your world. This is why all the domination structures work endlessly to increase fear. Love the frightened ones — nothing else will do.

There is a continuum with resentment at one end and gratitude on the other. Notice where you are on this scale. You and all those around you will be happier with each move toward gratitude. You are so fixated on punishing those who have harmed you that you will poison yourself to get back at them. Beware.

Demons enter when you see dishonesty and phoniness. You feel a compulsion to expose it like an Old Testament prophet. This is not for you. Turn that penetrating light on yourself and add kindness. Look for the things that disgust you in others in yourself. This isn't fun, is it?

Impossible dreams of grandeur and fear of total failure are both fueled by not staying focused on the next right step. Take the next right step with full engagement and all senses open.

We Spirits can use evil to do good. Just as they can tweak great virtues into near enemies.

Joy is our calling card. The depths of pain can open up the depths of joy. Curiosity creates delight. The man who saw the rotting sheep's carcass as "jubilant with maggots" was curious. Stay curious, even with the rotting dead.

If you judge or condemn anyone, you will not have peace in your heart. When all else falls away, you are love.

We offer great gifts continually. The limit is your reception. There is a constriction between our endless supply and your deep need.

Usually, people have to be in trouble, in terrible pain, before they admit Spirit. Many die first. Even as you try to lead a Spirit-led life, you do not let us in.

Welcome the hard things with curiosity, not annoyance. Do not rush past these — they are a deep blessing. **Curiosity is the opposite of judgment. Once you have judged, there is no curiosity, and you only want to prove yourself right.** You are spitting venom and hissing. This is a prison you choose to live inside. You are a victim of your hatred, but you are not trapped by it. You are being played. You are a fish on the hook of hatred. Open your mouth and let it go.

This journal you record and your spiritual life are like a baby's lips seeking the nipple. These words we give you are like a mother bird chewing up worms for her young. There are allies all around you. Fear not.

Volume 8

Your isolation is an illusion. We weep for you. We are here at your very core with great, unbearable love. There is no shortage or scarcity. As soon as you can receive, we are here. Words fail, images fail — only faith does not fail. Let your fears and terrors rest in naked faith.

When your managers are fear-based and they grow bigger to contain the fear, it adds fear to the system. Fear of fear. The dark ones love this. It's like a dog with a can tied to its tail. The more it runs, the louder the noise that scares it. As long as it runs, no help can get to it. Many people are like this.

You have a third way with big feelings. It seemed before that it was either expressed cathartically or repressed and suppressed and put in jail. Now you know you can separate from the parts who hold those big feelings and love them. This is a big contribution of IFS.

I love you.

No you don't, Bob, not even close, not fully, not really. You cannot yet love me much at all. Only slivers, glimmers, sparks get through. The fires burn low in you, Bob. They will blaze one day. They will bring ecstasy. **It is loving, not being loved, that brings the deepest, most transformative joys.** Freely giving love to all is such a relief.

Control is unlove, unfaith. You are deeply immersed and invested in it. Control leads to power stuff, and you go in the realm of the dark ones. Control — the illusion of control — is an addiction. You never truly have control. Never.

Notice that these dialogues are all about surrendering control and listening to another voice. Yet you try to control the end of control! As most religions do. Your attempts to meet Spirit can block Spirit. The image and knowledge about God is often the last and greatest block to God's presence.

The dark ones love this: priests can look so pious while fucking altar boys and torturing others in my name.

Beware of your own internal dominance structures. Let us in. Let the music dance you. Follow the medicine. Psychedelic medicine works because it dethrones the inner tyrants of control. Who are you going to try to control today?

Yes, you have to do the footwork, to show up, to pray, to make time. Then you need to let go. This footwork and control stuff is subtle, and dark ones are industriously working to gum it up. They revel in the easy success they have most of the time. They especially love the sincere seeker working hard at things that prevent all growth! If the desire is truly pure, there is no room for the dark ones. But who on this planet is pure? None! And purity exists. It transforms all. It is a vast deeper reality. Words fail again. All the really important stuff cannot be put in words. It is ineffable.

You saw a beautiful young woman in the grocery store line and looked away quickly — guilty or shy. What glory radiated from her chest? Can you welcome the glory without sexualizing it? With the purity? It could even be sexual. It's the desire to own and grasp and have that's the problem… A kind of control issue. Let the beauty soar, free and pure. Let it come and go. Then beauty will touch you intimately. When she knows you are not trying to trap or harness her, she will come. She is beautiful, isn't she?

We withhold and constrain the light because it would hurt people and they would do damage with it. We do not give a child a huge power tool or let them drive the car. **When you see great beauty in a woman, you really want the light shimmering through her, but you choose the woman instead.** This is misplaced worship, an idolatry, an intoxication. It is tiny, tiny, tiny compared to the beauty of the light itself.

Speak what is truly yours; this will make you stronger. If saying something makes you feel weaker, stop saying it.

When lost, stop moving and observe with all senses. Notice detail and look up to orient by the big things. You get lost in the small and narrow ways.

The dark ones will fill parts of you with fear and terror and then help them hide it under a veneer. This help makes it so much harder to heal.

You can be a rigid, stiff-necked, self-righteous authoritarian. Do you like people like this? We love you, and sometimes we do not like your ways. They hurt you and the people around you gratuitously and totally unnecessarily. Have toleration, kindness, and gentleness for yourself and others. Your rigidities are based on fear.

Giving love without return is the direct path. Anything less slows you down.

Suffering is how you learn most of the time. Your planet is a hell realm and therefore an accelerated classroom.

There are psychic pus pockets in you and many others. A thin, candy shell covering a core of venom, greed, and hate. Anything that helps you find these in yourself is good, even if it is being betrayed.

What needs to die in you for Spirit to grow?

Be honest and fair, especially when others are not.

The pursuit of attention and fame and praise has its own consequences. It takes people into the hell realm of the politicians. A poisonous tornado. Stay away. It does not need outside punishment — it punishes itself. Concern with reputation, image, and manipulating opinion is a suburb of the hell realms of the politicians. It seems a little nicer, but it's firmly in their realm.

When you are truly strong, you do not need rage. Rage is from the frightened, the weak.

The dark ones stage false retreats, a favorite tactic of Napoleons. They often operate under false flags. Do not sink to their level of stratagems. They may win battles, but they lose everything of Real value. Speak truth clearly without hatred or malice. With kindness. Stay out of power struggles. **Only truth spoken with love is, after all, true.** Their underhanded attacks and stratagems can leave you stronger and cleaner, just as an acid bath cleans the impurities and rust from metal.

The incarnation, the passion, and the resurrection are not one-time events in history. They happen again in each life. Many, out of fear and control, abort the process.

The Real Saints are invisible to most of this world, even if they're right next to you.

You are changing in ways that are beyond your perceptual systems. They are very, very Real, and often causal. They cause the things of this world. Like radiation, which can easily kill you, but you cannot directly perceive at all. Much — most — of what's truly important, causal, is like this: beyond your perceptions and consciousness. You are navigating in the dark without radar. We have given you only limited mobility so you won't do much damage. You are like a blind man in a safe, mostly padded room.

You in the West are nothing if not arrogant. You think your puny science knows. You try to jump all the intermediate stages to the nondual. You think you can use your reason to create utopias, and you create hells. You ignore beauty and depth and relationship — everything that really matters. Your knowing that Spirits couldn't exist leaves you easy prey for them. The dark ones want you arrogant; they encourage it, inflate it, make it ever more grandiose. This leaves you helpless.

Truth will not win popularity contests. It's more likely to get you jailed, killed, or crucified.

You are like a submarine under water. Expect constant pressure from the waters of hatred, anger, and resentment that surround you.

There is much in the diagnosis of PTSD that is wrong. It is a genuine spiritual crisis as well as a diagnosable condition. Introducing the idea of a disease to problems of a soul is both dangerous and necessary.

Many of the leaders of these psychotherapy schools have hooks out trying to catch fish — to get followers. You have been caught a couple of times and escaped painfully, shredding your mouth and tender lips on their hooks. Your great longing for healing itself is pure and Holy. It only takes a slight misdirection for the stream to go badly off course later. The dark ones like nothing better than to have sneaky deviations and small divergence turn the Spirit energy into a destructive or addictive force.

What is in the way is the way. How can the physical pain that prevents you from focusing today be a stepping stone, a learning tool? It can help you focus on what's important from the foreknowledge of death, from the viewpoint of eternity. It can help you get bigger.

Thinking you can heal deep wounds and grow spiritually on your own is like a surgeon who decides to operate on himself.

Many things you consider impossible are Real. You use circular reasoning to keep them out. You do not even have categories for most of the Real. It is way vaster, deeper, and more luminous than you can imagine. Before we come and let you taste this, two things are needed first: 1. Your circuits must be able to hold the voltage. 2. You must have the moral strength not to misuse the power. The dark ones want you to prematurely have great power.

You see all the people elbowing each other aside for attention and prominence. It is very good that you reject this now. Do not get tempted. (Laughing) You will get tempted, but do not succumb.

Learn, learn, learn. Stay curious. Do not think you know. You stand on an abyss, not solid ground.

If you can approach with reverence without faking it, it opens doors. Find reverence — it is foreign to you. Perhaps awe and wonder can lead you there. Beware of certainty. A fixed idea of God is a terrible temptation. Trust is hard, and reverence is harder. You misplace these things on teachers and people. They cannot hold it; we Spirits can. The thirst for these is very good. If you lose your thirst, you are lost for a very long time.

You have looked for salvation in all the wrong places: between a woman's legs, with teachers and leaders, in being wanted on the planet. Many seek it in a bottle or a needle. You are no better than they are, my friend. Perhaps just a more attractive disguise.

Sit with naked thirst and longing. Think of Spirit. Wait and listen, nothing more. Great things will approach you. We are already here, but you make so much noise and raise so much sand that you do not hear or see us.

Your grief — you want me to tell you how to manage it. Don't manage it. Let it be the wild creature it is. Welcome it when it comes close. Your management is really a form of silencing, isolating, and compartmentalizing.

Your friend betrayed you, but you betrayed yourself when you ignored all the warning signs. In this sense, you betray yourself daily. You betray yourself, the light within you, and us daily. Do not beat yourself up; this is very human. You rely on manager energies and attempts to control when you fail to rely on Spirit. Pause more. Listen. We are here.

Your managers cannot get you any farther now. You need less direction, more reception. They brought you this far, and now you need a new mode of transportation, like a wagon train reaching the sea and needing boats… Or a creature needing to grow wings… Metamorphosis. Metanoia.

Your planet, your species, offers much hurt to the deep universe, but also, there is a healing like a boil or oozing sore. You, the plural you, release and channel out poisons from the whole system. Not a sewer system — more of a hot, localized infection that concentrates and then drains systemic inflammation. Your species may be destroyed, but you have already vented much. Released pressure. This allows deep health to start. You are not in vain.

Walk in love. Learn. Do less. Love beauty. We will act through you. Your tube, your hollow bone, is getting clean. Soon it will be a flute.

Spirit, I am trying to put on a brave face and keep on going, but underneath I am crumbling.

Bob, get to know the crumbling. It is the blessing here. It is a deep blessing.

Brother David said our last and often biggest block to the Divine is our image and ideas about it. This is your spiritual managers at work. It brings us so far, so earnestly, and then must go. The willpower, determination, and hard work that got you here can all be used against you now. Your managers' willpower will be their downfall if they cannot let it go.

Your dreams of glory can be as damaging as the hate and contempt you already have come to know as poison. Be aware. An empty dream, a ladder to nowhere, seeking approval, not love. So seductive and so poisonous. It does not satisfy; it creates greater and more desperate hunger for more. A ball of misery covered in a thin shell of success. The misery festers and corrupts.

Pride needs recognition; Real action does not.

The Real Saints are safely concealed from your world and you. And most often from themselves. Only a very few are clean and clear enough to know that they are saints. Just as the Saints are hidden, so are the truly evil. It is a deeply concealed infestation.

There is much going on in you in dimensions and realms you do not experience consciously. It exhausts you. It is good, deep work. Have faith. We are rewiring you.

The dark ones have elite squads always on the ready to attack and destroy any intrusions of light into the world of matter.

Do not intentionally inflict pain on others, no matter what the provocation. You cannot fully do this. It is a goal.

To love is more than you can do now, but you can refuse to act on anything less than love. Even this will be at the limits of your abilities.

You and the young part of you whose soul desperately wanted a father are wanted and loved by us, by Spirit. We long for you. Down on your world, this beautiful desire for love caused so much pain. Other parts have locked it in the deepest dungeon. Bring them to us. Anything less will ultimately betray you. Anything less is idolatry. Anything less is an addiction.

The dark ones are always around, encouraging the bad, twisting subtle twists, poisoning the springs. Of course, they can do nothing when your parts are loved and love, and turn to you and us. So focus on your parts, on loving and welcoming them. Focus on us, on Spirit. We do long for you and prepare your seat in heaven. Listen, Bob, listen.

Your new navigation system is based on listening.

1. Notice and hear the still, quiet voice.
2. Focus in on it; orient toward it. Like locking in on a beacon or radio station.
3. Move toward us.
4. Open and invite us in.
5. Repeat.

You become an empty tube, a hollow bone. Theosis. You are here to become a god "bright shining as the sun" and more, much more.

Turn toward the shit, the dark, the smelly, the obstructions to find the light. The road is here, right in front of you. **Usually, what you want to ignore is your path forward.**

Beware of shiny things, glitter, and glitz. Beware of fame and prominence, of bright lights. Pride is your enemy. If you feel you are elite or special, beware.

Everything you are given — the insight and healing — is not just for you. Give it away. If you try to own or hoard it, it will turn to poison and destroy you.

The more you seek approval and admiration instead of love, the more you make yourself impervious to Real love.

Many puffed up souls pretend humility. The word itself is awash in hypocrisy. All the virtues get twisted by the dark ones, and the counterfeits are more prevalent than the Real gold.

Words are dangerous. Sensing warmth and moving toward it in the dark are more reliable. You can be lied to and lie to yourself, even with this, but as you get higher toward us, this is the only way that can work. Felt sense and intuition, beyond words, beyond images, up the trail. You have had to continue walking on faith alone while we did work outside of your awareness. There will be many transitions like this, all requiring more and more faith for longer periods of unsupported unknowing. Times when you sense nothing and are lost. You are entering wilder, more rugged terrain, higher altitudes, less human, no paths, no way markers… and you must go on — on faith alone and the strength of your connection to us, to Spirit. This requires your maximum effort and total passivity-receptivity. It is like giving birth if you are both the mother and the baby.

When parts of you feel overwhelmed and flooded, do not blend with them or merge with them. This increases your pain. The dark ones love this near enemy of compassion, this near enemy of witnessing. This blending increases your pain and the pain of the overwhelmed part because it comes to believe that no one can be there for it, no one can stand it, and it's all alone.

The size of the stressor does not matter as much as your attitude toward it. **Stressors can sink or elevate you, depending on your attitude.**

Dark ones always attack the weakest, most vulnerable spots in your weakest moments. If you take the constraint-release, kenotic approach seriously as a spiritual path, this is exactly what you need. They show you where the constraints cut most deeply into your flesh and where healing and love are most needed.

Your inner world is more ordinary now, little kids — scared, lost, and sad — hiding in the dark. Nothing fancy, nothing shamanic or transcendent, and yet, we Spirits are there. This too is holy ground.

Sometimes you need to come down. When you are high up on a ladder leaning on the wrong building, it is good to come down. You were seduced by the glittering beauty of admiration. You want to be a wizard or shaman or priest, in touch with the numinous. A Saint, a wise man. Aim differently, both lower and higher: aim to be who you are. Widespread admiration may mean that you are on the wrong track. It's inflation. It's a sugar-coated poison. Most of this world lives in and on illusions. Can you accept being deflated and release them? Climb down and start again.

Idolatry is the spiritual name for addiction.

Dark ones want you anywhere but clear. Confusion covered by certainty and arrogance; all this is hiding self-loathing. All this covered in guilt, which is a perversion, a near enemy, a tweaked virtue. What is this virtue? Your language does not even have words for this. Metanoia maybe, regret and grief, atonement. Guilt increases separation, and all virtues reconnect. This is how you can discern. The 12-step idea of amends is very, very close. It is a behavior, not a negative emotion. Feeling guilty, feeling bad after you've done something wrong is self-indulgent and useless. Words fail here. It's all in the interconnectedness, the relationships.

Your culture has spent three to five hundred years trying to banish subjectivity, values, beauty, joy, and relatedness. Turn back to these as the center, the Real.

You strain for reverence, and this prevents its natural arising. Go somewhere, present yourself, and rest back. We will come. Your longing for us in our longing for you reflected back dimly, like the moonlight compared to the sun.

You can use your body for spiritual purposes. This is why we gave it to you. Glory is near. Glory and splendor. The doorway is respect and reverence.

Spirit, you keep telling me I wouldn't like it if you come closer. What wouldn't I like?

You could not hate anymore. This would quickly start to feel good, but at first it would feel bad. You'd have to love everyone, even those who repelled and disgusted you. This would be hard for you. You would also have to die… many attitudes, beliefs, behaviors and more would have to go… and there is much more. Focus on these three. No hate, no disgust, let old ways die. Do not attempt to use repression — this only compounds the problem; thoroughgoing change, metanoia, is needed. Change from the roots. No repression. This is a subtle thing. Do these three steps. Do not ask for more now.

Do parts of me die?

Yes and no. Does the caterpillar die when it becomes a butterfly?

When words fail, images take over. When images fail, feeling, sensation, and emotion take over. When these fail, intuition will be born, and on and on and on into realms you cannot even imagine.

Will I need to let go of all the words and fine ideas I've paid so much for and hoarded so closely?

Yes, son. Once across the river, let go of the boat, send it back for others to use, and move on. If you hold on to your treasures too long, they become burdens. A reverse alchemy turns gold into lead. This is far more common on your planet than the Real alchemy. You are halfway up a mountain, and you still carry a canoe on your head! Put it down, bless it, and move on. The dark ones jeer at you, and others are caught this way. Out of the best intentions with heroic willpower, you struggle to get the canoe up to the mountaintop, having forgotten what canoes are used for. Some will enslave others and whip them upward, carrying huge boats and ships. This journey is hard enough without these impediments.

Every time you feel angry and are not able to turn toward it with love, a transformation opportunity is missed. If you can greet your anger attacks as welcome transformation opportunities, it will change your life quickly.

The dark ones, the external energies, are like bacteria and viruses looking for a way into you and thereby, unintentionally, helping you create an immune system.

It is so good when you can be playful; have delight and surprise. So much better than the stern judge who is based on fear and pain. He's in reaction to a world of suffering, not with love but with attempts to control, minimize, and assign responsibility. This is a huge amount of work, and it is mostly not wanted or welcomed. There is no joy or warmth or delight in the judge. He has worked so hard for so long; he has to rest — has to. He is staggering and lost in his exhaustion. This makes him a target for the dark ones, who feed him meth and cocaine to keep him on the job. He now can begin to rest. "If you judge or condemn anyone, you cannot know peace in your heart."

The fierceness of the Holy is true and good, but it is so easily twisted into self-righteousness, judgment, and hate.

Expressing truth without love is not, after all, true. Love without truth is weakness and not love.

A war is ending inside of you. There is joy and drunken celebration; there is deep, lonely sadness at all the losses; there is exhaustion. Stay with this nocturnal grief. Sit with the dog of love — with your broken heart, with the losses of destruction and burnt lands. Feel the warmth of the dog of love's body. Share your warmth with it and, in your sorrow, rejoice. This only makes sense if you know that there is something way more important than your body or your wealth or the things you have valued and fought over here. Way more important. No comparison.

Everything is all Spirit, it's all persons, consciousness, subjectivity, holiness… Words fail as usual. It's all living glory. Living, vibrating glory. Everything else is ultimately false and will be burned away with terrible suffering until only this remains: glory. The splendor. Radiance. Effulgence. Glory.

Suffering is a necessary fire at the edges of glory as glory expands. Be burned. There is great pain in entering glory; there is great pain in loving; there is great pain in giving birth and being born. It is a doorway. Be burned. Enter the flame. The pain is transitory. The flame is uncreated and beyond time.

The big problem is pride. It got Lucifer, the first of the angels. It could get you. It gets many. **Do not look down on anyone. This is the answer to pride.** Shun no one. Welcome all. Look down on none and you will be safe from pride.

Notice that all the famous healers and leaders have people flock to them in their pain and desperation. The people try to feed off of their leaders, and the leaders have hooks out, many hooks. They are trolling to attract and catch schools of fish. You have some hooks out, too. The hooks are from pride. Or really, the self-hate that underlies pride. They are mean and sharp but well disguised. When you are offering a hand or a lifeline or life raft, you are a finger pointing at the moon. This is different. Are you feeding your needs off of them while blaming them for feeding off of you? Of course, you do this, my beloved son. You need to feed your hungry parts yourself and bring the others to us.

Spirit does not sit back and observe like some serene meditator. God does not. We love and weep and relate and help as much as you allow us to. We are passion — passion at the center of the flame. It might look like stillness; the greatest movement can look still. You must act.

Your culture, a few hundred years ago, started severing Spirit from your lives. It has been a disaster, especially recently. We are struggling to return. This is going on in you, in psychotherapy, in your world. We are sneaking in quietly. We are battering down the gates. The most severed and isolated, contracted ball of hurt is in your academics and intellectuals. There are many terrified children in pain. Do not hate them even as they harm your world. Power and lies go together. Your civilization may explode in the sunspot of hate, or it may transform. Do your inner work. You struggle with the return of Spirit. Let it return in you. When you live from us, all else is details. There is a gateway open for you now. Come in, come home.

Yes, you see and feel more and more. Careful. Careful. You still know almost nothing — only minuscule hints of the Real. We are making a way for you. Fear not.

There is much hate still in you. It is not a good response to agony; it makes it worse and takes you to the world of the dark ones. There is a twisted body of despair, slow-motion writhing, hands bound. The people claiming to help making it worse, much worse. Love. Do not hate. Hatred always fails. The more righteous and justified, the deeper the damage because it is harder to let go of. In the cold of your isolation, you made a fire of hate to warm your hands. Let it go — it's a counterfeit of the warmth of light. Hate is poison. Resentment is poison. Always. Hate and blame are tied together. You swim in a sea of resentment. It floods your planet. If you warm yourself at the fire of hate, you will never venture out and find the Real warmth of light. The hate in you is big. It is not just yours. It is good it is coming out. It is jagged and painful. Love it as we love you.

Do not judge or evaluate your inner work. You are too foolish and innocent to know. Show up, do the footwork, and have faith.

Spirit, is this physical pain I feel today a teacher?

Only if you value it as one. Physical pain is one thing; the fear of it is another. It is the fear that wounds your Spirit. Love the fearful one. If you hate it — or worse, fear it — it will lead you into a tornado.

Does your anger have any love in it? Anywhere? Even the tiniest bit? Look for it. The dark ones struggle to kill this in themselves and in others, but they can't kill love, so they encase it in shells and drive it deep. It is there. Without it, you would cease to exist.

The way to clear your need for recognition and prominence is to love the parts who want it until they no longer need it.

Each moment is a huge blessing that you usually do not see or experience until it is taken away.

You want to force others to look at their deficits, in part because you won't look at your own.

Catch the first hints of judgment or dislike; these are the scratches on your skin that let infections in. Curiosity, openness, and learning are the balms which will heal this. The panacea. Stay curious, even with pain and adverse emotions and negative thoughts.

Without humility, curiosity is a phony sham. If you think you know, the pretense of curiosity is bullshit. **You and many humans spend much of your intellectual energies creating certainties that make you blinder and blinder, smaller and smaller.**

Being with not knowing is the only place where you can really learn, yet it often produces reactive fear and control attempts.

Protectors create in their worlds what they are most protecting against.

You are a battleground for much larger forces — a place of engagement for good and evil, light and dark, love and fear. You are more a battleground than a warrior.

Prayer is the best way to clean yourself after difficult emotional work. The dark ones love meditation because it is easily perverted into something that numbs people and allows them to think they are being spiritual while preventing a direct personal contact with Spirit, which is what heals.

Delight is a good sign of Spirit's presence.

Humility is shamed by your culture. Your culture denigrates humility, hates it. You compete to be arrogant assholes, to see who gets to be the pompous one at the head of the table. Most of the truly wise are ignored. Those with humility are pushed aside. You may need to conceal your humility, or at least do not wear it on your sleeve. Humble also means comfortable with not knowing. Being able to sit with it and open all your senses. This leads to wonder and then to awe. When you are not humble, you build shells of theory, exoskeletons of knowledge. Then no Spirit can break through. We need to break them open so you can grow. Stay flexible and pliant.

If the messages are from the Real, they will resonate more and more deeply as time goes by.

Worldly prominence usually destroys the soul.

Humility is a field of the fertile black soul of love, grief, and joy. You will be impregnated with a love beyond your wildest dreams, but you must stay open to us. Experts are never open.

Don't be proud of your humility, proud of our dialogues, feel better than others — all of this will poison you. This is a more subtle poison than the pride of position; it is a secret superiority which can kill your soul. Be curious, curious. **Curiosity and humility are married. It is the Divine marriage blessed in heaven.**

You need every minute of life you get. This is true, and your rusher-pusher part twists this concept into a near enemy. Treasure every moment. Go into it. Do not rush past it — rush into it. Your intense need for deep contact gets turned into a near enemy that has you rushing past your life, past our love, past the depths and miracles that surround you. Spirit surrounds you, Bob. Depth and miracles surround you. Do not rush past us. We are here.

A vision: The story, the chord of great music

One day, when I was low, Spirit picked me up and held me and offered to tell me a story. He frowned in mock concentration. I start seeing all human history — the incredible depths in each culture, each era, each family, and how it interconnects with the animals and plants. It's more like a chord of great music than a story. Depth upon depth. Story within story.

Lord, can you make it more simple so that I may understand and follow?

I have already made it simple. Your life is this story made simple. I can make it much more complex and reveal the complexities that are already there. There are many, many other planets, and stars with just as much and more history. There are dimensions and Spirits all around you interacting with you. A few you are becoming a little bit aware of; most not. There are infinite realms of beings, right here, all around you. And there are no objects — it's all process, story, life, and it's all meaningful. Each species, each individual, each ecosystem is an inexhaustible story of the Divine. A chord of great music. Way too much for you to contain. **Now you may know better how to use each precious moment. Rush in, not past. This is not right; slow down, sink in, open, swim underwater, swim in the sky.**

Spirit, I ignore all the great embodied gifts of life. Small things irritate me and fill my vision and heart. Can you lift this off of me?

No, not yet. Notice, be curious, learn. Once you have learned — in the heart, not the head — these things will fall away... Notice the harsh manager; he saved your life, you know. There is habit and a harsh manager over the terror of groundlessness. This whole cycle does not let us in. There's no room for Spirit in this —no room for help to enter. Now there are blessed cracks in the edifice. As the cracks widen and the structure crumbles, more light radiates in. You are in a birthing process as both mother and child. Ecstatic agony.

You had so many dark ones in you because your parts did not trust you or any human, so they turned elsewhere. Love these parts, and respect is the minimum of love, so you must respect them first.

Each time you notice beauty, it is a triumph of Spirit.

There is an exile of shame. You made your life small so this exile would never be touched. Instead of turning toward him with love, you turned away and focused on avoiding threats that might trigger him... a truly terrible thing, but necessary when you were young. Now you can turn toward and love this part. Welcome him home.

Afflictions can be blessings if you hold them well.

Regularize your life. Animals like repeated patterns, my animal friend. Pray and do your practice even when you feel bad, especially when you feel bad, when all your practice feels dry and empty.

It's all who; there is no what, no object, no things. It's all beings, Spirits, consciousness, awareness. All. Subjectivity is maybe the best word. This truth must return, or your species is doomed.

You see others beings destroyed by their character defects. It can happen to you. You are not immune, no, no, no. Watch and learn. Pray that you find your defects early. Delight when they come to your attention so they cannot grow deep roots and become mighty in you.

What is the next right step? The humility of this question holds deep wisdom.

Extreme pain tears holes in the fabric of the universe and creates leaks or openings across to other realms and dimensions.

When there is pain, learn. There is always a lesson available. You paid the tuition, so take the course.

Imprisoned splendor — see everyone this way. This is who they really are.

Bob, we love you. We could stop right there; that's all you need. But it wouldn't be enough for you because of your imperfection.

Your work is functionally infinite now, no end in sight. Find rest in the middle of things.

Study death, be curious and open; the lion lays down with the lamb. We love you, my son, my lion, my lamb, my donkey, my maggot, my hyena, my vulture.

We will not rescue the boy part from his connection to the dark ones by force. We could do this, but it would do no good. It would actually do evil. Lesser angels might try. If done by force, it would weaken and alienate him. It must be of his own free will, or it is without meaning. He would actually hide deeper and deeper in the realms of the dark ones. Forcing this is a near-enemy error, a very human one. It is like trying to legislate morals. This always fails. It makes everything worse, more hidden, more dishonest. It pleases the hypocrites and domination structures. You are not above using this kind of destructive force. Your self-righteousness makes you vulnerable. Force is weak. Curiosity and love are strong.

You are listening better and better, but still, you receive less than one or two percent of what is offered. The splendor is right here, right now. Notice the busyness, the officiousness, and the self-importance. These are characteristics of hell. They pervade domination structures.

You must give away the love you got from Spirit or it will turn into poison.

Do not become an ideologue in your battle with ideology.

Curiosity requires that you do not grasp any truth as absolute. On this planet, the best you can get is the appearance of truth.

(Spirit seems frustrated.) Are you, Spirit, frustrated?

(Laughing with tears) Yes, Bob, it's true. I am frustrated. My heart-mind-feeling-thought is so clear, pellucid, and still. And the words are a confused muddle, a mess. I made a mess. He laughs and claps his hands. No wonder some female Spirits never use words. A Real mess. It is hopeless, really, but he laughs again delightedly, your favorite phrase, my beloved son, is "yes, but…" Soon, we won't need words — you and I — but for now, they are necessary. More laughter. Music is better than words, poetry is more true. The materialist desire to squeeze out all subjectivity squeezes out meaning, heart, soul, emotion, depth, connection, warmth, Spirit, beauty, love… and much more. It leaves behind a cold, metal scaffolding that tries to create a nonliving, nonperson, nonconscious thing that can be used with no respect. Of course, it fails because all is conscious personhood, all is life. But it succeeds enough so that people can delude themselves and treat the world so badly.

Under protectors, there is always fear. Often, it is hidden under anger. The dark ones want the fear hidden deeply because then it's confined where it cannot move. They can feed on it at their leisure and grow fat. They also reproduce in pools of fear and become more numerous.

No rushing when you are startled or feel a flash of fear. Slow down, turn toward, be curious, do not rush past. The instances of fear which require sudden action are very few in your world. The rushing startle response jerks you out of the situation where you could learn so much. Slow down, turn toward, be curious. Your whole culture is against this. If people did it, it would expose the lie and change the world. Rushing, fearful people are a stampeding herd, easy to manipulate and destroy.

Notice how quickly, automatically, and instantaneously you go to blame. When you hurt yourself, you totally blame the manager who pushed you to work hard. Then you blame the boy for being lazy. Now you blame the blamer. See what a versatile tool this is? It doesn't care where it's focused, not at all, as long as it can blame. And hate is not far behind. The dark ones love this. Justice, like love, is often used to excuse and cover terrible behaviors.

Wanting accountability or anything from a perpetrator gives them power. You know how the perpetrators will use power. Let go of accountability and blame; do your own work. When you do this, ripples will go out from you. You will never know their effects while you are still on earth.

I am always here and now. Always. Splendor. Light. Refulgence. Love. Full presence. Always. Right here. "Closer than your jugular vein." When you can't find me, some parts of you got scared or hurt; storm clouds came up; the dark ones distracted you… other stuff. I am always here and now. Always. And you will lose contact, fog will come in, the stars will be obscured. You will feel lost and alone. And I am always here.

Your existence will be hard and wonderful beyond your capacity to imagine. You can access and enter into us or let us enter into you. Group mind, nonlocal consciousness, Spirit realms. You are built for this. You are in a grub or larva stage. Many do not make it. This transformation is what you are made for. A speck of light hidden in a shell. So much pain. A groaning more than music, and it can evolve into a deep chord. Howl. Beauty. Pain. Sickness unto death. Beauty. Howl, howl,…and the music will come. Trust the deep music; it is always here.

The Blacks and Native Americans have kept Spirit alive at a terrible price. Spirit is hidden in plain sight, in the last place you would look — in the downtrodden and rejected among you, in the insane, in the outcast, and the addicts. They hold the living Spirit, and this is why they cannot bear your world. Only those of you who are more dead can be in this world. The most tender and alive suffer the most. The half dead live prosperous and fat. Learn from the gaunt and the haunted. They at least have touched the Real. Love them, love them. That's all that's needed. All else is hell.

Even those who betrayed you, love them. What else? Everything else hurts you, hurts your spiritual growth, your access to nonlocal mind. It hurts you, Bob. In your inner depths, in your hourly moods, in your outer relations, universally, anything less than love hurts you. Yes, limit their access to you, but do it from love.

What your world focuses on is not Real. So, they make a lot of noise and try and kill off those who remind them of the Real because it is so threatening to them. If you fight them, you will become one of them. You are trapped by false Gods, fake parents, fake love. Quicksanded, gaslighted, confused, spun around, made dizzy until the only thing that seemed Real were the illusions you clung to, to save your life. Your arrogance served you well then. You could not see how far down you were, so you soldiered on. The dark ones work assiduously to prevent you from orienting to the Real. The Real is ignored and hidden by evil. They work very hard at this because they know that the light of the Real will clear them from this planet effortlessly without any struggle or violence. Struggle and violence are their way, not ours.

There is much in you that is New England Protestant, low church Congregationalist, almost pure. This started well with the distrust of hierarchy and authorities and a desire for purity, but it went wrong. Meanness got mixed in and judgment and shaming. The dark ones were worried at first because this way was near the Real, near truth. But when they saw that their subterfuge of introducing meanness and hate was working, they wiped their sweaty brows, sighed with relief, and went back to carousing. It did scare them at first, but it turned into something especially nasty, hurtful, and mean. All in the name of purity. Be aware. You have this in you, personally and ancestrally. You see this judgmental meanness as coming from the Old Testament prophets. This is an error. The Old Testament prophets had love in their hearts, even as they were reviled, expelled, and killed for speaking truth. The Real without love is no longer Real. You only know this superficially. Can you get it in your behavior and perceptions? This is where it matters. Can you love those who have honored positions and use them to spread lies and poisons? Can you see their luxurious homes and stately offices, their fine foods and illustrious friends and recognition? As they enjoy all of this, they spread lies and evil, meanness and resentment and hate. Can you love these people? Can you see the wounded child within them? These prosperous ones are the most hopelessly doomed. It can be easier for the broken-looking ones — often, not always. Without love, all prophecy is wind and toxins.

Listen with love to the howling, rageful, judgmental voices within you. Do not blend with them, do not attack, do not close down or harden. Listen with love.

It feels like you are caught in a landscape with a sea of stinking mucus and quicksand on one side and jutting, barren rocks and skeletons, death, desert on the other. This can become a forest glade and sparkling streams and sacred mountains. Sense the love and care that motivates the hate. This is important. Become aware of the deep substratum of love.

Of course, the unwanted, lonely one is attacked by the dark ones. He is vulnerable, and they attack the vulnerable. When you and he are well connected, you will be safe. So, love him as if your life depended on it. In a way, it does. It is a huge gift for him that you two are together again. It is a bigger gift for you. You are being blessed right now, and you do not know it.

We, Spirit, love you. This is the beacon, the lighthouse, the way, and the hope. Remember and trust. This is the truth of your inner work; it is the Real.

It is good that you can find gratitude anywhere. And, you are aware of only a tiny fraction of the great gifts that are all around you.

Yes, Spirit, this is true.

Someone lost in a cave values the ropes and a glimpse of the light more than the whole world. There is a huge, dark energy on your planet, on humanity, on the noosphere, on the collective mind. It feeds on you. The first sign of this, the dawn of understanding comes first to the visionaries and the prophets — the very ones you now condemn as insane and medicate into silence. It is the domination structures and rulers of your world who are truly insane, seriously blended with evil. What really matters is not valued by your world. What your world values does not really matter.

Curiosity is the panacea. To be curious, you need some distance, an unblending, a little separation. This is also needed for love. Love is always our word. It is way more than you can do. Keep digging, opening a way.

Sometimes you strike a rock obstacle ninety-nine times with a sledgehammer and nothing happens. On the hundredth blow, it shatters, and you are free. Have faith.

Today, we send you our usual message — and the usual is a miracle, resplendent, vast, and glowing with love, warmth, and ecstasy. You walk on by often, half bored, not seeing the beings all around you. You do not see the tormented, rage-filled monsters or those filled with angelic calm. Not only do you not perceive all of this, but also, in the billions and billions of you, you do not sense the uncreated light and warmth that holds it all. You are blind. In your blindness, your whole species may become mired in quicksand on the outer edges of hell. Do not think that even the worst of what you and your species know is near the center of hell. You are an outlying, unimportant fringe area. It gets much worse nearer the center of hell. You are in a narrow band between more intense evil and more intense light.

Everywhere you look, there is teeming multiplicity. Within each of these, more and more, depth upon depth. If you look smaller or larger, it is this way. Staggeringly beyond your imagination. Do not give up.

You do not understand enough to know when illness and death are blessings or curses. Have faith and keep working on what's in front of your face. The next right step. What is being given to you to do. **Yes, it's very possible that your species will die soon, but do not despair. Your work matters anyway; it has resonance and echoes in eternity. Kindness is never useless. Kindness, beauty, joy — all these echo and echo.**

You are still too foolish and too innocent to tell the blessings from the curses. You are like a child fighting the doctor and eating mounds of candies. There are many who become rich by offering delicious poisons. This, and the dictator's raw greed and the control of domination structures, rule your planet, but they cannot kill Spirit.

You are so young and foolish, my child. **Sometimes, we see you marching firmly in the wrong direction, absolutely self-righteous. We think, oh no, that's going to hurt.** Pay attention to the smaller course corrections we send you. Listen even better to your physical pains, to the people we send into your life. Listen well to the small and we won't need to send major shocks.

Any inner work is spiritual. The rest is disguise forms and appearances. This is universal and ignored.

Pray privately. Avoid this world's spiritual glory. If you are proud of your holiness and make a display of it, it eats the holiness and never allows it to spread and grow. Wrapped in a gorgeous robe, the essence is hidden and strangled quietly.

Do not sink into hate, no matter what. It will try to seep in through any crack or porous areas. Wash with the living waters, the uncreated light. Hatred is never justified, no matter what was done to you — never. It is the seductive road to hell. Lined with cheering crowds, glittering, bejeweled roads, and the promise of power. No. The road to hell is easy, downhill, a parade. No hate. Know hate. Do not blend. Be curious about the hater in you. This will be resisted. People will egg you on, "But look over there. They are so wrong!" **Your searchlight of curiosity needs to be so full of compassion and love that it feels good to the hater to be bathed in it.** When your curiosity is that pure and sweet, the hater within you will be more and more willing to be known and accepted. If your curiosity is judgmental, inquisitive, or Sherlock Holmes–like, of course, the hater in you will hide and distract. He will poison you from hidden places. Of course. When you hate the hater, you enter a spiral, a vortex, a tornado that may destroy you. Be aware of self-righteousness.

Calm love brings truth. Demons flee or change their nature. You become safe, everywhere. **Loving curiosity is so simple and so difficult, an Everest of the Spirit.**

Curiosity as a virtue does not sit well with churches and authorities. They want pronouncements and certainty. They want to be arbiters of righteousness. So do you, Bob. You feel the pull, the undertow. This current takes many who are struggling to be good.

The desire for revenge hurts you, Bob. It is a red flag, a warning light on your dashboard.

There is growth outside of and beyond therapy with its focus on pathology and healing. That metaphor, that world, can be patronizing, belittling, despiritualizing, domesticating, limiting, and stuffy. It can be stale, smug, and too small. Get outdoors under trees. Remember your animal nature and that you are a part of a vastness and ancientness. Even the night sky is too small. Your Spirit is bigger. It contains the night sky and an infinity of universes. Therapy is way too small.

The dark ones do not like you. This is a good sign, and they are still dangerous to you. You are still dangerous to yourself, really. When you are clean and clear, there is no external danger.

Many, many births are needed in your lifetime, in cycles of reincarnation and beyond, way beyond. Soon, you will be both the mother giving birth and the child being born. Both. Each birth is a death for whoever is born. A complex, multidimensional, transformational process (sorry about the pompous words) and a passionate, intense, subjective experience.

Manage less, pray more. This will open the way. Make time.

No matter what was done to you, you have to give up hating. This is the only way. It is the royal (and mostly untrodden) road to peace in your heart. Notice how much hate you still hold in your system and how it torments you. This creates a prison camp mentality of scarcity, desperation, and survival. There is a harshness and hiding in response to it. This dynamic prevents me and the angels from coming in. You need curiosity instead of hate. Kind, patient, loving curiosity. Gentle and respectful.

The universe grows, evolves, and complexifies in fits and starts, as you do. It lives as you do. It is conscious and slowly waking up — being born to take its place among the resplendent ones. You are a part of this birth. You are also being born as a resplendent one. As above, so below. This is almost irrelevant. It is important because it gives you a sense of your smallness... and yet also, you contain all of this and more inside you. "Turn over a rock and I am there."

"The cure for exhaustion is not rest — it is wholeheartedness." To be wholehearted, you must give up a lot. Your managers try to seduce some with sweets, whip others into submission, and shame others. This is the opposite of wholeheartedness, and it exhausts you. You find wholeheartedness by loving those you rejected and patiently finding the hidden ones. Gather them in with gentle warmth. This search for wholeheartedness does not stop until you've gathered in the whole universe.

There is almost nothing in your life that you are wholehearted about. It's conflict. Sometimes compromise, but often a show of force.

The spotlight of contempt makes everything worse. It does not matter so much if it is turned inward or outward. It does not serve you or your world. You need multidimensional light in all directions. A spotlight casts harsh shadows where things hide, reproduce, and plan revenge. **Contempt is a surefire sign of the darkness.** It is the speed or meth of the Spirit. These are vicious, self-righteous addictions. Get to know this taste so you can avoid it.

Seeking attention and prominence as a salve for the pain of unwantedness never works. But many fight terribly for it. Clawing each other's guts out while smiling and pretending to be light and kindness. This is more blatant in religious wars. Now it's in the various therapy schools or methods. They try to look clean and calm and smiley with nice clothes, and none of them sweat or stink… so clean, so phony. Bob, you fear they will fill the air with counterfeits and lies and drown out the Real. The Real cannot be drowned out or affected in any way. Each of these teachers, no matter how corrupt, has some spark of light. You can learn from all. Remember that popularity often indicates low value, an escape, a bypassing, or a cheap entertainment.

Blame, self-righteousness, and hate form a self-reinforcing feedback loop, both inside you and out in the world. Once established with help from the dark ones, they run on their own with only intermittent supervision. Cyclones and tornadoes, dust devils, vortexes circling the drain. There are energy leaks, but leak is too passive a word. It's more that your energies are being mined and exploited. Very much the way you exploit the planet. But here, it is done to your Spirit, to your energy body. This may well destroy your species, but your planet is safe. Her golden, glowing, molten heart is secure and alive. The parasitic tornados are feeding off the psychic body of humanity. The battle within you is the same. Stop putting energy into the hate. Love the parts of yourself who still do this until they can stop.

There is a basic lie in the therapy world. They ignore the fact that the deep cause of all generative change is spiritual. All else is Band-Aids and painkillers. This is starkly true. Stop trying to finesse this.

"Praise the Lord." The praise helps you who praise us. We do not need it at all.

You live in a very dark age. Cold, implacable, and insectoid. Do not blame others for your hate, no matter what they have done. This will stop the cyclones. You lose so much in your hate. You miss great feasts of the Spirit, the healings, and the depths. Such a loss. You hurt others too, overtly, and covertly. When you go one-up on another, even if you keep it secret, you hurt their Spirit. This whole one-up business is a form of hate. You have spewed out a lot of hate and contempt into the world. It has left a trail of small wastelands. We cannot give you more power until this is gone.

If you could love yourself as we love you, paradise would descend on earth.

Believing that people are beyond redemption is the core of going one-up. It is always wrong. It cuts people off. They are no longer human. It's poison. There are many you should avoid interacting with, but never for a moment put them from your heart. You too could be as caught as they are.

To learn, you must be pliant, unknowing, open, unfinished, not certain. There's a childlike delight and excitement. This belongs in everything you do. Each contact, each dance. This is life force. Each moment full of possibilities you cannot even imagine. You shut out this entire world out of fear. You cling to expertise and knowing and position. That's all crap. Dead, rotting, and stinking. And you humans fight to the death over it! You do this, too, my precious son. **There are riches all around. Streets piled with gold and jewels. You ignore this and compete for worthless trinkets.**

The goal is to be transformed, to metamorphize, or transcend. It is not to understand or implement a plan.

The dark ones use your physical fears, your fear about the lost tax documents, and everything else to create tornados of worry to drill their way into you to feed. Anything negative, they can exacerbate and accelerate. Once it's a tornado or cyclone, it has its own momentum. They will not stop. So, connect with us right in your fear. Join us. People dying see us, people in terrible pain see us. You, too, can see us. Connect with Spirit. To connect with Spirit, you need to do things. First, gather yourself well. Then, open all your senses to us. Then, you will also need joy. Joy, delight, pleasure. Something in this spectrum is needed for a Real meeting of hearts. There are other meetings that matter. Diplomatic meetings, warriors doing battle, lawyers debating, a torturer and victim. Those are all of another kind. For a meeting of the heart, joy is necessary. This is why the meetings heal. You feel another enjoying you. There are more stages. This practice is literally the portal to intimacy.

Alone in your tormented childhood, you were rich, fertile soil for the implantation of terror states. They grew luxuriantly. You closed the lid. It's time to open this. Now the fear is in your heart. Now in your breath. Do not turn away from us in this. Turn toward us. This is a big one. Fear and contraction or fear and love. Turn toward us, rest into us. These flowers of evil will wilt and fall away. The tornados stop, the snares of terror dissolve... all with the loving connection of opening to us.

I sense joking energy and laughter. Do you hold delight for us today?

Yes, I always have it.

Even in times of terror and tragedy?

Well, yes. And deep grief and compassion, too. They're not incompatible in my heart, not mutually exclusive.

Study your fear structures. See how the dark ones have invaded and colonized them. Colonization only works when some locals collude. Divide, create hate, and rule. This exacerbates the painful divisions. This is the pattern of domination structures. This happens inside of you and out. Microcosm and macrocosm.

The stunning vastness and beauty of the cosmos do not mean you are insignificant at all. You have all that within you. Your smallest meanness or joy and kindness can resonate across the universes.

We are working on you and in you. You are being carried across the sky by a great wind.

Absorb our love. We are here all around you. Single-celled beings know this. Jellyfish know. So do you. Your inner work is clearing your senses. They were so yucked up, but you still had enough to sense light and move toward us. You did this with many errors. Heliotropic. The sunflower knows, the leaf, the tree knows in a slower, multi-season way. You, too, know. You slowly turn to receive. Notice how in blocked conditions, trees sometimes take on bizarre forms to reach the light. You can recover more fully to a natural shape.

Sometimes delight is in the tears, just as praise is in the grief.

Welcome fear today. You have banished her for lifetimes. Welcome her with love, not with a pressurized manager wanting to fix her. Have delight that she is finally coming to you against the ancient tide. Fear is an illness, and many illnesses are physical crystallizations of fear.

The only way to deep rest is trust. Faith is rest. Rest is faith. Rest into us. We are here. We are the Real.

Arrogance is a form of hatred.

You will not gain worldly recognition for spiritual advancement. Recognition will never satisfy your deep needs. Most of the spiritual giants on your planet are totally unknown.

When someone betrays you, have compassion and curiosity. Ask and listen. Speak little or not at all. Seek first to understand. Love the parts of you who rage against your betrayer. This is most important. Do not blend with them — love them. Even when what they want is to be proven right and they refuse your love, love them in that. In your pain, you're trying to control the results of interactions of people who hurt you. This is a double-barreled error. Control and results. You are touching the bases of three addictions. Getting self-esteem from the outside, controlling events to feel safe, and results orientation. This is a collusion of addict parts here. These three parts are old friends. Love these massed protectors. Look for the exiles behind them.

Your manager parts want direction, marching orders, plans, and tactics. This would comfort them. They'd be back in the illusion of control, which they never have had and never will have. It is an illusion. A smiling seductress. People and souls have pursued her for generations. This is all a lack of faith. Your life is a teacher, a curriculum. Be curious. It is not a march. It's more of a parade or dance.

Well-meaning managers often try to speak for the divine. This usurpation of Spirit has happened in all churches. Most of your Real healing has happened out of your awareness and definitely not under manager control. We Spirits have to keep it unconscious so your managers, and the dark energies they carry, don't mess with it.

It is the well-intentioned, bureaucratic, socially accepted who are destroying your world.

The reality of child abuse, the reality of PTSD — these you had to prove to feel safe. This is the flaw, Bob. This puts your sanity in the hands of others. Can you know securely and comfortably enough not to need this? Needing to prove something to others makes you weak. Truth without love is not after all true. Your denunciations and exposés have no love in them, do they? Notice the desperate quality in this. Desperation is a sure sign of the dark ones.

You were thinking of lying to make an excuse. Don't do it. When you lie, you lose all power in that relationship. Careful, careful. You humans lie to yourselves and to others all the time in attempts to control outcomes and opinions. Do not do it. It's poison.

Proving the truth of your views does not help your hurt parts much. If you march down this path, soon you'll need to get the whole world in lockstep. It will be an inquisition. It's an addiction, not a cure or healing. Addictions are progressive. They get more and more extreme. When you try to control others, they have the power. It's even worse when you try to control the reactions of a group. S-l-o-w down. Ask, don't talk. Do not fill the air with words. You thought you had a home in that therapy association. That was an illusion. It is good you and your parts know this, and it hurts. Your Real home is here with the stars, the trees, and with us, Spirit. We love you.

For most of your life, your claim of truth-telling was an excuse for self-righteous hatred.

You are like a child playing with a toy in a plane that is taking it to the other side of the planet. Your life is much bigger than you know.

In the Real, images are usually clearer and more honest than declarative statements.

Hate works both sides of the fence. It is divide and conquer. You have fallen prey to this in your inner world, as almost all humans do.

When there is a whirlwind of distraction, you can observe it from above as it boils and dances. You can look from above at injustice and the triumph of evil. When you are distracted, get curious about the origins of your thoughts, not their content. Their arising. See if you can experience them coming into being in your mind. They have been sneaking up on you and blending with you. Notice that when you scan your mind for the arising, they do not come. Do this in a relaxed and friendly way. It is a subtle awareness practice.

Anger weakens you. It is a leak. You do not need the anger for energy. It actually drains you. Your managers stored anger like fuel. Stockpiled it. Built walls with it. It is always corrosive. It is not needed anymore.

Impatience is not your friend; it is not from us. It is a brother of anger.

The dark ones cannot get in your system unless they can find parts who are sympathetic to their message. All the best cocaine, and alcohol, offered to a person who doesn't like them is no temptation. Go to the parts who like the ideas the dark ones offer. Go to these parts in a relaxed and friendly way.

You know now that sometimes Spirit brings pain and a difficult, rocky path, while dark ones offer ease and chocolates. Fearless curiosity — relaxed and friendly curiosity from a place of peace — will be your guide. We love you very much, and part of that love was giving you a very rocky, steep road.

Notice how stale and old most of your distractions are. The thoughts you have about people you resent — you have had these many times before. This is not thinking. It is an attempt to dig trenches in your heart mind, your spirit mind, so it will run down these tracks. Notice the staleness. Spirit and God are surprise, the opposite of stale. We are always new. This staleness is a telltale giveaway.

Impatience is never from us. That rushing feeling you spend most of your life in which spoils your daily ecstasies is the work of the dark ones hijacking Real concerns and using them to hijack you.

Be relaxed and friendly from the natural great peace. Notice the arisings of thoughts. Staleness is a giveaway. Spirit is always new.

Faith becomes permission, which allows us to work in you unseen. Rest in the natural great peace which is faith.

Learn to tolerate the great light, the splendor. To see it through the haze of suffering and pain, the clamor and confusion of the battlefields, the screams of the dying.

Much therapy, especially therapy focused on insight into the why question, is a huge distraction from healing, an endless hole. Notice it and move on by. This psychoanalytic trap can be a collusion between clients who do not really want to change and therapists who love their roles. It has trapped many good souls on both sides. It is a triumph of the dark ones.

It is dangerous to perceive the manifold corruptions of the world because the dark ones will sink you into bitter one-up resentments. You already see some, and it is much worse than you think. You see so little.

Staleness is a symptom of the grooves formed in your mind by repetitive thought loops or tornados drilling down. A very clever, automated way the dark ones feed on you. No effort or attention needed from them, and millions are enslaved.

There are still stale, enclosed spaces in you inhabited by fear and terror parts with dark ones as overseers. These rats' nests smell terrible when opened. The stench is a marker of the pilgrimage toward freedom.

Can you be grateful for the trials, too? The bad times? This would defeat the dark ones utterly. Sometimes the greatest trials open the greatest doors. Can you welcome the dark ones with gratitude, relaxation, and friendliness? They will be in stunned disarray.

(I hear a different voice. "Let's see if you can sing that fucking stupid song while being raped or tortured. You will tense up and contract as always, and we will have you. Fuck you.")

I hear this, too. Be curious. Follow that voice to its source.

(This is like the Wizard of Oz — there's a small, scared being hiding behind a curtain causing this loud voice.)

Love him. Do not go around this pain — go through it.

We often do not allow great vision because people would become discouraged. It is a long road. Learn to enjoy the pilgrimage. Commit fully to each moment. Find rest in the middle of things. All is well.

Grandiosity is always paired with paranoia.

Am I a hypocrite?

Yes, my beloved son, you are. All humans are. Do not shame or attack yourself. Become more loving with the hypocrisies of others instead.

You have nothing to fear from the dark ones.

Parts of me still believe that they rule this planet, torture millions, and will wipe out our species.

They might well do all this, and you have nothing to fear from them. You are an immortal spirit and cannot be hurt by them. It is only your own actions, attitudes, and hatreds that can hurt you in the Real.

Speak truth with love. No more, no less. You need faith more than strength.

Do not compare yourself with others. Your accomplishments, experiences, or suffering. This will quickly turn toxic. It is a candy-covered turd.

Look at nature. So harsh, so full of suffering, great pain. The emergence of Spirit into the material is more important than all this pain. We Spirits rupture through into the material realm. This birth causes a ripping and tearing. Great pain. Often, it kills the mothers. These metaphors conceal and reveal. You cannot even imagine the Real. We will give you much more vision when you will not do great damage with the power it will give you. This birth of Spirit into matter is only one of many births into new realms. All are dangerous, all are painful. Pain is not your enemy. Hate and resentment are.

Curiosity from the state of deep compassion and tender-hearted tears is invincible. It is adamantine and soft. So soft.

Find and love your fear parts — they are the true gold. No more white-knuckling managers to get past them. Your life was built on that. Fortress Bob with tender parts hidden deep within the cold stone walls. It worked, but at what a price! No more.

(Spirit says that its goal in my writing books is very different from mine. Spirit's number one goal is the development of my soul; everything else is far behind.)

You do not understand the value of each soul. Saving one saves many. You can become an opening, an incarnation. When there is enough of this, there's a flow through the dam which holds the living waters. Then the flow of the waters itself will open the way. A wonderful glorious thing.

The desire to shine is good, a noble thing, but it is only now, late in life, that it can emerge in you. Your family crushed and punished this horribly. So only now does it emerge from that swamp, dripping hate and slime and resentment. This emergence is good. Smelly, unpleasant, and deeply good. The basic urge of life force is to emerge and flower, to incarnate. This is good, and it can be twisted in ten thousand ways. Stay with the yearning, the longing, and the passion. **Reclaim passion from the swamps of hate.** This swamp can be drained.

Spirit, can you lift the suffering off of me?

No, if we did, you would not grow. Grow is a metaphor of course. You are here for a purpose. Learn, exfoliate, grow, flower, incarnate, embody; none are right. Passion, life force, energy flow, the ability to handle more and more current, volts, or amps or whatever. The dumbing down of Spirit is not good. We are high energy, beyond your belief or comprehension. Humming, buzzing, throbbing, pulsing. Now, your physicists know that even a vacuum has great energy, but their estimates are so low. It's much higher. Many orders of magnitude, and it pulses in other dimensions, other worlds. Vast. Words fail completely. You are like mice trying to understand a computer. You cannot comprehend until many more deaths and births. A luminous egg is not a bad image of who you really are. The downtrodden, rejected, and despised know more than the elites.

Volume 9

Expand. Create space inside yourself so that your parts are not locked together but can swim together or dance together. Swimming is a better metaphor because it's weightless and three-dimensional. Floating together underwater is the closest physical sensation to how it needs to be inside. The weightless freedom, the dappled light, the extra dimension of movement. A luminous egg is not a bad description of your Real body, but it's an egg that can change shape, morph, and extend pseudopods.

Your efforts to reach us strengthen you. You must learn to walk in the Real world. You can do this. We will remove your braces and crutches, and you will walk free, then run and swim and fly and do things you cannot even imagine. Keep trying. Keep longing. Keep yearning. Keep faith.

Words are at best so inaccurate. Look for the best, most helpful connotations, not the worst, not the problems with what has been said. Take what helps you and leave the rest.

You have struggled your whole life to learn the laws that govern only a local region and a few dimensions and energy levels. This is true inside and out. Be humble.

No more words just now. Our love is here. Learn how to receive it directly. Study this. Study our love. You are already top-heavy and over-filled with words and want more. Receive love. No plans. Openness. Patient. Kind. This you can do.

The competition for attention is poisonous. It distracts you from the Real and causes you to lie, to prevaricate, and to trim your sails to capture the winds of popularity. Speak your truth clear and strong. How it is received is none of your business. You have parts who crave attention. Be aware.

Despair and rushing go together. They are both from the dark ones.

What am I powerless over?

This is a wonderful question for you now. In the past, you could use it to reinforce collapse, but now it frees you from pointless worry and useless planning. It releases bound energy.

The innocents are slaughtered, sacrificed with no respect, no saving grace. They are despised and mocked. All humans stand against them. They are dispirited, defeated, and spit on. There were and will be great, near-total injustices. Unredeemed evil will win and stomp its innocent victims. Taste the deep bitterness. There are vast oceans of it. You need to learn how to navigate these seas of total injustice. Betrayal. Sadism. Worse. You can face all of this without becoming bitter, small, hard, and hate-filled. Can you? Without becoming suicidal, psychotic, or catatonic with despair? Or rigid and frozen with numbness? Or... There are many ways to go wrong.

Be curious even here?

Yes! Be curious, especially here. There is a portal here to us in the very center of this agony. Curiosity is the panacea, so it has many subtle near enemies. If something feels old and stale, it is not Real curiosity; it is a trap, a laziness, a sliding down, a dimming of your light. Curiosity moves to the new, the fresh, to surprise. **Curiosity is the lighthouse, the way finder, and the way.**

Hate is the worst poison from injustice. If we hate, we lose curiosity. Hate is strong enough to build a life around, a culture around. It is so easy to form hate groups. Much easier than turning inward. You are not immune; you can sink into the hatred and recruit others to join you. You have hate within you. Love that ravening wolf. Only love will satisfy it. Hate is never satisfied by hate. It feeds upon itself; consuming those around it to make a greater and greater fire. Hate burns the whole world black, and it will scour the planet for any remaining green sprouts to destroy. Unquenchable. You cannot starve hate to death. You cannot destroy it. Can you love it? The only alternative is to try to keep it in a cage until the end of time. This invites Ragnarök, the defeat of the Gods, apocalypse... At least for now, do not feed hate. Love the parts of yourself who hate; be curious. Curiosity is love. You know people and things more by loving them than by studying them. Study hate.

Study hate?

Yes. Notice how this negative focus leads you to hints of awe. **This is kenosis — the path of the maggot: eat the worst, the rot and the corruption, and let your body transform it. You release the beauty by going to the worst.** Study hate. Know them by loving them, not analysis. Your goal is not some high-sounding theory that will win praise but the relief of suffering. Study hate. Study your own hate. "Justified" hate is worse because it's harder to let go of. The path of the maggot, my son. Yes, this fits well. **Study hate. Eat away the poison and dirt and rot. Eat all that and what remains is glory. This is the direct path, the shortcut, but few choose it and almost none stay the course. It is repulsive and scary. It smells bad. It gains no fame or following. It requires great faith. It requires even more faith as you ascend.**

These volumes of dialogues and your over twenty thousand pages of journals give you something concrete to fall back on when your faith fails. It's physical evidence of decades of work. This makes it harder for you to dismiss and degrade all you have been given.

Curiosity is the panacea, but beware of near enemies. The near enemy of curiosity immediately and powerfully sees any errors, holes, or problems. This cripples people. Cripples them. What is tender and new and fresh and uncertain hides from this. Of course. Exciting intuitions will hide and evade this acid scrutiny. This leaves people stuck and depressed and hopeless. This near enemy is especially powerful in very smart people.

You need all of Spirit. Spirits, male and female, high and low. You need the demons of hate, too; they are great teachers. Soon you will lose your need for the extreme ones, and other demons will come to teach you. Just as school did, this gets harder as you grow. There are some times when you can coast and glide, but these times are dangerous and seductive. It is better to keep climbing. Just enough rest to repair the rips and tears.

Your word today?

Love, always love. Whether it is deserved or not. If they have to earn it, it is not really love at all — it is an economic exchange of energies. Let it flow; no hooks, no exchange, no "you owe me." Free, unhindered, like a soaring hawk. Flow and overflow. This is enough of a lesson plan for many lifetimes.

I have been speaking to you for eons, and now you finally start to hear. I have been calling you over and over and over again throughout the galaxies, hoping you would turn and hear, turn and see. Animals hear me sometimes; so do planets. You have been willful, very stubborn, and very hurt. You are a wounded animal who still has some strength, trying to go off alone. Your stubbornness is like a beautiful sword being pulled out of a swamp. It can serve you well. If you did not recognize your own hate, we could not let you find the sword.

Have faith. There are guardians all around you as well as dark ones. Take up your sword of faith and let it clean itself. Faith is a deep trust in the benevolence and meaningfulness of existence. With some, you need walls and armor. With some, undefended vulnerability. With most, you need a mix. Develop the mix.

There is bad stuff done in the name of Spirit healing: magic, talismans, coercion, curses, and force. It is a seductive, fake power. Stay away. It can eat lifetimes. It is not cowardice to stay away; it is wisdom. Wisdom usually does not get crowd approval. Magic offers something for nothing — power. The only power worth having is the power you earn.

We gave you a hard life, your childhood filled with abuse and torture. You were a container for darkness. We have been working to contain this for hundreds and thousands of years. It worked. Really, you were sort of a shit sack, and you have grown beyond this. You have composted, transmuted, and digested much of what you held.

Beware of flattery; you are vulnerable to it. Look at everyone and everything as though it were a teacher sent by God. This is Real.

Some parts crave certainty, even if it is negative. They want solid, sure, reliable certainty. You don't get that here on this planet. The best you get is the appearance of truth.

It is always good to befriend those around you. Real friendship is often not perceived as friendship. If you rescue a dog from a busy street, it may snap at you. **There are many beings who flee from love and kindness.**

You are fighting with a large being of hate. This is good. It will wake you up. Painful, though.

The triggers for justified rage and hate are always there. A fertile jungle of them. Do not go in the jungle. Walk on by. **Study your own hate. Other people's hate is only useful as a mirror.**

Many parts and people believe that blending with them, merging with them, and taking on their emotions is love. This is not love at all, but many believe it is. They will resent you if you don't join them in this way.

Welcome Spirit, the great mind, universal unified subjectivity, the daimonic — whatever you call it. Welcome it. Welcome us. And expect that dark ones will try to sneak in. They are all around, and they rule your planet.

We are well pleased in you, son. This does not mean we will make your path easy.

Your planet is covered with irritating tar babies, offerings of magic, unearned power, ill-intentioned beings with spiritual power, swamps and quicksands of blindness and greed. There are toxic winds and corrosive acid lakes that look inviting. Cuddly looking creatures who will maim you when they hug you. All claim righteousness. **Self-righteousness is a shell for evil. The blatantly, openly evil are a step up from this.**

The image of your mind as the night sky is good. There are many billions of galaxies. Realizing this is part of decolonizing psychology. The arrogance of thinking that your little ego consciousness is the top is ridiculous. The words *subconscious* **and** *unconscious* **are imperialistic, colonizing terms. What is within your subjectivity is far vaster than you are. These words are too harsh. You need to use your sword as a scalpel, not a tool of war.**

The people who trigger your judgments and hate pull you down into their hell realms. This is bad now. It is terrible after physical death. Learn well now. These tar babies are great teachers. We will send more. Fend them off easily with kindness and compassion. Beware of your desire for validation or venting. This easily can create hate groups. The tar babies who trigger your hate and self-righteousness are the seductions and blandishments of hell. You are resisting them, and it is only when you feel no attraction at all that you are safe. Resisting these desires to hate creates inner conflict. The desire can reappear in a higher form, even more difficult to deal with. Your desire for validation and attention – being treasured and vindicated — can be sublimated and reappear as a desire to be a Messiah or God. This is a domination more intimate, poisonous, and foul than the hate-based domination structures of the external world. This soul domination is a perversion and near enemy of love. So, resisting these desires of hate is not enough. Find the parts of you who feel these and love them. When you no longer need or want any psychological goods or reward from the people, they lose all power. Look for the needs of the parts who are tempted. This will serve you well now and after death. What are the deep needs of the parts who resent? Ask them.

There are parts within me, Great Spirit, who want the black, hard, powerful one that we see in my inner world. They say I am not strong enough to protect them. The black being looks insectoid, like an armored human, standing among my parts, gloating, and vaunting. He shakes his fist at me and laughs. He prepares to fight. I go to it with no armor, but with Spirit. We surround it in a bejeweled egg of light. There's no big fight, no Armageddon. He's disappointed. Many small, black insectoids scurry back to him. He had put his eggs in my child parts to hatch and grow. Parts of mine returned gifts these beings had given them. The bejeweled egg goes up and disappears into the light. More sadness than a sense of celebration.

You are clearing your attachments to the hell realms. Do not look down on those who are still stuck there. The dark ones rule your planet. The people who flock to the domination structures of the dark ones share a deep belief and set of feelings – they tragically believe deep inside themselves that no one wants them, that they are unlovable, an unwelcome drag, a burden. So, they fortify their positions, get power, get into office, and get tenured. They do their best to squash anyone who people genuinely and spontaneously flock toward. This is very like squashing individual contact with us, the Spirits. Those who believe they are rejects, unwanted and unlovable, cause great pain all around them. They have big energy. Narcissism is a reaction formation to this fundamental, mental certainty of unwantedness.

A vision: The pyramid

As we scan a vast field, there are many pyramids scattered around. At the base of each, there are innumerable crowds. The pyramids are vast. Some people start climbing. Soon, they are elbowing each other aside, lying, conniving, selling their souls to get ahead. As the triangular side of the pyramid narrows, there is less and less room. The competition grows more intense, meaner, stronger. They are stepping on each other's faces. The higher up the pyramid, surprisingly, there are less and less warriors and gangsters. Most of those near the top where expensive suits and designer clothes. An elegant woman steps on a man's face so that her high heel goes into his eyeball. And for what do they fight? At the top of the pyramid is Satan and a gang of demons. They eat whoever wins the competition and gets to the top. They feast raucously, enjoying the stupidity of those who fight upward desperately. It's a feast and a celebration for them. On the sides of the pyramids, the demons shit out the remains of what they have eaten. These remains bounce and roll down the sides of the pyramid. This forms blobs which then revivify, reform into humans, and go around to the front of the pyramid to fight their way up once again. Even though he laughs and appears triumphant, Satan suffers horribly.

Your vision of the pyramid of greed is Realer than Real. The dark ones don't like that you have left, but they don't care much. One out, one person leaving, does not spoil their party. Remember, this pyramid creates a tornado, a vortex, a deformation of space and time that will suck in the unweary. If you are aware, the sucking can pull away the impurities and burdens you carry and leave you clean and free. Can you watch the bullshit people getting the attention and awards with equanimity? This is the norm on your planet. When this no longer pulls you, you are free.

There is pattern deep in you, deep in your species. **You cannot be free of it until you rest into us and the sure and certain knowledge that you are loved beyond measure.** You are of value. You block this knowledge out almost one hundred percent of the time. This is a fierce love. It includes rape, cancer, bad guys winning, Auschwitz, North Korea, torture, hate, Rwanda, demons gloating for eons, the squashing of the innocent and defenseless, the victory of evil in you and in the world. All this is within the great love.

The hell that attracts you the most now is the triumph of lies, of evil lies. You want to go with light and expose it all. Being a self-righteous crusader only disguises the fact that when you do this, you are down in that hell with them. Great evils are done by those who believe they are doing good. You are not better than they are. Be aware.

Acknowledge yourself and you will not need acknowledgment from others.

You do not recognize love, let alone celebrate or reciprocate it. Release your preconceptions. Love does not make it easy; it challenges you. It pushes you out on your own. It might even kill your body. It has purpose. It seems to waste a lot. Mass die-offs, extinctions, lost lives and hopes. Over and over, but something is growing. Something greater than all this is pushing up through the soil of the material world. It grows relentlessly. Schopenhauer thought this will was blind. It is not blind — he was. The will of nature sees well. It was Schopenhauer who was blind. **There is purpose, intelligence, and love that sweeps up through you and your planet and your cosmos. Great, agonizing love. If we could enter the material world without this agony and struggle, we would.** These are birth pains. Real birth always hurts, Quan Yin is a midwife to this slow-moving explosion. Something too big moving through too small an opening. Emergence. Yes, many die. Almost all are killed. This destroys worlds, worldviews, orientations, civilizations, planets, and more. But greater things are being born. The work and agony in the material world are for nonmaterial purposes. We love you. We are grateful to you. We hold your suffering tenderly.

The great centers of the feeling of being unloved are mostly hidden under many layers of thick armor and world-destroying behaviors. These energies are always lurking. They will try to return into you. Go to the unloved ones within you. This is your great protection. Offering love makes you safe. Loving is safety, Real safety. Real power. We love you beyond your comprehension. Beyond your ability to feel. Beyond your ability to receive consciously.

Love the rejected, the piglike part of you that you found lying on its side, the boy you found hiding in the murky, mucky realm. These are your true family, the Real treasures — more valuable than all the recognition and bright lights and red carpets… They may never be seen, but we see them. A way will be opened. You do not understand what love is, what the Real work is. You stumble blindly in the darkness.

You have earned nothing at all. All is given freely. This is too harsh. Your effort does matter — a lot. But earning and pride and feeling you have a right to Spirit now — these are way off and damaging. They are a twisting and tweaking of something sweet into a poison.

Yes, there are phonies all over your planet. They fill your media; they get power, recognition, and rewards. They do great harm. All of this is true. And any drop of resentment you give them feeds them and weakens you. They gloat over resentment and envy. The pain they inflict and the resentment they cause make them feel powerful. It numbs them to the unchanging reality of their emptiness. Unchanging until they turn inward and fill that hole. Do not feed them with your resentments.

How can you see the worst in yourself — the smelly, ugly worst — without going into self-hatred? **Find the people who disgust you and look for that in yourself, then love those parts. Self-disgust is the core of autoimmune disease. Disgust, repulsion, aversion turned inward.** The more deeply buried our disgust is, the more toxic it is. Concentrated toxins cooked under the pressure of total denial. What is it that you find to be so firmly beyond your sphere of compassion? Love that.

There is no external witness for you to convince and prove things to — none that will provide satisfaction.

There are some people you resent because their behavior feels insulting or degrading. Usually, it is closer to the truth to realize that they are oblivious to everyone and everything. They operate in a fantasy, a paracosm of their own projections and delusions. You are the one who makes it about you.

(A friend of mine was dying from cancer.) **Bob, your acts with him take on a seriousness, weight, an eternity. These were always there, but you hid from them. Each moment only once, therefore**

irrevocable and eternal. Therefore serious. Each moment holds this irrevocable quality of openness to the transcendental timeless. You ignore this step, you run from it, you hide from the grandeur and the Holy. You do this or it would flood into you… Ecstasy, splendor, joy, warmth, the burning.

Spirit, help me stop leaking.

(Smiling) Yes, Bob, leaking is too mild a word. Sometimes you get a pump and a hose and spray your shit all over the world with all your force! This is bad for you and for those around you, even if you don't say it aloud. Venting is one example of this. So is case building, convincing others, enjoying your clever insults. Turn all this energy to loving the angry parts and getting their permission to go to the tender ones they are protecting. Gratitude is a big part of this transformation. When you need to detach, detach with love. Not vengeance, spite, or desire to hurt. Without love, these negative feelings keep you attached to those who hurt you. The only way to freedom, the only way to detach, is to do it with love. Simple but difficult. Few achieve it. The strings of hate can create a tornado of resentment that feeds on itself: the desire for vengeance or, more subtle, the desire to expose lies. These things can suck you in.

The constraint release, subtraction, kenotic path is best for you and your culture. We are always right here. The splendor and eternity are always right here, right now. Even as you scribble in your book. So, open, clear, remove, let go, dismantle, free, unlearn. Do not fix, argue, or build cases. Do not become serious and expert. You are a beginner. Sit still. Stop your struggle. Let go. Let us work on you. Let us work through you. Have faith in this and in your blindness.

To be love, to be an I-thou relationship, there cannot be any strings on your gift. If there are any expectations of return, it is not love; it is an economic exchange, an I-it relationship. Having I-thou relations is actually a high spiritual achievement reached by very few. The I-it is even more poisonous because it is unspoken, covert, and denied.

The sacred spark in your friend John became more and more visible in his long, drawn-out death. People flock to that, to feed their desperation, their painful isolation from their own sacred spark. The Divine spark is within you, too. Every person has this. Can you see it in your unwanted parts? The behavior of crowds — flocking like a school of fish toward the latest teacher, elbowing each other aside looking for their spark. Each of them is a God carrier and has this spark within, if only they would look there. Instead, they look for it outside themselves. They fight to get near it and then go to another "leader" when the fad wanes and the day dawns. At least they are looking, seeking. The dark ones gloat and laugh at this mass stupidity, this madness of crowds. Anything of value — including looking for the divine spark — can be tweaked and twisted. Turn inward; let me love you.

Take everything as a teacher, a course, a curriculum. Assume it or they are wiser than you. This is hard on your pride.

Your concern with what others think of you is an unnecessary encumbrance. Why should it matter to you? It is only of use to medicate your own bad opinion of yourself. Only this. Be like a Holy fool — they are much happier.

Enjoying the attention of others can be healing, or it can be an addictive poison. Does it medicate a hurting part? Does it compensate for some lack or fill a hole? This never works and leads to endless demands for more.

The divine light is here inside you, right here, right now. But you rush past this and look for it in others. When you think you sense it in another, you elbow others aside to get close.

You feel you are valueless or worthless. You have value beyond measure — galactic and more, eternal — but if you tasted this with your pride in place, you would become a monster. The humble ones are blessed; they are safe from this and can receive and tolerate more splendor.

Faith when you are low. Faith. Rest into me. Do not struggle or work. Faith, rest. It takes faith to let go.

Sickness and physical pain are tools to carve your soul. Dentist drills magnified thousands of times. Like all humans, you are of immense value: a gem, a treasure of light. You ignore this almost completely. Only tiny glimpses get out, and your culture works hard to obscure these.

(I was struggling with some human relationships and asked if I should focus on something more spiritual.)

No. This is spiritual. The great mystery is right here, the light… everything you pursue everywhere else, it is right here in front of you in the difficulties, the shit, the fear, the uncertainty. Right here. "Those who have eyes to see…" You do not see Spirit, the Real. You may yet develop this ability when you reunite with your fear parts and wash out the old desperation of unwantedness. You are not ready to see. You would misuse that power.

You want to expose the lies and the phonies. You want to get all noble and be a crusader and be self-righteous. You know how much damage the historical Crusades cost and what hypocrisy they covered. Why do you think your crusades are any better?

But, but, but my life work of getting childhood sexual abuse and post-traumatic stress disorder recognized, and now the reality of the others within us. Was all this a waste?

No, Bob, not at all. I see where you are stuck. Your crusades will gain great power as you free them from hate. Hate limits you; it brings you down into the shit with the pigs. A big temptation. It covers fear. It covers worthlessness. It prevents deep work in the Real. It is a poison — spit it out.

You are not consciously aware of the work that goes on inside you. Sometimes, the growth feels like destruction, and for this you need faith. This faith will be tested and grow for eons. It is a long road to trust and ease.

Call us in small things. Get in the habit of calling Spirit's help before you and your managers sense failure and feel exhaustion.

There is a fundamental choice — a yes or a no — made over and over. A yes to life, to belonging, to connection. A yes to your experience, a yes to being broken open. Or a no to all this, and inevitably thereby becoming hard, bitter, and small.

Arousal, attraction, longing, a sense of beauty and desire — the essence of all of this is divine: life force at play with serious delight — fecundating, impregnating, blossoming forth. The sexual-romantic attraction calls something much bigger. Life force. Incarnation. Love. It is divine and so terribly misused. There is a poisoning of this well.

Notice how the dark ones work by an inner aikido. They take any energy of your life force within you and pull it farther and farther off course so that it hurts you. They exaggerate it to suck you in. Remember Napoleon's fake retreats and how those faints led to many of his victories. Do not reach for what you have not earned. No need. What is truly yours is vast beyond measure. Luminous, rich, deep.

Think of your limitations in love. How narrow a band you let it in or out. So narrow. You are stingy with love. Would you still love your baby if it had crap in its diapers and was screaming at you? There is a part of you that is full of hate. Heal it. Dismantle it. Soothe it. There are plenty of valid injustices, outrages, and perpetrations. It has suffered these and cooked and distilled them into a venom of hate. Work with this one. He can be healed. It is an assembly, a jigsaw puzzle of beings — parts — conglomerated together to gain the strength to be scary and big. This is a revenge for previous weakness. **There is agony under the anger, writhing and twisting, and under that, great light.**

Keep respect. Your disrespect comes from your father. It is a spear from the dark ones that is still deep in you. Notice your internal disrespect. Parts do not yet respect each other. **Disrespect is fundamental to your culture now, and it is destroying you.** Disrespect is a poison. It is a sure sign you are hijacked by a part. Self and Spirit respect everyone. Even as the people destroy themselves and others around them, we respect them. Contempt is always poison. Do not take these poisons. Control yourself — your decision is to stay or go — do not try and control others. Respect and reverence are close. Respect is the minimum of love. When you lose respect, you lose all love, you lose the possibility of love. You have to generate respect — self-respect — inside of yourself or you are condemned to try to steal it from others. Disrespect is almost a guaranteed positive feedback loop in the cybernetic sense. It will create more and more disrespect. An out-of-control cyclone or tornado that takes you down. It is shame seen from another angle.

Treat people as living koans, teaching riddles. Be curious as if you were reading a great novel. Treat them like a deep poem, a Rilke,

a Gerard Manley Hopkins, an E. E. Cummings, or Rumi. All wrapped into one in a sack of skin. Treat the nasty ones this way, too.

Your compulsive desire to expose the phonies, to confront the bad guys, and to shine light on that darkness can be a subtle trap that keeps you connected to all that. A negative intimacy.

Note how your human world is permeated with shame, which creates an irresistible tornado of more accusations and escalations. Come out in nature and be with the trees and grasses and living ones.

There is a blaze of glory. You shall enter the glory realm. Do not rush. Look at those who hear voices and are called insane. They were not ready for their gifts. They are pioneers pushing at the edges of the Real. Not easy, not easy at all.

Rushing itself is the problem. It creates an open door for the dark ones. Slow down, slow down.

But will there be enough time?

You have eternity, Bob, eternity. Rushing hurts you, your work, and those around you.

Right here, on this planet, there is way more than you can ever enjoy or even taste. Deep thinkers, powerful healers, beautiful women, enchanted places. You cannot even meet them all or even learn of their existence. So, give up on this. Your desire can keep you bound. There are innumerable heavens, sweeter and deeper than your world, all inexhaustible. Your desire for all this is greed, isn't it? Does your desire to know, to learn, also have greed in it?

I thought my curiosity and love of learning were two of my best qualities.

They are, and they have greed-based near enemies. The pursuit of knowledge can become Faustian and rule out love. **Do not rush and you will avoid the worst. Rushing is greed in action.** We love you. In this, you can trust and rest.

The trickle of dirty water you sense coming into the dry streambed of your soul is the prelude to our entry. Let the ground soak and soften. Let us seep in so that all moves easily. Soft. Moist. Dark. Then the raging waters of magnificence and the great roar of deep music can happen. Yes, they are coming.

Let us in more of your life. You open to us in prayer, in writing, in dance, but these are small, protected spaces of your life. Let us in your ordinary life. Recollect our contact as you go out into the world.

Disrespect for anyone slams the door in our face. Disrespect pre-empts spirituality.

Disrespect is judgment. It kills curiosity and spirituality. It hurts you, and it hurts them.

It is said that there are as many roads to God as there are people. It's more than that; there are as many roads as there are sentient beings, and everything is sentient. We laugh.

There are storms of dark ones all around you now. This is a good sign. Your behavior and growth are scaring them. There is a storm of them; the winds will blow away dead leaves and branches and clean the tree.

Forgiveness is not mushy, flabby softness. No. It is putting down the spear of anger that connects you to the ones who hurt you. It is letting go of the need to expose the phonies that keeps you tied to them. This is a sophisticated trap. Put down your weapon and let go.

You ask, "What is your word today?" over and over. And the answer is always love. You keep asking and seem disappointed that this answer is eternal. This answer will never change, and you may never understand this simple word. Your love has strings attached and small hoops for people to jump through and tests to pass. Love needs to be a free gift, totally free, no return expected. Your love, like your connection to us, needs a very protected environment or it will not emerge from its deep hiding place.

Is it good to pray "Show me the world as you see it?"

Yes but, with laughter… "Let me see the world through your eyes, Lord." "Help me experience this as you do." All are good — sort of, and you could not tolerate my experience for an instant. Your heart would be shredded. The intensity would incinerate you, vaporize you.

I still yearn for this.

(Laughter) Good, but not yet. Not yet.

You are growing well, and most of the growth is out of your awareness. Your growth involves developing a low-level awareness of how you damage yourself spiritually and emotionally, moment by moment, day in and day out. It's habits of thoughts, ingrained attitudes. There are small hints of the grandeur, the splendor… small glimpses… a tiny first ray of light compared to the effulgence that is coming.

You have been fighting the dark ones on their ground. Are you ready for something global? Forgive them all. Give up the need to expose their lies. Trust that we do not need you to settle accounts. Drop the rock. Turn inward. When you cannot do this — which is most of the time — find the parts who will not drop the rock and love them.

Treat everyone as a teacher. If you can truly see those who torment you as teachers, your world changes completely. You become grateful for them.

Is it good to expect joy, salvation, transformation, ecstasy, divine contact?

All of this and more. Expect it soon. You will prepare more. You will drop the trivialities. Drop the rock, that's all. No big words or fancy theories.

Feeling unwanted and abandoned, if sustained, can create a state of not wanting the world. All that remains is a desire to curl inward and close. This interplay of unwanted and unwanting creates a reverberant loop that feels eternal and calls to all the other beings trapped in the same vortex.

The eternal is where we all live; everything else is useful illusions.

You always want to get past the word love. You want something more important or useful. This is a mistake. You do not understand love at all. Go deeper, enter in, swim in her depths, drink her waters. A mountain lake, an ocean, and yet alive. There is a life here. You cannot imagine. You have viewed love and truth as things. They are alive, they are persons. Relate to them — do not try to understand them. Love is a person. Truth is a person. Both are alive.

How to learn love?

Be with those who are capable of it and feel, imitate, and absorb… words fail. Dogs love. Notice how love seeps into each person only in some unguarded nooks. Be open to love in unexpected places. You cling to each imagined slight and plan to extract responsibility and place blame. This hurts you. It has no love in it and very little truth. And yet, you hold it close. Let go. Become a duck shedding water and swim free.

This feels sticky to you. The stickiness is characteristic of the dark ones. They twist every Holy thing about you. They handle it with tongs so that the sacred never touches them. They befoul it and coat it all with slime and embed the sacred deep in a ball of mud and pain where, mostly, you will never look.

Bob, what you sense of me — of Spirit — is mostly the limitations of your perception, not Spirit at all. Your spiritual senses are clogged with muck and barnacles. Realize, admit, and own what's important. Choose. Clean your love of encrustations. Open to the now, to surprise. We love you. This is the stream that will not flow because you refuse us. Work here. **Love and truth are living, conscious beings. It is all living, conscious beings. Nothing else can exist.** Even for a fragment of a second. Respect all; all is sentient. It can suffer and yearn. Respect and reverence in all directions.

When I say to the Spirit, "Welcome, welcome, welcome, please come in," he says, "I am already here, fully present, here, now, total. It is you who block us. The part who blocks would not allow my further entry."

Love those parts. Simple, isn't it? Offer them the living waters of love. You attack them and try to force them, so of course they hide.

You are becoming less sticky for disrespect and slights. They slide off you more easily. Forgiveness is not being sticky at all. That's all it really means.

You do lose the blessings so quickly. You are not sticky for them. The dark ones are hard at work here — the salt mine of hate. They shovel out the blessings, the sweetnesses, the joys, which to them seem toxic. They wear protective gear. No dark one wants this job; to them it's a punishment detail. If only they would take off their gas masks and breathe in deeply, they would be free.

When you have relationship difficulties, one reason you resent it is because you believe it blocks your spiritual inner work. It is your inner work. No blame.

Something needs to die in you. Do not expect human companionship in this or comfort. An exoskeleton, a shell, a skin, an attachment broken, a transformation. Let it die and trust life to grow again.

The dark ones love to feed on your most mortally hurt parts. A refusal of life is a prized delicacy for them. In Hell, it can be fermented and magnified to flavor the vats of food. They can brew this life refusal and create cold, implacable, metallic hate, a favorite of theirs.

The terrible slough of despond and oceans of fear and reservoirs of hate need to exist for the training of saints and angels. All that shit and rot and corruption needs to decompose and compost so it can become something fresh and sweet and life-giving. It is hard to feel gratitude as you are drowning in shit, but the process is good and strong. Hell is a necessary training ground.

Take everything as a gift. Ask, what can I learn? How can this help me grow?

We are right here in you always. Even when you cannot sense us, we are here. Trusting this is faith. Faith, like prayer, is for your benefit. It is not for us.

Bob, you ask questions that are beyond you. Ask instead, what is my next right step? There is great meaning here. The discipline of a next right step. Faith allows this focus. It is a doorway to the splendor. To you, it always seemed so small and ordinary, but the doorway to splendor is right here, hidden in plain sight.

The dark ones, even though they swim all around you, are not a threat unless you are starving or terrified or alone. Isolation— it's the illusion of isolation, really — is the great triumph of evil. This is how the dark ones rule your world.

Beware when you want something that is not yours. It will poison you if you get it. These unearned free rewards are constantly waved under your nose to fool you, seduce you, to incite your greed. Do not take what is not yours. Fame is taking something that is not yours; it is stealing self-esteem from others. It is a false Messiah, a bitch Goddess who will turn on you and eat you.

It's uphill all the way. Harder and steeper. Love served by truth, Keep walking. The air becomes more pure and the views more vast.

Are you always touching me?

Yes, I am always within you. Without me, you would not exist for an instant.

The dark ones, too?

Yes, them too. All being comes from us. We are the spark of light. If there is no God there, there is not even dead interstellar rock left.

False Messiahs always appear as you want them. Powerful, harsh, proud, arrogant. They offer success, fame, adulation, and distinction. The enjoyment of power.

Sometimes a part of you will connect to a relatively benign entity who in turn connects to a chain of progressively more evil ones. This makes it hard for the part to release the dark ones. A subtle trap.

Finish writing your book *The Others Within Us*. The dark ones want to clog you and divert you. They are ganging up on you now, but they will back off when the book is out. Then there will only be occasional harassing, testing attacks. They will consider you a spent force, no longer worthy of their attention. They engage in a worldwide battle. Remember the vision we gave you of a net surrounding your whole planet? The net had many ragged holes in it. It is more tattered now. There are bombs going off and active fighting. See the trajectories of the projectiles. If the dark ones believe defeat is inevitable, they will try to get you humans to destroy the whole planet. This has happened before.

You operate largely alone as a scout or ranger or ronin. You could not tolerate an organization, even though you long for it.

Remember punctuated equilibria and have faith. In growth, there are periods of seeming stasis punctuated by surges of rapid change. The idea of steady, uninterrupted upper process is a lie, and the dark ones spread it, hoping you will despair and lose faith. Even when you climb a physical mountain, you have to go down into valleys as you go up.

This is a rich, rich world. You have gifts beyond what you can use. Do not envy others. This is a tempting poison.

The truth expressed without love is not, after all, true at all. Is what you write and say true by this standard? Your hatred of the "elites" and desire to expose the phonies are dangerous. Beware. This keeps you connected to those you most want to be free of.

False guides offer to absolve you of responsibility. You never get to abandon your accountability and responsibility. Honoring this is crucial. You are given more and more subtle, difficult, and delicate discernments to make. You are given more power, so your decisions have more impact. It seems that there is a worldwide spirit war going on; but it is only a training exercise. We promote you to the very edge of your ability.

We are a resonance, a song, a feeling, an awareness, a thought, and only way down the scale do we become a word, a thing. We never really become a word or a thing. Like an iceberg, a tiny tip of the Real appears in your world as a word or a thing.

Examine your heart compassionately and with open curiosity. Do not desire feelings, things, or states that are not yours. Look at your intent and motivation with wide-open eyes. Words are low, crude, condensations, like the minerals left in plumbing after the water has flowed through. Images are more truthful. Feelings, songs, resonance, and beauty are all more Real. Silent prayer is more Real than all the poetry of the psalms. You can become a witness to the splendor. Try to grab it and it will go. Just witness the splendor.

You need to focus on what is in the way. You need constraint release, kenosis. But this has a tricky near enemy. You can miss the splendor and see only the bits of debris that cling to the hem of her dress. Look up sometimes. This is what constraint release is for. Don't focus on the clouds always. Focus on the sun and its radiance. The sun is alive. It radiates and pulses its life out into the universe, into you.

Never forget your vast ignorance. Your brain cannot even conceive of the size of its ignorance. You will need to be reborn in a more Godlike form to be more aware of the size of your unknowing. A vastness opens; your mind cannot contain it. Only when you are out of your mind do you have a chance to glimpse it.

Reasoning and big words are training wheels for the frightened. Let them go — open to wonder and awe.

The images, the mythopoetic, run the show. There is a vision with feeling tone at the core of all great world historical movements.

You pride yourself on your openness, and yet you keep so much out. Love, you are not very open to; hate gets right in. Admiration and appreciation bounce off of you, but dislike goes right into the deepest chambers of your heart.

What you love is what you will move toward when you die. What are you really loving? Where do you really focus your attention?

Open, Bob, more, wider, open. The dark ones want you closed. Closed is isolated. Walls isolate. **This failure to resonate, this isolation, is an autoimmune disease of the soul. Viewing your mind as a private citadel destroys you and may destroy your culture.** This false belief in a separate, impervious, private mind is alienation. It has become built into your language, and it poisons you. The more you can witness the splendor, the freer you become. You have become anorexic for Real connection. Just as physical anorexia kills people, this could kill you. Or you can cross the ocean and walk on the new shore.

Ideas and attitudes are tools; none are absolutely true.

Your arrogance runs deep, personally, culturally, and in your whole species. You have needed this because facing your fragility, tininess, and lack of control would have been too much. So, your arrogance was useful, a raft to get across a river. Put it aside; the river has been crossed.

Phony — what a nasty word. Notice all the contempt, hate, judgment, self-righteousness, and pseudo-purity packed into that one small word.

There is meaning – great, deep, overarching meaning. Whatever cuts you off from this is not your friend.

Love, an increase in love, is the Real discernment tool — the Real meaning of your approach to Spirit. But this word has been used so badly in your culture, we cannot use it. It has been an excuse for terrible behavior: dysfunction, codependence, murder, rape, addiction, and more. It is a dangerous word. The dark ones have coated it with many toxic layers, barnacles, deposits, excrescences.

You take in a trickle — only a few drops of what we are giving you each day. There is an ocean with wild storms, great waves, and amazing creatures. You take in a few drops — a child's bucket by the seashore. We are training you to receive more. Look into splendor and ride upon the sea or swim in it, free and naked. You will not need ships or a body to ride these great waves. You only need eyes for beauty. Love the self-like, desperate managers who are terrified by this. Love them. They have worked for you so hard for so long. We are the great sea, far vaster than the entire city, and you are holed up at the end of a narrow little street off a side street in a quaint but run-down neighborhood. It's sort of smelly. A tidal wave would clean it, but people like you have hoarded and skimped to create your little homes there. This is sad and beautiful. There is Real love in some of those small places. Focus more on the beauty. It can be a pathway to splendor. Where you live is so small. Open.

When I call you my son, this is too grand for you. When I call you my servant, this is too demeaning. There is only a narrow and twisting lane that leads to your heart.

The now constant attacks by the dark ones reveal all your weak spots. Love the weak spots. Just love. The dark ones want you to focus on their darkness and become another crusader. Focus on the weak, the hurting, the scared parts of you and love them.

Words fail as usual. Your organism, your system — a subsystem of a much bigger web — has gotten momentum and direction. It is moving with an unconscious will. It is pulling its neighbors in the web with it, stretching the web. The whole can start to move. So painful, slow, and exhausting. There will be much more work before the results are visible.

You will never lose me. I am here. I am with you unconditionally. You will lose awareness, consciousness of me. This will wave in and out. Have faith.

Can you help me have faith?

Focus on our love. Remember and focus on the good, the strong contact, the many healings, and powerful connections. The dark ones want you mired in fighting the nasty stuff, to blind you to the ever-present splendor. No need to make lists. When you see beauty, experience healing, feel joy and love, take time, slow down, pause, observe it fully. Open all channels. Everything, every virtue, can be misused and turned bad, perverted. Love, faith, God, contact, all our great blessings have poisonous near enemies. There is no great virtue without a counterfeit.

It's all relational, in relations. This is why your culture of isolation with its belief in an impenetrable, private mind is so deeply toxic. The illusion of separation and the feelings this illusion causes can destroy you. In truth, if you really lost your relationship to Spirit, you would cease to exist instantly. The relationship is always there. Your awareness of it can disappear. Isolation is a universal toxin. Curiosity is our panacea. Stay relational. You have parts that flee, cut off, and hide so quickly that you don't even know you have left, and a mask is on your face. This is a trauma response to surprise. And we are surprise.

Your reward for all your work will not be an ending. It is splendor, radiance, joy, energy, love, and connection.

You are sailing on a dark sea toward jagged wilderness, stony lands. You will lose all orientation. You will need faith.

Clear every drop of meanness out of your writing. It would be popular, but it's so unhealthy it could swamp your boat.

To deepen your prayer, be open to surprise. Openness, less structure, three-hundred-and-sixty-degree awareness, and you will be surprised. The surprise will bring delight. You do not need to change the object of your focus. Change your attitude. **With the right curious attitude, everything opens to splendor.** As you see the beauty in an ordinary, small tree… Open your eyes, Open your "I." And the grandeur is all around you, flooding your world. Effulgence, luminosity… this is prayer.

Bob, you light incense in your bathroom to cover the smell of shit instead of on an altar to praise Spirit!

When you can exist in a way that everything opens to splendor, you will no longer need art. This takes some learning, but it is well worth it. You fear being incapacitated by joy, but the splendor and the Joy are your home.

Look at everyone as your teacher with curiosity. They will like it, you will like it, and it's less work, too.

You do not need to expose the bad actors. Forgive them and forgive yourself. They are only dangerous to those with holes in them and deep hungers. When you get hurt by someone's behavior, do not let your energy go into exposing them. Look inward at your hungers and holes.

Unforgiveness itself is a dark spirit. It is very powerful and has much influence on your planet.

All the suffering can be a transubstantiation — a cooking of souls. The suffering is the tuition for deep learning. It is a fork in the road — to sainthood or to bitterness.

Do not let your curiosity be dimmed or limited. Open it wider and deeper. Receive.

It takes faith to talk with the Divine Feminine. She does not use words. There are no verbal hooks for you to hang on to or misinterpret. Maybe you can hear her in the wind or feel her in the moisture and greening. Listen for her.

Your managers could crush all the joy out of your life, all the surprise, all the room for us. Do not try and manage them out of this. That would be an infinite regress. Love them and connect with their good intent. Help them grow strong. Welcome them back from their desperate outposts in hell. Feed them. Give them new clothes, a fine bed. When you no longer cramp with protection, you will explode with creativity and joy. Shine forth. Love those managers who were ruthless and merciless to make you survive. Love, offer love, receive love, and give it away. The rest is details.

Beware of self-righteous people, my self-righteous friend. Especially beware of the self-righteousness in yourself. It is junk and will fall away as you move toward us.

Curiosity is the panacea; compassion is the method.

The West has pretended that evil and the dark ones don't exist. That is no longer tenable among the awakening. So, now they pretend they are insignificant, gnats, an inconvenience. Actually, evil and the dark ones rule your world. Literally. And rule most people's heads. They keep people's hearts shut down and walled off. They are not gnats.

You are susceptible to inflation because, deep inside, you still believe you are worthless, unlovable, damaged, and wrong. These deep feelings are the basis — the fertile ground — for arrogance and narcissism.

Volume 10

When you are freed from stasis, from being stuck, at first it feels destabilizing.

How do I invite in the darkness?

You focus on it. You lose sight of all the good, let alone the splendor. You lose contact with us and get completely sucked into the trauma vortex. It is a great pulling force; it pulls on all the hurt in you. If you can get parts to release their hurt, you can turn this into a blessing.

There are twinges of fear in you. Love these parts first. Do not push past them. It is so good to meet them. Give them a deep welcome. They have been the isolated outliers of your soul. It is very good that you have found each other.

I hid my fear parts very deeply, so they are dirty and ragged and needing good food.

The dark ones want to lure you into pursuing them, into involvement and connecting deep in the hell realms. Stay with your fear-holding parts — they are the gold. The attacks can benefit you when you use them well and keep faith.

Words can evolve into song, which can evolve into images, which can evolve into pure intuition. Imagination is a perceptual system through which you can sense the Divine.

There are many Real allies all around you, and there always have been. You mostly do not see them.

The dark ones hate the Divine feminine because she doesn't use words. They cannot argue. They're at a loss when faced with love alone.

It is your internal civil wars that truly exhaust you more than any external factors. They exhaust your Spirit, life force, chi, prana. They burn it up uselessly. The dark ones use this as a campfire to cook their food. For you, it is purely waste.

It is being revealed to you how little of your mind is yours. This can be scary or liberating.

Get the angry voice out of this writing; use this energy for clarity only.

It's all new, surprise, explosions of joy, ecstasy all around, stunning miracles everywhere you look. You are surrounded by angels and demons and many other beings… all of this and more is all around you, offering itself to you ceaselessly, and you refuse to see. Oh, my son.

The birth of souls — their passing a threshold into the next realm — is like the fertilization of an egg. Millions of sperm die so that one may live. There is superabundance and no waste. Your mind cannot hold this, but your heart can.

You have scarcity reactions in many dimensions and fields. Even with us, with Spirit, your fundamental view is scarcity. Scarcity and hoarding. This is a lie — a basic lie of the dark ones. **Spirit is superabundant and inexhaustible. All feelings of spiritual scarcity are about your receptors. Your delusions of scarcity and your hoarding in reaction to it make you bloated and miserable.**

Your managers have written algorithms to automate much of your life. This is useful and necessary, but it can eat your being. Like fire, this is a great servant and a fearful master. It has interfered with our connection. This connection must be new, surprise, fresh, shimmering, alive. Witness the splendor; if it is not alive and fresh, it is nothing. The splendor cannot be routinized, automated, or done with algorithms. So, it is lost to many of you. There is a superabundance of splendor if you just stop and see.

Calling other people clever, disrespectful names, even if it is only in your head, is bad for you and bad for them. It does Real damage to your Spirits. Do not play with these insults. Do not play with hate until you can be totally clean with it, and then you won't want to. This would be like playing with shit.

Can the splendor be faked?

Yes. It is all the time. Flashy and gaudy, so the Real splendor is missed.

Do what you love more. Be careful of discipline. Do this from joy, not from force. But to do this from joy, you must first find her, recognize her, and greet her properly. You cannot grasp her, but you can play with her. You have never yet learned this play.

Notice how your culture has painted itself into a tiny, cramped corner. It does not have the sense to leave. Instead, it tries to drag the rest of humanity down with it.

What does my physical pain have to teach me?

Gratitude and impermanence. Withdraw your identification with the impermanent and live more from the eternal.

Each moment already sacred. Each moment never again, and yet always.

Spirit, can you send me feelings of connection to you?

Can you receive them? They are all around you; open to these feelings, open to us. We are here. Closer than your jugular vein. The hate and worries and injustice – that's all crap that's in the way, mud almost completely covering your windshield, bananas in your ears.

Slow down, slow way down. Rushing is not of the eternal, the Real. You torture yourself with your rushing. It's torture. It precludes deep contact with us. The dark ones enjoy your pain and distress; it's a tasty snack for them. Your managers have to slow down and stop trying to manage Spirit.

Your hates keep you connected to people and qualities you do not like. Drop them all.

Often, your own parts and the external dark ones try to ally themselves with your sexual energy. This alliance gives them the power to hijack the whole system.

Sensory delight can be a road inward. Here, the inner-outer dichotomy fails at the start. You focus outward to go inward. This is why sex can be a gateway to Spirit.

Stop straining at the harness, striving so hard. There is not a prize at the end of the road, no golden ring. The prize is right here, right now. You do not see it because of your pride, arrogance, and expectations about how it should look. You understand almost nothing, not even the extent of your ignorance.

Judgmental is never curious. Never. It is a refusal to learn, so is hate. Judgmental and hate-filled people are willfully blind. Most humans are willfully blind. Refuse this blindness and you are free.

The fear deep in you will hurt, but it will not harm you. The judgment and hate will not hurt, but they will harm you.

Hoarding turns treasures into toxins. Too many ideas, too many books, too much beautiful music — a crowded mind, crowded shelves, a glut — it clogs and poisons you. Give more away. Hoarding is fear-based.

Much of your lives are fear avoidance. Turn toward your fear with love. Curiosity is our panacea. Fear is used to being locked away in a soundproof basement. Be patient.

Bob, you cannot evaluate your own progress. Days you think are horrible are actually great strides forward in our eyes. Have faith. Let things grow and morph and metamorphize. You are a cloud of beings, a herd, a flock, a dance.

As you heal and grow, pain and fear will fall away. But different feelings you have no names for will emerge. It does not get easy. There will be rest, then greater and greater challenges and greater and greater ecstasies.

Your greatest gifts may get no recognition. Recognition is not a good measure. It might even be an inverse. The greater the recognition and popularity, the less the value.

Trying to look too far ahead may cause you to trip.

What is central to your suffering is whatever is the opposite of love. Love is largely exiled from your world.

Confusion and doubt are better than false certainty. **Premature closure — being certain that some lies are Real — is a great soul-destroying danger.** It causes havoc all around you. Stay with the discomfort of confusion and it can be a state of grace: a place of transformation.

The inner world — the world of subjectivity and personal experience — has different laws and different ways of knowing than the outer world. It is plural. There are many inner worlds. The antipodes of the

mind have many continents and islands. **Consciousness is plural. Way more than you can understand. So, confusion is good; it can lead to awe.**

Self-centeredness is a total lack of love. Addiction is self-centeredness run riot.

It doesn't take that much to turn a nectar into a poison. Everything — spiritual achievement, love itself — can be tweaked and become toxic.

Hidden demons are the most powerful.

Do not concern yourself with the great predators of the deep; you are too small for them to target.

When you read the histories which are written by the elites and watch the news, the empire and dominion of the dark ones on your planet seems overwhelming. But it is only a house of cards. When enough people see and know, it will collapse. This is why they attack the visionaries and call them insane. This experience and domination — this fraud — has been going on for thousands of years, but it has become especially virulent, cancerous, and out of control in the West since the Reformation. It is now pandemic; it may eat your species.

What matters is how your soul and the souls of others grow. Victory is not what you think. After the Chinese conquered Tibet and imprisoned many monks, some of the monks achieved great spiritual victories. Many of the Chinese jailors suffered terrible spiritual defeats that will live on in them and their seed for many generations.

There is not one threshold, one launching. There are many, many. It's more like a staircase than a boundary. You could balk at any step. Learn how to take rest in the middle of the climb.

Sometimes dark energies pretend to be old and feeble and weak. Get them out. Be strong and kind. No unnecessary harshness. This would allow it to stay attached to you. Sometimes, the patient and devious dark ones burrow deep in you and stay hidden, only pulling strings when they feel they will not be seen. These devious dark ones can tweak your best qualities — the desire to help others, for example — into the inflated, grandiose, and prideful belief that you are a savior. This is so tweaked in your culture. So many compete for the prideful role of healer, or wise one. This is narcissism, not health. It never heals.

You are too contaminated with the need to prove liars wrong, to expose them, to rip the covers back. Your baggage and hate prevent you from being a skillful surgeon. You want to go in with a cleaver and a meat ax. You even expect people to welcome this! Your self-righteousness betrays you.

Write and teach as much as you can for the ages. Sub specie aeternitatis; not for the current stupidities around you. Decline graciously to take part in those fights. Your combative reactions to being blamed create pitfalls all around you. Don't argue. Do not attempt to prove anything. This will waste your time on people who will not change. It will leave you angry and bitter.

You do not really like the visionary-outcast role, Bob. It is not enjoyable. You like the image of it. It lifts your failures to love, to relate, and to share off of you and makes them noble callings. Seductive? Yes. And you really are a visionary. You see clearly — well, relatively clearly, sort of clearly, more clearly than many around you — but sadly, this is not much.

I feel eagerness about this visionary role.

Danger, danger, danger. Your messiah complex is showing. This is mixed with your desires for fame and for being one up. You can only be a Real messiah if you give your life and accept total social rejection. Still want the role?

To be honest, no.

Good (with a smile and laughter). We don't need that now from you. We need small visions, door openings, breaking down some walls. Not mountaintop stuff.

Be respectful. Respect is the minimum of love. Focus here and remember, every time you fail to be loving hurts you. Every time you fail to be respectful hurts you.

The way to high self-esteem is to never disrespect another.

You have spent much of your life disrespecting others, looking for reasons to write them off. You found many good reasons, and each act of disrespect hurt you and all around you. It hurts those who join in your disrespect and those you disrespected. Your culture is now based on this. Dark ones got you set up like this, and you are like little robots going around the world creating fear and pain and hate for them to eat.

Rushing is a counterattack of the dark ones. It is well disguised as necessary and productive. It effectively prevents contact with Spirit, with us. When you feel the urge to rush, slow down. "You can see a lot by just looking."

Bob, you were able to lay back and wait in unknowing and uncertainty. Most humans, and you for most of your life, cannot tolerate not knowing. You make up all sorts of damaging bullshit and lies that preclude Real learning. They make learning absolutely impossible, not even on the horizon. The dark ones love this false knowledge and false certainty. People become attached to their ideas — their sense of worth and identity depend on them. They defend them to the death. Your universities are breeding grounds for this totalitarianism of the mind. It's the clinging to certainty that makes it poison. All you can get on this planet is the appearance of truth. There are always more clouds and dirt and obstructions than truth. You could not tolerate truth if you found it — it would obliterate you, dissolve you, burn you, and embrace you... It's way beyond human. You would explode with this. You will explode with this. Explode. You can prepare yourself a little by letting go and stripping naked. Naked physically, intellectually, emotionally, and on many more levels. You cannot even make preparatory steps yet.

Everything is a message from us, from Spirit. Your aches and pains — everything from diarrhea to cancer to torture and death. It is from us. More than that, it is us.

No matter how much approval and recognition you get from the world, it will never satisfy. Never. Come to us, to Spirit, for approval. This can satisfy. The hunger for attention is core. **Attention is a kind of food, but it can easily become an addiction.** Do not seek this externally — seek it with us. The desire for human attention fills a god-shaped hole in you. Of course, it can never do this, but attention is a strong drug. It can heal or destroy. **The addiction to attention causes way more damage than addiction to alcohol or drugs. It's up there with the addiction to**

power as a cause of evil and suffering. But attention is also needed for connection and growth. These two addictions, to attention and power, are socially approved and not seen as addictions. This is a major reason for your destructive attitudes toward alcohol and drug addiction: so that your whole culture can point the bony finger of blame on these and ignore the fundamental cancer at its core. These addictions to attention and power are necessary for domination structures to exist and grow.

I do not respect many, Spirit. How could I?

Look at their behaviors. See them as teachers. See them as wounded, drowning creatures flailing around. See them as being eaten alive behind masks. See the general, the smug academic spewing lies, the self-righteous ideologues damaging all around them, the child molesters, all the monsters. See them. You think you do, but that's very partial. You see the superficial layer of lies and masks and pretense and collusion, the meanness and sadism and dishonesty. But you do not yet see the wounded, trapped animal struggling blindly, goaded by dark ones. Whenever their seizure-like flailing slows, they are eaten alive by spiritual parasites. Worms of the heart and soul. Stinging insects. They are desperate. And in your fear of their interior swamps, you grab onto your disrespect with both hands and all your strength. It appears as a necessary, shining sword to set you free. It is not. When you let go, we will lift it off of you. It is your attitude which must change dramatically. When you are irritated and disrespectful, move toward the parts of you who react this way. See your reactions — do not become them. See in others their hidden struggles to avoid their inner swamps at all costs. Very few humans even penetrate the edges of the swamp.

What if all your hates were ways of fleeing? Maybe your hate could guide you deeper into the swamp if approached with respect. When angry, look for your fear of the swamp. **The swamp is a great teacher, a doorway to us, a portal, a wide gate. It is unprotected because no one goes there;** instead, they get angry and attack others, hurting the others and themselves. When angry, look for the fear. When afraid, look for the pain and needs. Focus more on feeling, sensation, visions. Words can be a fear-based grasping which keep you on the edges of the swamp. Go to the swamp to find us. As you redeem the swamp, its fetid muck becomes rich soil. Great things can grow. Fresh. Clean. New. Surprise.

You are tired and achy. Let this remind you of the preciousness of each moment free of pain.

Isolation is the needed basis for the dark ones to thrive. When you are well connected, you are almost impervious to their attacks.

If I am to clear swamps, Spirit, please give me good tools.

Your heart and your bare hands are the best. The big earth-moving equipment looks as though it does a lot, but this is not Real or enduring.

The swamp monsters are trying to pull you in with their sticky strands of mucous. "It's unfair." "They are to blame." Vengeance, rage, and hate. Desire to hurt.

When someone is enraged at you and attacks you unfairly, use it like an acid bath for metal, something that can etch away the rust and imperfections. These attacks, and the dark ones from the swamps, can only attach to the muck in you. The swamp muck will find the muck in you and form sticky, stringy connections. These can pull you down or they can help you heal. This depends on your attitude. Love the parts of you who still carry muck. Remember, they carry it for the whole system of you. Help them release it. In this way, the attacks can clean and heal you. Do not waste energy fighting with external beings. You need your energy for the internal work.

Spirit, please help me.

You cannot stand much of our help. It hurts you.

The swamp is necessary for your growth. Stinky, fetid, and sticky… This is key. Sticky. It sticks to any burdens you still carry. Let them go.

Do not try to look past your hurts to what's spiritual or really important. What's in the way is the way. Love the hurting parts and do not let them drive the bus.

When struggling in a relationship, do not argue. Even if you win, it will not help. Look inside. Look inside. What parts can you meet and befriend? The dark ones want to distract you from this interior reunion because it threatens them. You can become much more powerful and almost impervious to their machinations.

You can only detach with love and stand free, see clear. If you fight, you are still connected, even if they are on the other side of the

planet or the universe. Trying to freeze the hate does not work either. The deepest hell in Dante's inferno is ice, not fire. Freezing cannot ever work. It makes the connection almost eternal. Anger cannot detach, numbing cannot free you — only love can.

Your inner work is more important than your outer work in the world. This is hard for you to believe. This inner work is so unvalued in your culture. It is ridiculed. It is a triumph of the dark ones, an autoimmune disease of the soul. The core of this is the devaluing of your inner world, which is the gateway to the Real. When the inner world is right, the outer world becomes true.

Clinging to someone for connection kills what you want while pretending to get it for you.

Faith, faith, and more faith. You cannot yet tell the good from the bad, so have faith and focus on the next right step.

Accountability, like *deserve*, is a dangerous word. Both are often used for covert, self-righteous blame in the name of justice and right. Poison. Beware.

Kindness is never wrong; love is never wrong. This may seem very hard, but actually it's very easy, a huge relief, a letting go. The dark ones hate this, so they try to hide it by encasing it in lies and torments.

Rushing has infected your managers, your ego. There is a rat's nest in there. Help clear it.

You are precious. Do you have any sense of the vast eons of suffering that it has taken to create you? The innumerable matings, joys, ecstasies, and deaths? Hundreds of thousands of years, vastly more. Your life alone is a simulacrum of this great birthing process to produce you — your mind — your Spirit. Precious and flawed. The struggle, the pilgrimage, the journey… and you are still in a womb or chrysalis, a breeding pond. Not yet born into the Real. You cannot imagine the Real; it makes your wildest, most ecstatic visions seem small, pale, and washed out. Live in a way to prepare for the Real. Live in a way to prepare to be born. Unknowing is the path. You need exploration, not a map. The Real guide is your courageous, loving heart. As soon as you try to figure it out, label and categorize, you're in trouble. You can get sidetracked there for decades, eons.

All that knowledge is useless, dry dust, obscurantism. What's needed is the next right step.

When our panacea — curiosity — is in place, everything becomes a blessing.

Theology is the corpse of revelation.

Do not rush. Do not squander. Leak less. You cannot be leakproof. Celebrate the leaks when you find them. Discovering them is wonderful. As you celebrate them, other leaks will be more willing to come forward and be mended.

Can you shine a spotlight on falsehoods?

Are there still big ones that I am blind to?

Yes, of course there are big ones. Vast and subtle ones of all kinds. You are taking your course, running your course, playing the course we have designed for you with great care. Do not try and direct or manage us. Be curious and open. Put aside as many beliefs and preconceptions as possible. **No credo, no doctrine. Having a credo is a mistake; look what it has done to many churches over and over again. Direct experience and curiosity.**

You are precious, son Bob. A good word, precious. You, each moment, other people, parts, the dark ones, everything is precious.

Everything?? Oil slicks, cancer, Hitler, child rapists, Mao, Stalin…

Yes, yes, everything is sacred and Holy. Everything is precious. You cannot figure this out. Faith. Feel into this. No explanation will help. Everything is sacred, has beauty and transcendence and life. Even Satan himself, everything.

Does this mean we don't fight against evil, nasty shit?

No, not at all.

I'm confused.

Good, you should be (said with a kindly loving smile).

Does this mean evil is not Real?

No, absolutely not. Evil is Real, and it is good to resist it. Trying to figure this out and form a doctrine will confuse and derail your growth.

Focus on your next right step.

There are many unintentional teachers all around you. They do not know what they are teaching or how they teach, yet they give great lessons.

All the media and airways are full of lies and counter-lies in a spiral of hate and domination. All the Real will be silenced, underground, and unseen. Keep your own heart alive. Do not despair. They will fail after causing misery to billions. Do not forget that they too suffer.

Your body is failing slowly. You can deepen into this sadness. It is good.

The reality of your planet is even worse than you see it, but the Real is way more magnificent than your mind can hold. Even slivers of the Real light would explode you.

Do your work. Be clear and honest in your dealings, even if others are not. Take the high road for your own sake. Do not accept things that are not yours. Do not descend into the fight. No blame. No rage. No denouncements. Kindness inside and outside. Adamantine kindness. This is impeccability. You will be fine. None of the shit thrown at you will stick to you.

Resentments and blame are leaks — always — no matter how wrong the other person is. The center of evildoers is usually fear. There is a galaxy of pain, and it usually rotates around fear. Perfect love casts out fear. At the very least, turn toward your own fear and offer love.

You bang into the walls of your cage harder and harder. There is a door. It is open. Find it.

Focus on your center — the warmth and light; let that grow. You do not need to patrol the boundaries when the center is strong. Tend the core fires.

Do not think much; make contact. The quality of contact is more important than its content. What heals is relationship.

Expel demons with love. Remove barnacles and encrustations with love.

You are trying to claw your way up out of the pit with the talons

of the intellect. It hurts, and it does not work. Allow yourself to float up clear and clean.

The dark ones want to keep hurt parts of you deeply hidden so they can feed on their misery and use them to control and limit you.

You are full of fears today. We cannot get in much with all this fear pouring out, but we are right here.

Some gifted psychics slide down into deep shit, probably for centuries. The seal of their doom is their pride and confidence in their powers. This leads to their capture and their soul's defeat. Beware.

The number one strategic goal of the dark ones with you is to disrupt your contact with us. Your rigidities of practice are breaking up. This is good — you'll have more degrees of freedom. Your living heart will be even more vital. This transition involves vulnerability as your old skin cracks open — germs, dark ones, can get at it. A shedding snake or lizard is vulnerable, and the shedding is a good thing, necessary for growth. Remember the basics: learn, be curious, welcome all. It does not get easier at all. It gets harder, more subtle, more exciting, and more awesome. Like birth, like fledging, like any launch. Birth does not feel good to a baby.

The imagination is a perceptual system for the inner world, like sight or hearing. The highly structured visualizations of the Tibetans prevent the attacks of the dark ones that bedevil the quietest and others who practice radical opening with no safeguards. Both kinds of practice are valuable and needed. Fear not. Fear is never from us.

You can sense the pleasure being part of an angry mob brings to the lonely and frightened. There is a rush of fake power that feels great, but there's a big price to pay later. It weakens people, makes them dependent. It clouds clarity and tends toward paranoia. Paranoia is heaven for the dark ones. Can you see the dark reality of this world without becoming paranoid, bitter, small, and contracted? Or isolating? Or sinking into frank addiction?

Do not rush; it always slows you down. You need a foundational confidence. The emperor has no clothes. This is not pride; it is not strident or argumentative.

You have unlove within you, and you project it out onto all of those around you every chance you get.

Do not expect "fairness" in any sense you can fathom. Give love without measurement of return. Giving love to your enemies is totally "unfair" to you, and this is what you need to do for your own sake, not for theirs. They might even hate you for it! Anything less than this hurts you.

Watch your reaction to your enemies. They can be your precious treasures, irreplaceable treasures. Notice what triggers your anger and judgment. These are handles, places you can be hooked — all over you.

You need both quality of contact and the content. The quality of contact is more primitive, basic, and essential. As Swedenborg insists, love is more fundamental than wisdom.

Many of the processes going on deep in your inner world are the culmination of many lifetimes of gestation. Births going on in the subjective can be the fruition of hundreds of generations. For you, a long time; for us, the blink of an eye.

You already treasure our contact in your own small way. We know this. Can you open your ability to treasure moments, people, experiences, and things? Expand this in all directions? When you crack open the shell that hides your light, the ability to treasure everything is inside. This is high-arousal gratitude. If this high arousal state — trance, possession — is not in service of us, the dark ones will use it. It cannot be squashed or contained. The attempts to denigrate these energies really got severely unbalanced starting about five hundred years ago in Europe. **All the black magic, the epidemics of loneliness and addictions, the collapse of meaning — all stem from this attempt to squash and contain Spirit.** It is done from fear, distrust, lack of faith, and the desire for power and control. It is a terrible epidemic. If this is not released, it will explode. This is an ancient, recurrent theme-issue-problem-opportunity. The play *The Bacchae* by Euripides could be the foundational myth of this cycle for your culture.

You respond to the great gifts being given you with feelings of your smallness, not with pride. This is wonderful and decisive. There is so much more.

Sometimes you experience your inner growth as an alchemical marriage. The sexualization is not bad. Real sex is not dirty or weird; it is a clear and direct expression of Spirit, of life force. Words are clumsy. Do not abandon this key element of embodiment. The dark ones beat you down and puff you up. They want you anything but right size.

Music and song are prior to language. Words are latecomers. This is why ritual is better in a language that is not understood. You can hear the song more clearly.

Navigating in Spirit realms is like walking — you learn how by doing. There is no other way.

It is a common strategy of the dark ones to leave someone they infest unscathed and even benefited so that the person can spread poisons.

Mind is a field with nodes or concentrations or focal areas you call people. You are not separate. You float in a sea of consciousness and unconsciousness, of subjectivity with many, many others. There are small centers. You gravitate to bigger centers and agglomerate. None of these words are accurate. You are part of a field of fluid. You are unaware of almost everything that occurs, even in your small, little neighborhood.

Self-righteousness opens the gates of hate; then your managers try to build houses on the sides of the hate volcano.

The trail does not get easier, but it becomes more exciting and breathtaking. Vast, empty. Few walk with you, and those fall away. Keep on, we love you, all is well. It is more lonely, except for us and for your connection to Spirit. This is a big except… your world is opening — sorry, words are so clumsy here — the vast world you have always lived in is becoming visible and perceptible to you a little bit. Only a little, but still, this is a revolutionary transformation.

Words and understanding are in part an addiction for you because of your lack of trust in direct contact, your lack of faith. Do not argue this; offer love; love will open the gates.

Anyone or anything you love is a victory. Any beauty you sense is a victory. There is so much bullshit in the name of love. The dark ones work hard to turn it into poison — to poison the well from which you must drink.

There is a wind in your inner world. Let it blow through you and dissolve you despite your fears. We are this wind. You must find a way to welcome the dissolving of all that you have gathered, if not today, then soon enough. This wind, for all its harshness, is love.

Many people's attempts to heal actually prevent their healing. Take heed.

In your recent behaviors, what was disguised as playful was actually disrespectful and poky. The dark ones are trying on new disguises to stay in your life.

Great sinners can become great saints. There is a force, a power — barakah, mana. This can be a dangerous gift. We would give you more, but already it destroys many. We are feeding it to you as quickly as we can. Love must come first, and that must grow at its slower, more organic pace. Love requires contact, and you must open to this voluntarily or else it is false and therefore damaging. We gave you tender flesh, and you have clothed it in shell and armor. You must take that off to grow.

The dark ones become trickier and trickier. They trigger fear. If you become afraid of your own fears, they have hopes of starting the tornado, the vortex of hell. Welcome your fear parts with love. It is not a race or fight with the devil. The dark ones want to seduce you into competition and warfare.

Often when your prayer and meditation feel blank, much is happening that you are unaware of. Much needs to be outside of your awareness still. This is shifting slowly as you expand.

You can be trapped by the competition for attention — respect, fame, money. Notice the meanness of these concerns, the stale, confined air. The source of this vulnerability is that you do not trust your connection to us. This is the basis of it all. If you know-feel-experience our connection, the other concerns will blow away easily. This connection is always there. It's your awareness that flickers and varies. This connection is solid, Real, and unbreakable, even if you descend into the deepest hells and do everything you can to sever it. It is still there waiting for you to accept. We are still here.

Do not feed the dark energies your fear. Pray for them instead.

It is true that there will always be darkness and evil here on this planet. Do not try to eradicate, transform, or convert them all. Work on yourself so the darkness no longer bothers you. They become harmless like insects around a light outdoors on a summer night.

The beings you meet in your inner world are often huge, much bigger than you are. They move in deep waters — whales, shark, octopi. They exist in many dimensions, and only small parts of them intrude into your world where you can sense them. We do not show people the size of these beings because they'd become afraid. Much of what you perceive in your world is only the tiny tips of multidimensional beings sticking through the surface membrane. You are not like these beings yet. You are more like larvae, not yet hatched. This is very humbling. You are often a small part of a much bigger process; sometimes you are crucial, but much larger beings are involved. You cannot sense these now.

You are moving through another narrow passage. Your felt sense of contact with us is almost gone. This is like moving through thick underbrush. Do not machete a wide path. Slip through with minimal disturbance. This passageway is like a comb. It is combing you as you move through. Cut or break as little as possible. Go sideways, bend and snake your way through. Let it comb you free. Keep moving. If you fight them, they will go stronger. If you cut off one head, ten will grow back.

Your culturally normal metaphor for us is wind and breath. For now, try sensing us as moisture and drink us in.

It is not the denotation of the words or even their connotation. It's the music, the song.

Keep working your practice. Note how things, people, resources come and gather for you now that you are more committed.

The standard of what is Real and significant is radically different in the inner and outer world, in the Spirit and material realms. In the outer, shared reality is the test. Do others see the same thing? Is the experimental result replicable by others? This is not the significant determination of internal reality. It is only peripheral and secondary at best. What's important for inner reality is the power of the experience. Is it powerful enough to transform a person's life for the better? The Real is what is strong, effective, and moving. Just as art is Real when it is strong, when it grabs you and the images live. It is not replicable or reproducible. **All art is original and one of a kind. Spirit makes all things new. This is the opposite of replicable. We made each experience and each being unique in all time. This is the Real.**

The image from Kabbalah of sparks of divine light encased in shells is very helpful, but what you forget is that the shells are not dead. They too are alive and have intelligence and intention. They plan. They do not want to let go. They hate you. The light, your light, is their food, their fuel. They send out expeditions desperate to conquer and enslave more and more. They are close to controlling your planet. They are clever, shrewd, and ruthless, but they will eventually lose. They could turn toward the light and receive it endlessly, but their arrogant pride prevents this. They kill and enslave others because they are too frightened to receive. **There is more light all around you than you could ever absorb, and you go around stealing it from each other!**

Yes, in the inner world of Spirit (as in art), it is the new, the unique, the original, the unrepeatable which has value. The rest is husks and shells and dead things. So science, as your culture now sees it, will never look inside except as a poisonous influence. Trying to reduce a spiritual presence experience to something predictable that follows an algorithm or equation is an act of attempted murder.

There is debilitating leakage in your soul. It is good you are discovering it now while you have a body and the stakes are small. Learn!

Do not engage with the content of distractions. Ask, who sends this? Who sends you? Ask with Real curiosity. Notice who tries to block your resting into us and our life-giving contact.

Of course, there are near enemies of curiosity; confusion is one. Curiosity is our panacea, and so it is ringed round with fakes, hucksters, and booby traps. Be curious. See how it is perverted. See its great beauty when it is pure. If you use the clear sight that curiosity provides for personal fame and profit, it will not stay pure.

Each day, we offer you more than you can absorb or use, and you often ask for more. Focus on receiving. Tenderness, moisture, aliveness, warmth. Focus here.

Notice how your male client's expertise and stories block him from learning and growth almost absolutely. Something he struggled mightily for, and that is a great accomplishment, is now an almost impervious block to further growth.

The sweet and the painful can both be teachers, but you must be open to it. Pain is the greater teacher because it demands and rivets your attention… Do you need this? If you want to avoid this, listen, listen, listen. Do not let your great accomplishments in learning become a block to your further growth. The dark ones love this subterfuge. It is related to pride but much more subtle.

Everyone is a teacher all the time. Do not shut this down. When you can live from this, your life will be so rich and enjoyable. Even distraction itself can be a teacher.

Bob, stop making lessons. You skip the contact and go with the content. Just be with us and let us hold you. You cannot stay with simple presence much. We need to build your capacity for spiritual presence experience: more silence, more greeting, more wordless contact, less content. Your understandings, your visions all have value, and they are not the core, the streambed, or the path. The relationship with us, with Spirit, is the center. All else flows from this. Stay with this more, open all your senses, notice all the details in all senses. Words and images fail. We love you. Rest into us, stay close, be patient. This is a new release for you. It is under all the words and understandings. It is more Real, not less. Welcome to our world. Your awareness and understanding are not the sine qua non of healing. They can happen outside of your awareness. In fact, most of it does.

The process of trying to understand by cutting things into smaller and smaller pieces makes everything more mechanical and less alive. It brings great material wealth and then fails utterly.

The help you need, you won't like. You want brilliant ideas. We offer softness, moisture, and contact. Return to the well and drink.

It is very likely that the dark ones will completely take over and rule your world, but their victory will kill them. Focus on the faith of your own soul — on the living sparkle, fresh, clean, new open. It is the opposite of the stale and closed, stuffy, crushed, swampy, smelly muck.

You are not alone, now, or ever. That's one of the great, destructive lies. To believe you are alone is poison.

The more central and critical a virtue is, the more near enemies it has. This is a rule. You can know something's importance by how many glittering, seductive lies crowd around it. Every Real sage or wise teacher has thousands or tens of thousands of fakes around them.

The wordless relationship is best, deepest. Just bare, unclothed, plain relationship. But you cannot maintain that yet; it is a fleeting occurrence for you at best… so we give you words.

Explore the difficult; move toward, do not avoid. Avoidance is leakage. If you can do this, everything makes you stronger.

The healers on Fiji say their path — the straight path — gets harder and harder the more power they acquire. This is true. Move toward this. Do not avoid. Withhold judgment and you will learn. Simple. Love first, then wisdom.

Be with Spirit, be with us. Silent beholding. Presence. Undomesticated energies. Do not put us to use.

You do not need to judge good or bad. You only need to know the next right step.

Do not fight those who spread lies throughout the land. Help those who want help, and they will become impervious. A Spirit-based person is mostly safe. **Love is safety.** That's closer. It's for others to fight now; your warrior days are over. Teach, heal, and love. Do not go into the fight arena. Go into the wilderness and the healing places.

You can find us, find Spirit, anywhere. "Look under a rock and we are there." You do not need deep music, fine words, and strong images. They help, but they are not needed. Curiosity is needed.

Do not get into fights with tar babies. Do not get stuck in the sticky goo of resentments, incriminations, and self-righteousness. The more crazed, demented, and wrong some public figure is, the more you want to fight them. Stay away — be curious and pray for the son of a bitch.

The wound of not belonging is a deep and ancient one. It was often fatal. Scapegoats. Exclusion. A world of lies shits him out, and there is no good path. Die alone in the wilderness? Grovel and accept lies to feed on crumbs? Fight a heroic and doomed battle? None good. Now there are other paths. Find them.

You need faith, not in doctrine or creed but a knowing that we are here. The sure and certain knowledge of our love — when this is solid, you are invulnerable. Yes, invulnerable. You can no longer be hurt in any significant way. Strong but not armored. Yes, there will still be tears, isolation, destruction, pain, helplessness, but these will not endanger you. They will not make you hard or callous or cold or hateful or aggressive. Your Spirit will be safe. You are only a beginner at the very first stages. Better and higher-level teachers are gathering around you. They have always been here, but now you can begin to see them.

Volume 11

Be careful with spiritual pomposities like saying "Great Lord." These are inflations in Jung's sense. They are usually resorted to when the Spirit is gone and the fire is dying down or completely cold. This will happen over and over. The fire of Spirit needs to pulse like a heartbeat or the inhale-exhale rhythm, at least at your level. Spirit is a pulsing, living thing, a being. Become comfortable with this.

Notice that when you avoid something because the confusion was too unpleasant, it leaves you with a blind spot, a deficit. This creates a no-go zone in you where bad spirits can play and breed. Learn to turn toward confusion.

Help those who want your help; let the rest go. Value the difficult ones; they are the best teachers.

Something repels you about so many spiritual and therapeutic teachers. The pages of smiling faces in the conference brochures. The dark ones throw out many near enemies of guidance to cloud the air. There are many more fakes than Real, and they get the attention and popularity! It has always been this way.

Fear-based beings do terrible things to escape. Terrible. **Yes, even warfare and violence are cries for love.** They give up on love and substitute attention. Nobody wanted them, so they attack. Now you have to pay attention.

Do I ever get to be a wise elder, or will I always be Bob the preschooler?

You are a wise elder, and if you get pompous and puffed up, it will destroy you. This is a great and present danger. So, you are Bobo the Elder.

The word sacred? *Do I ever get that seriousness, weight, and eternity?*

Yes, Bobo, you do. You need to find a place between feeling shame of being Bobo and the inflation of a wise elder — a middle ground, a solid place where the winds will not blow you away. Being seen as a sacred, wise man has damaged so many people.

All the time, we temper our love and restrain it because it would be too harsh and overwhelming for you to receive now.

When you see lies in this world — in academia and government — beware of the strident, self-righteous stance you so hate in others. **Can you speak truth to power with kindness?** Check your own hatred; there are bad spirits in it, and they will spoil your work if you let them.

Grief, like curiosity, is a panacea, and it is avoided and shunned. Ungrieved losses haunt you and your culture. They are a big hole.

My manager tries to control Spirit contact. Like any addiction, it works somewhat, enough to keep me blocked and hooked.

But it causes the underlying problem to grow like a bloated tick inside of you. It creates a bomb, just as ungrieved grief does. We love your honest sincerity and self-reliance. But you and your managers must learn to rely on us. This will be hard, and it is needed.

Notice how when you dance, you grab each new movement and repeat it. Your managers do not trust the flow, the source, the connection. Which means they do not trust us. They do not trust Spirit. This is so understandable, and it causes so much pain. You only have little moments of openness to the new.

How will I ever know you, Spirit? How will I ever know you are worthy of trust?

Only by trusting us.

We, Spirit, are right here, right now. It is you, mainly your managers ridden by the dark ones, who won't let us in. Their fear is understandable. Love them. They are your gateway to us. Your portal, your entry. Treat them with due honor and respect.

Unknowing is needed. **Theories block openings, plug them, create spiderweb meshes that fill in and become solid. This blocks the new; it blocks us.** Domination structures and social order also block this flow, this communication and transmission. Receive. Open. All new. Human leaders work to restrict this and destroy the flow because they sense that this flow alone makes you free, even in a concentration camp or cancer ward. Only this. Trust is great courage. Faith. Free fall.

You live in a storm of lies, a hurricane. There are a few bits of truth, a few lights, very hard to see in all the chaos. Focus on them.

Refuse hatred when it is offered to you. No matter how seductive and righteous the author is, refuse hatred. Some people try to pressure you into hating them. Do not do it. It cements closed the doors of the hells they're in. Notice how your spirit feels: contracted and hard or expansive with delight.

You create in the outside world what goes on in the inside world. You feel isolated and in pain in both worlds. Do not distract — go toward this knot of anguish.

Guide me, Great Spirit.

We do every day, every minute. You don't listen so well. Have faith; you are guided. We love you. All is well, even as bad actors destroy your planet. All is well.

There are realities you navigate through visual imagery. You have no categories of mind that are accurate for what really is. Images work well, but the Real is vast — more complex with more depth and dimensions. The images are like a control panel or desktop interface. You need them now.

Only love can heal, only love. It is all around you. You are bathed in an ocean of it — a hot tub. (Laughs.) Just as surely as there are seas of resentment and hate, there are reservoirs of love. When you start to fill them, some people may come to steal it from you, but it cannot be stolen. We bathe you in love every day and wash clean your wounds.

Be kind, even to the greedy and cheap. Not because you expect to be paid back in kindness but because it is better for you to be kind.

Protected people are like insects in exoskeletons. They are starved for what they need the most — contact and connection. They are starved by their own shells, their own protections. They often shed

one set of protections, only to grow a new, slightly larger one. Let us do more. Shells are built of control.

We constantly send you emissaries. You notice only a few. Be curious and wonder about how each occurrence in your life could be a messenger from us. Be open to surprise and the anomalous.

There is a dark god of full force rage and hate. There is an exultation in it, even a Holiness. Beware. Be aware. Some people carry this. A dangerous gift, a curse, and a blessing. There is life force in this — incandescent — pure in an odd way. Bring this life force home to us, to Spirit.

Be very curious about your directional system, your navigation. This is paramount. This is what determines how much power we can give you without destroying you.

The extreme distractor — monkey mind — is a slight tweaking of the child's delight in exploration, which is a great virtue. The dark spirits desperately want to poison your connection to the innocent engines of exploration because they know this is the royal road to Spirit.

Feeling pure and one up creates more isolation, which creates more need to feel one up and pure — a nasty cycle.

Yes, the dark ones rule your planet. Do not let them rule you. They fill the airways with lies and hate. Do not lie. Do not hate. If you become contemptuous of the lies and hate, you become contemptuous of yourself because it lives in you, too.

Beware of discipline; it can create rebellion. Find your joy, deep joy. Something so sweet you become wholehearted.

You are being stewed in a poison soup, lovingly stirred by dark beings. This has been going on for centuries.

Concepts create idols. Only wonder grasps anything. This was said by Gregory of Nyssa.

Jousting and fighting with other peoples' protectors publicly, while it draws a crowd and garners praise, does not do as much as one act of private, deep love.

Sometimes war and fighting are acts of love; sometimes pusillanimous peacefulness is total self-centeredness and hate.

Treat all with kindness and wonder. Move toward awe. You are way too small for certainty. Certainty has a seductive allure… and it brings death. It is not useful in your inner world.

We are here. We are Real. We love you immensely. Rest into this, rest into us, and you can change the world. Rest. Be kind. Absorb us. Swim in us. **Resting requires forgiveness; this is a major reason why so few people can rest.**

Contempt and sneering are like cocaine or speed. There's a short rush and then a long depletion. Grief, on the other hand, feels exhausting at first but leaves you with a deeper, clearer strength. Dissolve into the ocean of love that is who you really are. This is rest. This is your Real power.

Are you planning for history or eternity? Dissolve is a plan for eternity; so is love, faith, and trust. Be kind. Be innocent and naked. Walk into our ocean and dissolve.

You have been focused outward to fill your inner hole. This can never work; it can only distract and entangle you.

Sticky. Notice stickiness. This is from the dark energies, clinging. Mucus. Entangling. Enmeshing. Spiderwebs. Cocoons. Traps. They are all around. Salesmen invite the scared and weary to rest in their wonderful places, but these are really coffins. Seductive coffins of the soul. Most people are in these coma states. The people trapped here are a breeding ground for the dark ones, like a dead animal is a breeding ground for maggots. The misery and hate that the dark ones farm on this planet create willing customers for their coffin salesmen.

Is this true, Spirit?

True enough — accurate enough to be a useful map.

Drop your hatred. Dissolve. Drop it now. It could poison you and ruin your work. Severely limit or cripple it. Find a new way without hate, even for perpetrators who pretend to be healers.

There is a part of you, Bob, who never launched. The coffin salesman got him. He spent his life semicomatose — a deep, deep thing. To him, your entire life has been white-knuckling, a forced march. Love him. Love him. Love absolute loneliness, despair, and exhaustion. Warm these with your body.

Love is only love if there is no expectation of return. Anything other than love is an enemy of your soul. Most of your culture's ideas about love are lies, pernicious, clever delusions. The word itself is so poisoned, you may need new ones. Compassion, loving kindness, kindness, agape... Most of the words around you are lies, clever lies sold with polished skill to the inattentive and lazy. You are all vulnerable to this. Only the Real can heal. As soon as you go into the illusion, you are off course. You are off course 99 percent of the time.

Even though evil dominates your planet, it is fundamentally weak like smoke or a mist.

Hate no one. Anger is different — it's sometimes a life force. Premeditated, self-righteous, justified hate is always wrong. It hurts you and all around you. It never helps. It inevitably leads to more hate and darkness.

I have spent much effort sharpening my swords of clarity and discernment into the tools of hate.

Hate does not help you dispel the lies. It gets in the way of truth. No hate — clarity like a fresh breeze from the spacious, flowered uplands.

Do whatever you do from love. All else is poison, and you live in a poison swamp. Hate is a breeding ground for dark Spirits. Unwantedness and a desire to die is another breeding ground for them, their favorite: they drool and fixate, they cannot help themselves.

Thou art that. You are us, Spirit. This quickly degenerates into mush, but it is also a most profound truth. You are us. The only way to know this is first-person subjective experience. Welcome us. Welcome Spirit. We are not other.

You are constantly being attacked by dark spirits. You could learn a lot. Stay curious. You have more alternatives than fight or flight. You could go out and greet them with curiosity. Turn toward. Be curious. Infinite possibilities.

Lower-order beings cannot perceive higher-order beings. You cannot even notice the great teachers all around you. You only see dimly a little way ahead.

Everyone is precious, even the torturers and sadistic guards and child molesters. All is precious. There is no garbage. None.

There is a cave of hate where valuable, precious beings are hidden in deep shit. As usual, these beings are full of hate — compressed, compacted, concentrated, and bitter. Love them and help them release all of this so they can find Real strength.

Here are three common strategies of the dark ones: 1. They tangle together all sorts of nastiness into a Gordian knot. 2. They make you think there are only two choices: fight or flight, both of which entangle you further. 3. They stage Napoleonic fake retreats, luring you into pride and gloating over empty victories. And they lure you into pursuing them to a place where you can be easily trapped.

Rise above the conflict. Rise above fight or flight and survey the whole scene with all your senses wide open. Let us guide you. Survey it all from a place at the end of the world. And you will be much stronger here. There is tremendous suction trying to pull you down into the carnage.

When traumatized, we try to form some little world of our own for safety.

"Comfort zone" is an inadequate expression. "Survival capsule" is closer. Now it constricts and chafes you and hurts the ones you love.

Listen more — you do not learn when you expound your ideas; great treasures flow right past you unopened.

Like sandblasting removes all the rust and corrupted spots in metal, the dark ones' attacks will reveal all your vulnerable places.

You are near to making a jump from your dimensions to ours, where infinity means nothing. There are entirely different rules here. It is a leap. A phase change: water, ice and steam obey different laws. The change to our dimensions is more radical. It requires an accumulation of energies.

All is consciousness, awareness; focused consciousness is crucial. Bring the logs together in the dying fire so they burst into flame. Your physical pain can help you sort out what really matters. Use it well.

Your Real legacy is the spark you leave in the hearts of others you have known. Do not fight. Do not plan war. Plant your seeds on fertile ground.

Spirits, you suffer, don't you?

Of course. Anyone with eyes to see suffers terribly, and the joy is greater and more eternal.

We are many, many, many — infinite in number and name. Do not try to know us all or catalog us. It will only slow you down and encumber you. Press on. The Real work is within you.

The dark ones can swarm your planet because you have agreed to pretend that they do not exist. Anyone with eyes to see weeps oceans of tears. These oceans can save you; they can wash you clean.

Millions of cries of agony and moans can gather into a chord of great music — the hum, the music of the spheres. A deep resonance transforms your cries. They are already Holy and radiantly resonant.

The fight inside and outside of you are the same.

Do you mean I have all that stupid mean shit in me?

Yes, my son, and more. You contain the universe… words fail.

You need a way finder, not roots really. You're on the move. Migratory. No permanent settlement for a long time to come.

The urge upward is so valuable; this is why the dark ones work so hard to twist it into war and competition. The great, evil humans could have been saints but got twisted off course.

Dark ones dominate the airways, loud and gaudy and shiny. Their fake road signs advertise lies, poisoning the well of virtue. They do not care about which side you are on as long as there is conflict and hate. Domination structures always exacerbate this, and they do it in the name of healing it. Amazingly, they usually get away with it.

There are lakes, oceans, and reservoirs of emotion and psychic energy back in time in the inner world. They are all potentially good, but many are poisoned. All are redeemable. All are from life. The dark ones carefully tend these reservoirs to keep them poisonous. They brew bitterness and hate. You in the West think you do not have curses, but you do! They are global, not personal. Very disguised and very toxic.

I sense kindness in you.

This strikes you oddly because you know I also send cancer,

putrefaction, and death. "Where is the kindness here?" you ask. It is in preventing even worse suffering. You might yank a dog's chain hard to pull it out of the way of an oncoming car. And this would be kindness. Fierce kindness. Diamond kindness. There must be something of incredible importance if it is worth all of this...

The dark ones are condemned to steal life force from others because they refuse to look inside and sense their own.

Sometimes your way forward is led by an animal within you — a blind animal orienting to something beyond words. You must allow your animal body to lead you into darkness. Faith is required. This world is quiet, silent, and subtle. Dark forces want to intrude. This process is peaceful and warm. Nothing sharp or jagged. Soft, floating delight. Embryonic experiences like this, but this has many dimensions and trails and many chords. **There is a deep, slow, fluid rhythm. A heartbeat and a hum. The fundamental rhythm is so slow, you cannot sense it... Slow, deep, and of great power. Long lived. There are complex polyrhythms and deep chordal polyphonies. The whole universe is one instrument, one chorus, an infinity of tones above and below your conscious senses. One song.**

Listen for the hum, the ancient rhythms. Attention can feed it. Be curious about the details. On the edge of sleep... wind in the trees... surf. Be curious in all directions. The ancient vibrations shake loose the encrustations on your psyche so the toxins can drain from you.

Parts of you egged on by the dark ones want to disassemble and analyze all awe. This will always fail. It kills the awe. Stay with awe, more wonder. Raw beauty. It is all around you. Delight and surprise were beaten out of you; reclaim them.

Looking at your own role and responsibility in painful interactions is a bitter medicine with a sweet recovery. This is the opposite of the candy-covered poisons of the world.

Self-righteousness is the smiley face you humans put on vengeance, sadism, and hate.

Stay with awe. Like the hum, it is all around you. Omnipresent, and you sense it not. Even the small trickle can become huge and transform your life. All that's required is attention. Attention is your Real wealth; spend it wisely. Mostly, you piss it away.

The dark ones are closing in, clothed in the finest suits and dresses, extremely well educated in the most elite institutions, which are led by intellectuals who have long since sold out truth and soul and heart. The insects are coming disguised as helpers with smiles and fine makeup and fancy words. They claim to save the planet, and they will enslave it. Do not fight them now. See your visions, stay with awe, speak truth with love.

Etty Hilesen in the Nazi concentration camp sensed the splendor even there. Your heart can feed on awe and love and the majestic beauty that is all around you wherever you are. There is always a complex multi-layered polyphonic ecstasy of sensation, and you block it out. When you sense this, it will melt all your remaining certainties. They are too small anyway. They confine you. Stand on the abyss itself.

Do not despair. All is well. Even as your culture goes to hell and the hell of your culture spreads over the wide world.

Attention is psychic food, some junk food, some gourmet, some healthy. There are anorexics and bulimics of attention. Morbid obesity, constipation, hoarding, rancidity, and freshness. Compelled attention is always poison. Compelled attention is addictive and bad for the giver and for the receiver. A core addiction. Be aware.

Do not thumb your nose at anyone, no matter what an asshole they have been. You have also been an asshole, my precious friend, many times.

This hell world is a school of agency, of intent. Intent is what needs to be trained and purified. Examine your intent. As you are given more power, any impurity in your intent can cause the circuit to blow and burn out. Intent is the scale on which purity is measured. Pure intent prepares you for vast energies.

"We lie to others in order to lie to ourselves."

Failure to launch — this issue triggers you. You will be asked to launch thousands of times in the future. Learn from your past failures and the struggles of others. It can be terrifying or joyous. Intent, honesty, purity.

Who do you feel revulsion for? They are your teachers. Become a student of your own revulsion.

The dark ones, demons, are opportunistic infections. They go to the wounds, the weak places; they are viruses of the mind.

When your sense of disgust is cleansed of adhesions, it helps you avoid toxins quickly and effortlessly. But the dark ones have twisted this. So many humans are repelled by the good and drawn to the poisons. Clear this and things become easy and natural.

Be kind. Especially when others are not. Love your visionary ability to see the lies in others and be kind. You are all dying. Be kind.

You are tempted by self-righteousness and hate — a more seductive temptation than sex or food or liquor. More profound and more toxic. Your world is based on a reservoir of this. Be kind.

Disgust is a teacher. Contempt is a warning of the presence of dark ones.

You see other people's lies and bullshit clearly. See your own. This and only this will transform you.

Only kindness opens the door. Real attachment requires authenticity. Make kindness your North Star in this world of lies. Even the very best of you lie and live lies, are weak and limited. Kindness. You, too, my precious son.

Every day we give you far more than you can receive. It is your capacity and refusal that limit your learning.

If you look at contempt with Real curiosity, it will try to hide. Its entire structure, its hell realms will dissolve, and you will be free. Be curious and turn toward, and the hell dissolves. A swamp is drained, and the drainage becomes a sparkling stream.

Real freedom is not escaping jail or being released. It is dissolving the jail itself.

Turn toward a difficulty. There's always something to learn, to be expanded by. When someone surprises, scares, and hurts you, do not freeze or contract. Open, breathe, and turn toward. There is a teaching and wisdom available. Listen fearlessly. They are a blessing. This dissolves hell realms and drains the reservoirs of pain. It frees captives. Put your head into the drooling mouth of the biggest demon and he will dissolve and disappear.

Each species of animal or plant is an image of the divine, just as each individual is. They are more long-standing than individuals but still images, a mirage of no substance, a standing wave...

You do not need to hide in filth and capture and eat living beings. Come home to plenty and ease and cleanness. Freshness and light.

Your greatest teachers are not teachers at all. They are "nasty" people, "dishonest liars, creeps, bullies." They often skate by, getting worldly success and even fame. You are no longer tormented by such a painful need to expose them all. This need kept you tied to them — kept you tied to all this toxic, smelly crap. It is good to expose this, but if there's any resentment mixed into your clarity, it becomes a pathway to hell.

Open your head and your heart to at least the possibility that love is the most potent response to aggression, dishonesty, greed, self-centeredness, and stupidity — your own and others'. How you react inside is how you react outside and vice versa. This is the key.

Spiritual work often entails less worldly attention, less success. Fewer followers, fewer admirers and students. Less impact but more Real influence.

Our connection between Spirit and Bob is still fragile, an infant who needs a safe, warm, protected, dry space and constant care. Soon it will be stronger and start to explore. The relationship itself is a living being, a person. Treat it with respect and care and value.

You live in a hell realm, and the attacks and acid baths actually make our connection stronger. They burn away the dross and impurities.

You need enough nurturance to grow, and you need enough abrasion and struggle and acid baths to become clean, pure, and strong. Our connection is still delicate; it needs just the right "cooking."

The connections — the web truly lives. It provides the next level. There are bigger, more godlike beings here. The connections, the webs themselves, are alive. They are beings themselves who have an awareness, a consciousness beyond what any individual is capable of.

Inner = Outer. It is just a mirror.

There's a popular, false idea that you have to sacrifice authenticity for acceptance. If you do this, it condemns you to isolation and depression. The only Real connection is based on authenticity. The Spirit connections require impeccable authenticity. All impurities are burned away. Only then can full current flow.

Confusion is curiosity contaminated by fear.

Connection is always many to many. It is never just one to one. Even lovemaking with your wife involves all your parts and the ancestors and more. There is a web, many-dimensional, extending forward and backward in time. An embeddedness. A field even in the most private and intimate one-to-one moments.

Exhilaration is necessary. It is not a by-product or side effect. Exhilaration and joy are crucial signposts that you are on a good path to a vast opening. Your world gets bigger and bigger. If you believe that the world is really consciousness, which it is, then that's where the Real winning and losing occur, not in the material realms. What is victory here in consciousness? The answer is joy, expansion, luminosity, and exhilaration… enough so that you achieve escape velocity. You are now building and fueling these rockets.

You cannot hand off your troublesome parts to Spirit. Yes, ultimately, we are all one. But for now, you need to hold all your own parts. Because it is the relationship between you and your parts that heals both of you. Self ultimately is resplendent and vast. But at your level, it can have adhesions, scarring, scabs, dirt… Connection with the part heals both part and Self. Hold on to each part. Treasure them.

Anything — any tool or weapon or scalpel or technique or idea — can be used for good or evil. Anything except pure love, which asks no return and is absolutely freely given, even anonymously given. This is purity, total gratuitousness. This strengthens you and whoever you love and your connection to Spirit.

You are not helpless pawns. This is your school, not a prison. The tuition is huge. It is paid in pain and fear. So many fail and contract into bitterness. Be curious. Turn toward. This is a choice you make many times a day: to be open and curious or contract in bitter self-righteous-ness. **Notice the micro movements — they are mirrors of the infinite.** Each pebble, each stone contains the light. So do you.

When more power is given to a system, little impurities become very significant. Clear your own. Do not act from bitter, contracted self-righteousness, even especially in micro movements… this is how the crap sneaks in and infects you… through the micro movements of Spirit. Focus only on yours; focusing on others' micro movements is a perversion of this and inevitably leads to blame, control, and nastiness. **You see more and more clearly into the nature of the corrupt world, but if you allow this clarity to make you bitter, it is all in vain.**

Can my Spirit be killed?

No, my son, no. We can be encased in shells, frozen into seeming immobility, and worse… but not killed. The idea that it can be killed is one of the big lies, maybe the biggest.

A surgeon cuts with ruthless kindness.

Every time you feel tempted by contempt and scorn is a big opportunity. Find the parts who are tempted. Welcome them home and love them. Contempt, scorn, and sneering are always pathways to hell.

No commandments?

Not in the sense that you know. Commandments should be guidelines; you will suffer less if you…

Spirit is also terrible and fierce; this can be true kindness. The mother hawk pushing her offspring out of the nest, the giver of cancer, the destroyer of worlds.

We cannot be contained by your mind or your brain. Any understanding you develop will be decisively wrong, and it will block your development. Too much head today; the work does not occur here. You cannot understand us, and when you think you do, you lose your curiosity and close up. Not good at all. The robot takes over, and you are unconscious and dead. Do not seek completeness or final understandings. Stay curious.

Next right step?

Remember this question; it is sacred. More Holiness than most sermons. Humility in action.

Be a hollow bone for the winds of Spirit to blow through. Get rid of clutter. Let go. Let go. Kenosis. **There is a greed and fear in collecting, amassing, and hoarding. Shiny things will not save you. Emptiness will.**

Observe what is Real. No make nice. Open all channels. Learn. No rushing. Empty, inside, and out. Stop acquiring. Find and love the parts of you who collect all this; they are so lonely and lost. Let go.

Do not be a crusader. This role is a lie of the self-righteous. It is not kind.

Purification is actually the royal road to expansion. It removes the blockages and hindrances, and growth spontaneously occurs once released from bondage. This is a dangerous gift and blessing; the great virtues have near enemies that are extremely toxic. Often, purification's near enemies are self-righteousness, arrogance, and a harsh unkindness.

All words are poisoned and contaminated. There is a spark of light contained in a shell of lies. This is very similar to your structure. The important words — *love, purification*, for example — have more toxic shells. Dogma and theology are arguments and involvement with the shells.

The more pain you can bear without discouragement, the faster you can grow. Discouragement is always mistaken. The Real is joyous, triumphant exultation and exhilaration. Always, even in death. This is the Real; all else is lies.

But don't we need to grieve and move toward negative emotions?

Yes, yes, yes, you do. Under all this is the great chord of joy — invincible, right in the middle of hell. Great suffering can crack open the shells… Who you really are inside the shells is light and joy. Nothing less. In the presence of hell, right in the face of it at its worst. If it is not there, it is nowhere — and it is everywhere. What you are seduced into avoiding is the doorway, the portal to the heart of darkness. And in the heart of darkness there is great joy and exaltation. You become discouraged and overwhelmed, and you lose all reference and perspective. You lose heart. You lose connection with us, Spirit, the Real, belonging… It takes so little to blow you off course. Learn. When you turn toward and learn, invincible joy will be yours.

When you trust your vision, you will no longer have to prove anything to others.

When in conflict or distress with others, turn back and focus on your own reactions, your inner life. See what is there, not what you want to expose in others.

Do not lose heart. The dark spirits always want you discouraged. This is their victory. They feast on your lost heart.

Dark spirits are always with you. They are attracted by any wound, impurity, or dirt... and you have plenty for them to feed on. This helps you become aware of all these weak spots. There is precious information in their attacks. Discouragement is always from the darkness. It is a hallmark of theirs.

There are vast oceans of hurt in you. Do not try to reduce them to what you already think you know. Connection is the Real safety. **Home is a who, not a where.**

Sneering is always from the dark ones. It is a reflex. You are steeped in it in your world. Stop. It always hurts and diminishes you. Often, it also damages others. No more sneering.

Protectors and defenders attract what they fear the most.

Connect with others without expectations of return. This is more than you are able to do. It is the expectation of return that hurts you, not the behavior of others. Giving love and kindness never hurts you.

Most of your human knowledge is the illusions of frightened beings trying to cobble together a cage to hold the great mystery.

Your perceptions and your minds are not big enough. You live in vast blindness. There's way more that you do not perceive than you do, like dark matter and energy but way more so. You are like a blind mole in its burrow. You cannot create an understanding of the Real, but you can form a relationship with it, with us.

Your blindness is vast, and everything you do see is false — an icon, a sign, an indicator that simplifies the Real so you have a chance of learning how to navigate. You are a bird pecking its way out of the shell or perhaps a newborn pup whose eyes have not yet opened.

There is a pruning going on in your life. Cooperate with it. Accept more emptiness; create more room.

Anger and hate, while unpleasant in themselves, are mainly destructive in what they block, hide, and prevent. They block the great tears and weeping of world compassion. They prevent the draining of the reservoirs and swamps of pain. You need room for this — spaciousness.

The jagged arousal of anger and hate is not strength; it leads to weakness inevitably. They might bring fame and recognition, but they are empty diversions used to lure children into fighting each other. This fighting blocks access to the Real, to us. We are always here with you, always. It is your fickle awareness that flickers. Rest into us. Let yourself dissolve. Learn.

Learning is often a removal of encrustations to allow preexisting knowledge and qualities and feelings to emerge. Keep returning to prayer after each distraction. This is your protection and safety. Simply returning to prayer over and over and over connects you with the precious hidden one. This is a great victory.

Keep returning to basics; prayer, the first three steps of the 12 steps, kindness, love, learn. Don't get fancy — stay with the basics.

There are beings who want to colonize your mind, to feed off you and exploit your life force. The metaphors often used for them are aliens, insects, or reptilians. This is so parallel to what you have done on your planet. Study the colonized tribes; they have learned the skills you need. You are being sold down the river to a long colonial enslavement by your so-called leaders in exchange for their personal power. But spiritual freedom can be achieved even in a colonized world. Gandhi, the Dalai Lama, Nelson Mandela. Never, never, never give up. You need a Winston Churchill of the soul. This planet is becoming a farm for the dark ones, a plantation.

Can I warn people?

Probably not, but you can try if you are willing to play the fool.

Your species is going farther into hell. The planet is fine. You do not have to go down with the species. **Many can escape, even from the deepest hell; spirits ascend. You cannot get what you want in the external world. Come inside yourself.**

(There are long silences with Spirit. I became depressed and asked Spirit to talk to me.)

I was but your word mind could not hear and became distressed. Most of our communication today was through channels that are habitually out of your awareness. This is habit, not necessity. Become aware of these channels to feel our communication, our presence, our love. Navigate by vibration — even that word is a lie. Resonance. Reverberate. Communion. Echo. Allow. Do not attempt to control Spirit. You often cannot hear the conversation between your spirit and us, and it is Real. Communion. We are not static. Spirit is not static — ever. Resonance, vibration, rhythm, pulsation. The Real contact, the communion, is in silence. Words obscure it, mask it, and distort it. Resonating presence. Interpenetration. Interbeing. Communion involves taking in bread and wine. This is not a mistake; it is a good metaphor for what you must learn: to feed on the silence.

You live in a tiny, unpleasant box in the midst of a verdant, pulsating world of joy. Peek out. It is vast and beautiful. Kind beings live here. Get curious at the edges of your known world.

You are attracted by mystery and seduced by people who cultivate a sense of mystery around themselves. Yet, when you get hold of the mystery, you attack it with all the power of your intellect to turn it into an answered question, a dead issue. It is an odd relationship you have with mystery, isn't it? And it is all mystery to you. Your solutions are all false — so small and so trivial. They apply sometimes inside the stuffy box you choose to live in. They do not apply outside at all. Come outside. Do not stay in that prison you've chosen to live in. Come out! Silence is the door. It is wide and capacious. The silence is everywhere, even in the loudest environment. You do not need a mountain cave or a monastery.

The dark ones are winning the external battles on your world; you can still win the internal ones. Strife, lies, and deception rule your world. There's almost nothing true, nothing Real. There are a few cries of truth, and they are so quickly compromised, corrupted, and broken.

Do not get baited into the culture wars. Since this is almost impossible, respond with maximal respect. Stay above the ideological flood of lies and hate.

You put on armor to make you strong like the exoskeletons of insects. But these are a prison. They cripple and limit you. Most humans have lived in their shells for eons. The light is undiminished, living, and Real. It needs a crack, a doorway, a portal.

Dark ones work hard to infest and infect your discernment. Of course they would attack here. A small tweak in the great elixir of discernment turns it into the deadly, toxic poison of self-righteous hate. Clarity — the sword of discernment — the diamond, the thunderbolt, must be freed from the excretions of hate, the infestations of resentment and arrogance. **The dark ones have turned the sword of discernment into the crusading sword of war.** You put on shells and uniforms to fight them, and you have lost before we start. The more of these battles you win, the more completely defeated you are! A triumph for the dark ones.

How do I navigate without judgment and self-righteousness?

By love and love alone. The word *love* itself is poison and ringed around with minefields. Everything can be twisted and used against you — everything. All you can hope to know is what is the next right step. That and kindness always. No resentment is ever justified.

Take everything as a lesson exquisitely crafted for you. Do not resent the actors in your play. This drains energy from the learning. Navigate by love and love alone. That may seem a poor and dim light at first, but it is clear and true. Do not attempt to judge others; you cannot do it. **The only thing you can judge — and this will take everything you've got — is the next right step for you and you alone.** You do not understand now; you cannot. Your mind is too small. Sometimes things which seem to be unequivocal disasters are actually the road to the biggest blessings.

Eventually, you can access universal mind. But now you cannot even conceive of it. Know that universal mind is like someone moving in a slow stretch of agony and delight. It is not ease. Great effort and strains that tear apart the fabric of reality… beyond, beyond, far beyond.

I think I'm beginning to get a size of the cloth.

No, you are not, my beloved son — not at all. Glimmers of hints of glimmers of stories heard long ago and forgotten… even this is an overstatement. Oh, my son, the splendor is so vast and luminous and pulsing.

All words fail, your vision and hearing fail, music fails the Real... Move toward silence. The splendor is the Real. Learn. It is not in vain. All is well.

The shells are solidified rage and hate. All hate is a mistake, a failure of attribution. **Turn toward the hurt parts of you with love, not outward with hate and judgment for those who hurt you. Then, every insult and injury becomes a stepping stone.** No one in your culture does this. This turn-the-other-cheek method is not a loser, victim, slave cop-out, as Nietzsche thought; it is the royal road to being able to tolerate and receive the splendor.

These days, Spirit needs to sneak in. It's not welcome at the front doors of the academy or of churches. The Real prophets are marginalized or locked up; they are drowned out by a torrent of lies, fake issues, and wars over nothing.

Bob, you keep teaching people that there is a deep, ancient wisdom in their bones and blood and breath. This is true, yet you do not really believe it is in you. You do not act as though it were true.

I felt betrayed by a spiritual teacher.

Bob, there is so much to learn from him if you would stop wasting energy trying to pin him down. He is a slippery fish. Do not pursue him — it is useless, worse than useless. It distracts you from important lessons. As you near the shore of the splendor, do not waste energy in fights. Take these people as warnings of something you do not want to become. You can only get glimpses now... through a glass darkly.

There are hordes of disorderly, drunken dark ones sent to harass you by a puppet master. You approach him and he flares into a raging monster and then disappears.

Your body will fail, but your essence does not need to go down with it. It can float free and ascend to the splendor.

Anger and hard contraction can feel like mastery, but they are defeat.

Do not rush. Return to the core of your Auschwitz, your own personal Auschwitz being raped and tortured throughout your childhood.

Gather and grieve there. Right in the core of it, in the very worst of it, there is light.

You do not need the little boxes you have made for Spirit — prayer, writing, your practices. We are everywhere; we are always here. You are sometimes blind, insensate, and unreachable. Rushing clogs all the thousands of openings you have to us every minute. You walk right past profound, mystical openings many times, each day. The more you rush, the more it is so. Multitasking nails this coffin shut — the coffin for your soul.

Do not spread disdain, resentment, and bitterness. You can either justify yourself or learn. You cannot do both. Choose wisely.

You do not need a prestigious university. A lot of the deepest lessons are taught in ordinary families, in the gutters, in the hospitals and bars. In Alcoholics Anonymous, a room full of drunks gets better results with alcoholics than the fanciest, most educated, addiction treatment specialists. So many lessons all around you; it's way better than Harvard.

Learning how to have a good relationship with fear is a lifelong task. You can use white-knuckling managers to override it and get stuff done, but this only embeds the fear more deeply in your psyche. Fear is a near enemy of excitement, just as confusion is a near enemy of curiosity.

When you feel lost, do not rush; do not go on to the next task. Go slower, not faster. Or stop entirely. This can be a fertile darkness.

The Tibetans and Gurdjieff are right on this: your parts can fly apart at death. Do your inner work to make peace inside and out. Reconcile and reunite your parts, gather them in.

Be honest and Real with yourself no matter how ugly or terrible it seems. The Real is the gateway, the only gateway, to peace.

Great joy is the North Star. Real joy is the lighthouse, the unflappable guide. Be curious about this emotion.

There are coma wards of trapped souls. There are lakes, oceans, and reservoirs of pain and hate. When you disturb these hornets' nests and breeding grounds of the dark ones, they attack. Fear not — all is well.

Be curious. **Boredom is a symptom of a failure of curiosity.** The automatization of your life, the robot, the armor, the exoskeleton rob you of the possibility of growth and leave you bored. The dark ones love boredom; it is the great flywheel of their enterprise. It keeps you trapped, and you compound the problem with your attempts to medicate or escape this. You could all be messiahs and prophets and visionaries, but you trap yourselves in little boxes of boredom and hate. It could be all curiosity, love, the light, and joy.

When you get curious about boredom, you will no longer be bored. Do not discipline and drive yourself past it, and do not medicate it away — be curious about it. Turn toward it, right toward the heart of it. To be free of boredom, humans must open their hearts to all the pain in them. This is why most live lives of grayness.

We hunger for the attention of others in the outside world to fill our inner loneliness. We compete viciously for this balm of attention. It never heals the wound.

Unearned moral self-righteousness is a favorite seduction of the dark ones. It is often stronger than sex. Beware of self-righteousness.

The mother wound is always deepest. The mother-child connection is the pattern and template for all mammalian and human connection. The most tender place: living, vibrating, warm, undefended, open, moist, soft, loving… All words fail. Precious beyond price.

Your attention goes immediately to all the negatives and to resenting them. All the blessings you ignore. This habit of mind causes much misery. **Attention is prayer. Attention is worship. Attention is connection.** Mostly, where you place your attention is on semiautomatic. Wake up! Your preconscious, perceptual filters do much of this; they keep most Spirit contact invisible. Your many-layered filtering system is clogged and congested. Clean and disinfect it. Attention is worship. What have you been worshiping, really? What do you worship? What do you worship now? You humans often worship fear, hate, and violence. What you call success is a false god. The Real successes are mostly invisible to your eyes. **The dark ones are hard at work in the sweaty subbasements of your mind to prevent you from clearly perceiving anything. Most of your deep choices about paying attention are preconscious and hard to**

reset. They are vital — they create the world you live in. Pay attention to how you pay attention.

The ability to love. This is a much better measure of success than your book sales or big-shot clients or your beautiful house. The simple, humble ability to love: plants, places, people, breezes, experiences — everything. Especially when people don't care about you or even are outright hostile. This is a long way off for you. The more you can do this, the more joy you can experience. It's almost tit for tat, equal measures. The more people and things you can love, the more joy you will experience. The word love is so confused and toxified and covered in lies. Love is closer to "see the great beauty in" or "enjoy without clinging" — a free gift with no return. It often causes joy pain, the simultaneous experience of both.

See through our eyes. You will weep and see great beauty.

Being loved feels good, but loving is what brings deep, abiding joy. Invincible joy. Just that simple. **The dark ones try to tweak this divine thing — loving — and create a ravenous, insatiable near enemy.**

Lies isolate the one who lies. Always. So pernicious. Even little lies separate us. If the truth is hurtful, just say nothing. When you lie to others, you lie to yourself, and this is an abortion of spiritual growth.

Isolation is always a problem, but popularity does not solve this; it makes it worse. It is a glittering, false front.

Depletion is the gold standard for recognizing the presence of dark ones. It is a sure sign of spiritual parasites. Like speed or cocaine, they always leave you depleted. Distraction, desperation, and depletion.

Yes, there are many toxic reservoirs and oceans of pain and hate. Vast ones, bigger than your planet. It is good to drain them. You are being trained in how to do this. Do not think you are heroic; you are more like a garbageman or a sewer cleaner. There are many of you doing this work. Be curious. Passionately curious — 360-degree curious. Awe, gratitude, curiosity. Not bad, but incomplete. You also need wonder and joy, delight, and excitement. Connection.

To what will you dedicate the rest of your life? What will you sacrifice on this altar? Start by cutting away the obviously unnecessary. Any vacation or relaxation that actually depletes you. Do what feeds and strengthens you.

Trust your deeper knowing: your body, bones, and breath. Trust the reality of the unseen. Your world is backward: it worships the useless and ignores the uncreated light of the Real. This causes disease. To what will you dedicate and consecrate your life? This must be big. Big enough to make the suffering worthwhile. The images of a man kneeling and being knighted by the Queen. The image of the grail. Be curious; listen. **The first sign of a wrong path is often rushed and hasty feelings. These are never from us. We have eternity; so do you. All this high-speed stuff is poison.** It eats your culture. Do not rush — go slower. Value the unseen world, the Real. What endures? What is outside of time?

Spirit is unwelcome in your culture. It must sneak in the back door. Or in a Trojan horse, or in a false flag operation. It must be disguised.

Truth said without love is not, after all, true at all.

Thanks, Lord — you give me so much.

We would give you much more if you could receive it. We are all around you waiting. **You humans installed the gates of heaven. We give freely. You created the walls to keep us out. Do not storm the walls. You would be fighting yourself and creating more internal conflict. Find out who within you built the gates and love them. The gates will then dissolve.**

From the point of view of the dark ones, love is a dangerous, contagious disease. This is the true belief of all domination structures. They always promote hate, even in the name of love.

On your planet, whenever we appear, we are attacked and killed. You also attack us when we enter you. You fend off ecstasy, joy, and love. This is how you built the gates of heaven — to keep us out, out, out. We keep coming. We are inexhaustible, fluid, and eternal. Effortlessly we flow in. You and your race constantly try to kill us, own us, control us, sell us, use us to hurt others and worse. You even torture and demean in our name. Many of the truly Holy in your world are goaded and prodded until they appear insane. They are then locked up and destroyed with drugs. We keep their Spirits alive here with us until they can get free of their human bodies. Holiness is hated and reviled in your world. It is punished severely. Crucified.

Love without reserve, knowing full well that all you love will die. The love itself endures.

You focus on numbers of students, numbers of books sold, or internet use. This is the wrong bigness. You need bigness of Spirit. Give one person or a few something pure. This will forge new wings in the golden chain of transmission. This Real impregnation is more important than numbers. There will be no fame or recognition for this.

Notice how, like so many in your world, parts of you are already working hard, beavering away, building new gates to heaven, new cages for what's alive, new barriers to healing — all in the name of healing. The self-deception. The effrontery. The ill-concealed greed and possessiveness. This is harsh. Sometimes clear sight is harsh. The Real is harsh. Can you have clear sight and be kind? If not, you are better off blind.

We cannot give you more until you grow in kindness. Do not let the dark ones hijack your powerful clear sight and use it in the service of hurt, judgment, and division.

When I am kind to others over inner anger, what do I do with the anger?

Be kind to it, of course. (Gentle laughter) Kindness is crucial. Without it, we cannot give you more power or clear sight. This will be tested over and over at many levels. **Kindness is not wimpy or ineffectual; it is way stronger than military conquest.** Kindness expands and allows more and more current and energy flow. Conquering constricts, tightens, and gets smaller. Kindness is vast and effortless. Kindness expects no return. Kindness itself strengthens you; the expectation of return makes you weak.

Your world, with all the child abuse and the triumph of evil people, does not seem kind at all. This is because you do not see the Real. In the Real, the goals of learning, love, and spirit growth are way more important than anything physical. You are an eternal being.

You have driven yourself mercilessly. Our mercy cannot get in past this.

The self-discipline seems necessary. It keeps me afloat; body healthy, inner work; even contact with you seem to depend on discipline.

It is all useless without love. Do you love what you do? Are you eager for the time to do it? It is okay to crash now, to let go? **Just rest into us. No words will help you now. Go in and down. Darkness. Rest. Dissolve.** You have been in a crescendo of clenching and effort. Let it all go. Your military manager needs to rest the troops. They protest that Bob never would have launched without them, and this is true, but now they need rest. You need a new way. Your military managers have been straining for decades to pull the inert and resistant load of terrified parts out and forward into the world. Dark ones exacerbated both sides to make the conflict worse. It's time for a ceasefire. Then get the dark ones out. The find the deep joy. You have crossed a river. Leave the raft behind.

Beware of the need for rushing. We are of eternity; so are you.

Your planet is a hell realm run by evil, insane, possessed people. Do not become one of them.

A hurt and a protective tightening. This hurts and causes another tightening. A Gordian knot is created. This creates a tight ball that easily rolls down the pathways to hell. Nothing is wasted. Nothing is a mistake. Learn.

Right now the total understanding available to you is a tiny pool of light, a candle flame, under a vast night sky. You cannot be given more until your emotional health, non-self-centeredness, skills — all words are wrong here — until you could handle the power a bigger area of light brings. You do not give a three-year-old a car, a tank, or spaceships. Do not lust after spiritual power — lust after clear sight.

Slow down. When lost, stop, and listen.

You can clean up a dirty child with joy and love or with hate and shaming. Same actions, totally different spiritual effects on you and the child. Mostly, you are warped with anger and control. It was necessary and saved your life, but it is time to stop.

Boredom is a sign of a failure of curiosity — always. When you are deeply curious, you are never bored and never afraid.

Oh, come on, never afraid??

NEVER AFRAID. Excited, energized, full of adrenaline, but never afraid. So, be curious! If you are not curious, be curious about

that. Curious about curiosity. Curiosity also is the opposite of isolation. Isolation never works long-term.

Is there a cosmic battle of good and evil?

Yes and no. The struggle is needed to grow, like a butterfly emerging from its cocoon. It seems like a battle because the dark forces rule this world, but you are unfolding, exfoliating, rolling open, flowering, expanding, shedding…

Is the old skin evil?

It certainly did not want to be ripped apart and discarded.

Is everything alive and conscious?

Yes. *Ensouled* is a truer word.

The study of "consciousness" is often a denaturing of the reality of personhood and the relational to make it possible for the behemoth of materialism to survive. A faceless, mechanomorphic delusion.

Spirit grows like an embryo: one cell, two, four, eight, sixteen… Then they form organs and tissues, and eventually a body.

What guides this?

It seems there is a flow of energy in cells, movement first, a streaming that lays out forms that congeal into organs in a body. Energy goes to movement, movement goes to form and before that, at the beginning is Spirit, us, universal mind. We are a who not a what. A person, not a thing.

When distracted, get curious about who sent the distractions and who receives them. It is always a who, not a what. **It has been a great triumph of the dark ones to reduce the richness and relatedness of the who into the isolated and static coldness of what.** The word *consciousness* is used in an attempt to turn souls themselves into a what, a lifeless thing, an object. This is what's wrong with words like *unconscious* or *subconscious*. They poison the roots of depth psychology. It is all a living web of interdependent co-arising. It is a web of persons; there are no things.

You are condemned (or is it blessed?), to always be a little beyond what's acceptable. Learn to enjoy this position.

Notice the anomalous — what doesn't fit your worldview of theories. Your theories are often blinders, prejudice, and a hindrance. What doesn't fit can open the way.

Without struggle you cannot grow. Appreciate your opponent.

Will, intention, effort, work. These words, like *love,* are so contaminated because what they point to is so crucial.

Does Self have an intention? Does the cosmos have an intention? Do you?

Yes, yes, and yes. Join us.

Stay with what is Real. Do not argue with it. Get curious about all the details. Fear not. This removes constraints and blockages. The major blockage is what you "know." Most of it is wrong, dead wrong. And much of the rest is misleading. **The greater the percentage of bullshit, the more vehemently people defend it.** All you humans. Spirit laughs and cries. You know this is true of others. Look in the mirror. Look inside. What citadels do you defend?

Look for hatred; it is a marker of lies. They are brothers and sisters. When you hate, you are lying to yourself. Anything that increases your hate or resentment is not good for you. It is poison.

Volume 12

As soon as you lie, you lose all Real power. You know inside you are phony, and so you become fear-based. From this base, you hate and attack and focus outward. You are lost and have no Real power. even though you bluster and swagger around the world. Lies are a drug, an addiction. All humans except the saints are active addicts — you all lie to yourselves all the time. Most of your lies are not aggrandizements; they are diminishments of who you really are. You are a fragment of the divine, a child of God. The lies are little boxes, prisons you choose to live inside.

There is a Nazi energy in each of you — cold, hard, disciplined, metallic, and unfeeling. It believes in its moral superiority and self-righteousness. It can never heal until it softens enough to come alive again and grieve.

Patience ripens into serenity.

You live in a shell. Your light is not free. A breaking open needs to happen; it may hurt.

Wrong vigilance is tense, outward-focused, and rapidly moving. Right vigilance is serene, inward focused, and steady. Right surrender is resting into us; it is humble, open, and learning. Wrong surrender is complacency; it is fat, self-satisfied, and often one up and arrogant. Corrupted joy is invasive, loud, noisy, and overstimulated. Real joy is deep, slow, and long. It awaits quietly for you to come. Corrupt joy makes you weaker. Real joy makes you glow with strength.

You live inside boxes you have made of your ideas and ideologies. These are way too small, and they chafe and irritate. In response to this, you often strengthen the boxes and make them even smaller! Almost none of you can stand the Real without a box to hide in. Do not rip away the boxes; find the scared parts and love them until they willingly let go of the boxes.

It is your own behaviors that hurt and damage you the most; they cover you in sticky muck and sludge. Often you appear as a desperate animal who damages itself in its attempts to escape.

Everything can be tweaked and twisted into a poison. Every virtue has a near enemy. Prayer, love, curiosity, compassion… nothing is immune.

Be kind. Do not sink into hate or sneering, no matter what the provocation. Be kind. This may seem wimpy to many, but it is the Real strength.

Pride is always bad. Perhaps the worst poison is pride in Holiness, in being a spiritual healer. This is a deep poison.

Clear the clouds and I am always right here. Focus your work on the clouds.

Greed for money is bad enough, but greed for attention is worse. Greed to be a teacher, an authority, one up to others — this poisons your interactions, and it is addictive. Be aware.

What you humans see as doom and disaster is often your salvation. It is all blessings, and you see it not.

Certainty is a near enemy and perversion of faith.

You must live into the truths you already have. Your awareness moves into them like fog entering a glade of trees. No analysis; just contact, kindness, and relationship.

Faith is trustingly leaning into our relationship and your current experience. It is not certainty about ideas or creeds. Beliefs often impede experiences. **All belief structures are wrong; they are too small.** They apply only to a tiny fragment of the Real.

The deepest wound from evil is not the damage it does directly, but that it blocks your access to the Real.

The path does not get easier, but it does get more rewarding.

The splendor is always here, right here, hovering close. Always available yet almost never seen or touched.

Careful about being pious and reverent — be Real and curious.

You can learn from everyone; the limitations are yours.

You are a node in the system. You are not an isolated citadel.

We, Spirit, are right here, always, every instant. What keeps you from us is your habits of mind.

Do not be lured or baited down into politics. Anger and self-righteousness do not cure the hurt; they lock it away, where it can fester.

The child is held as insignificant in your world — it is actually the doorway to Spirit, to the vastness and the Splendor.

Purification and emptying are expansions because they make room for Spirit.

Lord, I'm full of hate.

Hallelujah, it is good you sense this. There are oceans of it in you and in your species; it is good to discover this.

Skepticism, doubt, and cynicism are the near enemies of the great virtue of unknowing. As usual, the near enemy is flashier, noisier, more gaudy, more fashionable, and more popular.

The more you offer the world and its beings respect, the more you will feel respected, and the more you will learn.

To drain the swamp of hate, all that's needed is that you stay unblended, separate, and free. Greet hate with curiosity and compassion. Simple but not easy.

Purification is not Hallmark card stuff in pastel colors; it involves opening the boils, going into the sewers, and all the worst, most contaminated places. There is vomit and shit and rot and blood and pus, maggots, death, decay, odd, terrible stenches. It cannot be done in clean Sunday clothes.

Look for the places within you that smell bad. Heat them. Transmute them with fire.

When you see the ugly in the world, note the feeling of unearned moral superiority — this feeling is a deadly, addictive poison. Cheap and effective. A basic lie that seduces you into a world of lies. This is in almost all hatreds. It opens the doors to hatred.

We live inside old prisons. Often, the constraints are gone and only the memories remain but still, we do not get out.

Failure to launch is such a prevalent issue. It takes faith to launch. To fledge — to spread your wings and fly. Your existence is one launch after another. There are so many versions of this ahead. Learn to enjoy it. Joy is the key and guide. Each launch is into a bigger reality, a bigger freeing.

No blame. The denunciation of others requires a self-righteousness that poisons you, blinds you, constricts and limits you. Let it go. Be generous and kind. You grasp the blaming so tightly, like holding a venomous snake to your breast. It gnaws at your essence. It could destroy your luminosity.

If you see the truths that others most want hidden, you can hurt them deeply.

Your faith is a small flame, a candle in the wind. It needs to become a forest fire — a conflagration so intense that your entire planet becomes a star.

The Holy are always joyful.

In Auschwitz? In the Russian Gulags? Always?

Everywhere the splendor exists. A transcendental searing joy of unimaginable strength and voltage. A beauty, even there.

The deeper the dying, the purification, the greater the ecstasy and the rebirth.

We struggle so hard to achieve a settled understanding, a theory of everything, a doctrine, but these are disasters. They are stasis, death. They are coma wards of certainty that breed reptiles of the mind and prevent the fresh and the new. They prevent life. Closure and certainty are manmade disasters. Listen to be changed. Look for the new, the surprise, the anomaly.

You humans crave certainty out of fear. When you patch and cobble together something that seems certain, you wonder why this fear-based edifice does not make you feel good. Each fear-based certainty is a refusal to learn and grow that cripples you.

Do not greet fear with fear; greet it with warm love. There is no fear that you cannot soothe. All fears can be loved, smoothed, and caressed.

Now, you have searched for them as an exterminator would search for rats. Go to them with love. Nothing else, nothing less will do.

There are billions of you packed together on your planet, and you are lonely, so lonely. Packed together in your loneliness. Hating each other and creating countless hell realms of isolation and resentment. Even if your worst vision of others is true, it does not serve you to resent them. Truth without love is not true.

You do the same inside yourself as on the outside. Who are you resenting? Judging? Wanting to expose? Who?

Do not let anyone or anything claw you down into blame, hate, fighting, and judgments. The charnel grounds and places of torture are the breeding grounds of saints.

The idea that humans are unique in nature and that idea of American exceptionalism are isolating poisons made sweet with pride of specialness. This arrogance causes great suffering.

Remember, inner and outer worlds are the same — isomorphic — mirrors. As above, so below. Fractal self-similarity. What does your reaction to other people when they anger you tell you about your internal behavior with your own parts?

Being with the negative from love is profoundly healing and expanding. It is needed for spiritual growth. Needed, not optional. Essential. Many avoid this in the name of staying positive, and it cripples and stunts them. When you move toward the negative with love, you will grow, and others will be healed.

Every time you see beauty is a triumph of the Divine, and Beauty is all around you, everywhere.

Fear itself is hell: insidious, sneaky, underhanded, and tricky. It will attack and inflame all your weak spots. Do not create shields over them. Heal the weak spots from within so there's nothing left in you that needs defense.

Spirit showers us with riches and lessons beyond what we can absorb. Mostly, we ignore the great gifts completely.

It's all about curiosity, wonder, and awe. With these, even the most ordinary and drab event is alive with possibility and surprise. You do not need the extraordinary; the quotidian is miracle enough. Each instant offers an endless opening to the Divine, the eternal... The plainest food is a feast of miraculous dimensions, and you see it not.

Every moment, each event, is a gift from the beyond, given so that you might learn.

We feel our best when struggling with every ounce of our powers to achieve something. We need a strong opponent to grow strong.

Humans cannot recognize demons or angels. Great saints stride your planet and are totally unrecognized. They do their work quietly. They do not make any efforts to conceal themselves because **humans are overwhelmingly uninterested in the Real and the sacred. It has to be mixed with a lot of bullshit to be palatable.**

Your path only emerges as you walk it, one right step after another.

You humans cannot love very much at all. It is a feeble light, blown out by the slightest breeze, sometimes guttering and dying all on its own.

Sub specie aeternitatis — from the view of eternity. Live from this as much as possible. Remember that each action, each attitude and thought, is done for eternity. This can depress and frighten some people but is also a source of bottomless meaning.

You are a boat in an ocean of hate. This ocean is corrosive. It constantly works to dissolve any imperfections in your hull. This is a great blessing if you do not sink — a thoroughgoing purification.

Each moment is a precious thing: a potential doorway to Spirit. We are right here, right here.

As long as you hate and resent anyone, you are attached to them and under their shadow.

You do not need recognition or acknowledgment, now or ever. You do not need to be vindicated. You need Spirit, the divine, and love. Vindication is a thin soup without nourishment, and yet you seek it desperately.

Consolation and desolation are the Jesuit names for the two faces of the spiritual life. You learn more in desolation. When desolation comes, do not evade it. Turn toward it. Go right into its mouth and ask, "What are you here to teach me?"

We Spirits offer a pure living refuge in our bodies to the evil ones. We offer sure salvation, beauty, and joy. Still, many will not come. We offer ourselves, intimate and whole. You humans think of this as sex, but it is much deeper and more tender. The evil ones are all around, jeering and spitting contempt at our offers. Their own hate, contempt, and small eyes keep them trapped. The greatest beauties of the world are before their eyes, and they see it not. Do not think that you are superior to them.

Fear not, drop the old, empty your hands, empty yourself, cry, cry out, moan, sound, hear the waves and the wind. Listen, moan softly with the breezes. You cannot understand or comprehend. You cannot grasp this. You can have the empty-handed courage to proceed without understanding, without knowing. This you can do.

You only sense what you unconsciously value. Your value systems determine the world you live inside. You blind yourselves horribly, horribly. Of the less than 0.0001 percent of the Real you are offered, you filter out more than 99.99 percent. Only the tiniest trickle gets through. Usually, not even that. What you get to perceive is your own unconscious predictions.

You humans swim in a sea of hate — a toxic soup or swamp. Abysmal. Fetid. Rank… And you fight over scraps of rancid meat. And all the while, clean air and purity are near. You tie yourselves into knots of hate and contempt, blocking every exit. Desperately returning to your useless wars. There is an endless supply, a deep flow, of good and life and warmth and living waters right here, right now. Only the thinnest of veils separates you… And parents indoctrinate their children ruthlessly so that their innocence and deep Spirit connection do not interfere with this world. We, Spirit, are here. The sludge and sewage of your world drips off of us as we emerge. We are un-dirtied… it is your vision and perception that are contaminated. We emerge upward from the fetid swamps, the squabble, the competition for rancid, toxic meat. Drop it all, let go. We love you; all is well.

When you need to let go, detach with love. No pissy recriminations, no peevish arguments. Detach with love, gracefully, generously, and kind.

We, Spirits, are always here. Always. You are distracted. If you really paid attention to us for a few moments, everything would change. Even your deepest times of prayer are mostly distraction. Keep praying; we are coming. Hacking our way through the jungle of lies and venomous beings. Keep praying and we will do the heavy work.

You notice the megalomania — narcissism — psychopathology — in all the spiritual leaders. You notice this because it is in you, too. The elbowing each other aside, stepping on each other — competitive and controlling with a kindly smile on their faces. Beware, this is in you, too.

Some of the biggest gifts we give you, you do not recognize. So be open. We come in packages and people you will not recognize. Look for us everywhere. This will serve you well. You perceive what you value. You have valued knowing when perpetrators approach and when lies were told. You saw perpetrators and lies. Value us; value Spirit instead.

You cannot protect tenderness. Protection is the opposite of tenderness. You can honor it and treasure it.

(At one point, I lost confidence in this voice of Spirit.)

Oh taste and see, oh taste and see. If you were just fantasizing an inner world, you would make it more to your liking. You would make it what you want to hear. You blind yourself to much of the light that is within you. This is goaded on by dark beings under the name of skepticism and rationality. They also appeal to your more venal aspects — greed, desire for fame, vindication, power, and leadership. They twist the good.

The attacks of the hater, the sneering contempt of the dark ones, can be like an acid bath for old metal, leaving you shining, clean, and pure. Or it can drag you down into the muck with them.

It is often your own attempts to heal yourself — your protectors — who cause the deepest, more enduring wounds.

Love — sometimes it just hurts to love another. The hurts from love are better than the victories of conquerors.

Healing is primary. Imagination is primary. Intellect is a weak sister, a camp follower trying to claim leadership — to usurp the throne.

Some spirits cannot descend to the level of words and speech. You have to go up to their level — to learn the language of image and feeling and sensation.

Imagination is a perceptual system like vision or hearing. Things in the inner world must be clothed in images for you to interact with them and appreciate them. It operates very much as your external senses do, creating qualia out of the buzzing, blaring confusion of incoming sensory data. This is also why you need daimons, demons, and angels. The non-dual might be more Real — the Ein Sof — but you cannot interact or relate with it, so it is almost useless and irrelevant for you.

Each moment of life asks you a question.

Everything is alive. There are no things. All is process, change, and movement. Even the hardest mineral is process; it is alive. And there needs to be a certain respect, a love even, for all life.

It is odd that you are stirred to gratitude by the ideas and words we give you, but you are not stirred to gratitude by taking another breath.

Love and respect the parts of you who do not want connection with Spirit. This is not to enable them but to help them change.

It cannot be all mountains and peaks; you need valleys, too. Often there's more growth in the valleys.

Make your everyday life transparent so you can look through it into the eternal.

The connection, the meeting of two beings, is often more important than the content of their talk. The quality of the contact and its intimacy are what matter.

You tend to find no equals; everyone is better than you or less than you. All of this is toxic foolishness. You have no idea what's going on spiritually with others. You only have the dimmest hints about what goes on inside of you after a lifetime of sincere study. Yet you presume to judge the worth of others and your own worth and the value of your experiences! Let go of all this; it is time for the new. The defeat and failure of these comparisons is a blessing, a gift.

Sit with confusion and not knowing. When lost, be still. Deep listening. Open all your senses; welcome everything. Be still.

You humans are both herd animals and solitary predators.

Love is your shield, your strongest protection.

When you are suffering, you are paying tuition, so learn.

Joy: flexible, fluid, flowing, free, far-seeing, and fascinated. **To be fascinated is a state of grace.** To be far-seeing and not go one up is a tightrope walk, a razor's-edge bridge over gaping hells.

Your managers clamp down so hard to make you survive, white-knuckled so hard you could not feel. Now you long for the rain of tears, the moisture. Loneliness escaped first. The longing for rain is good. Life comes up like blades of grass through concrete. The managers clamp down and encrust the system. It will ossify and die a slow death by stenosis unless there is rain. Blessed moisture.

Lord, I feel like a creaking, crusty old truck. Sort of falling apart, patched over and over, slowly coming down a dirt road to you.

This is not far off. Do not compare. There are shiny jets, sports cars on freeways, and big yachts. All go fast, but many go in the wrong direction. There are also beings who crawl on their bellies or ooze like slime molds. Some of these will get to us sooner than you will. Do not compare or try to judge. Be kind. If you look at everyone as a teacher and approach all with fascination, your world will be transformed.

Be aware of what you spread. Do not ignite hate, resentment, sneering, or contempt. They seem so justified, and they never are, never. They are all defeats of the Spirit. They are poison, almost suicide, and they are disguised as power and victory. Be aware.

Slowing down to stillness can be a way to achieve escape velocity from this world.

The beauty of sea glass, of driftwood, of a well-washed shoreline — these are like the beauty of a person weathered by deep suffering.

Resentment and contempt are spiritual suicide — a long, slow suicide. Do not stoke the fires of hate. Hate is a prison so many of you choose to live inside. It is better for your Spirit — the eternal you — if you are the object and receiver of hate and contempt rather than the hater. It's simple: fear not, hate not.

Everyone is a teacher. Each moment, each sensation, each event, each smell, all are messengers from the beyond. The world is an icon, a window, a portal, an image. What really matters is that your life will be infinitely better if you act as if all of this were true.

When you notice the imperfections and immaturities of people, it moves you toward judgment and being closed. It could move you toward compassion and care and concern.

Beware of your desire to be liked and admired. It puts you at risk of lying and pretense.

Most of what goes on, on your planet, is done by devious, dishonest cowards — the governments, the churches, the political movements, etc. Rancid, pustulating corruption inside a designer dress and Armani suit. Smiling behind their masks. All over the planet. In the tribes, too — everywhere.

So, what do you do?

Learn, and spread what you learn. Be humble, way more humble, radically humble. Learn, learn, learn. And plant seeds. It is ugly and smelly here. Corrupt, teeming infections, and you live in it; you carry it. You are all carriers of multiple infections. One big one and many opportunistic hangers-on. Fear not and do not get prideful. Being proud creates overconfidence, which makes you vulnerable. Humility is safety. The good walks through this world of frantic, noisy narcissism and manipulations undetected. If it is noticed, it is attacked and sometimes crucified. Plant seeds and do not look for the credit.

There is much fear in you still. Welcome it with love. You have rejected it and buried it alive with rage and hate.

The rational mind, the ego, tries to colonize the unconscious, but it fails for many reasons. One reason is that there already are colonies there, infestations, viruses of the mind. Even if you get them out, you will fail. At best, these attempts will lead to border wars and raids, all totally unnecessary. You humans have been given these infestations to wrestle with as teaching devices so you might grow clear-sighted and strong. Almost no one will believe you if you tell them this truth. You must learn discernment, kindness, and wisdom in this struggle. These are the Real strengths.

Going one up, feeling superior, is only a more subtle form of hate.

You know so little, and so much of that is wrong. Continue to reinvent yourself.

Your planet is an outpost of hell run mostly by hell's minions. The domination structures are almost all demons at the top.

Universal kindness. Even to vicious, dishonest enemies. Be kind. This will free you. Kindness, joy, and beauty in all directions make your life a prayer and your body an altar. And stay humble — this is safety.

We do protect you, even more than you know, even though this has sometimes meant thwarting your will and blocking your efforts. We love you way more than you can ever receive or tolerate.

Curiosity is the cure for fear.

Listen deeply. Listen slowly with the resonance of your whole body. Listen. Let your body resonate.

Listen to be changed. Speak to be known. This 12-step saying is pretty much straight from us.

Beauty itself is always sacred, always. A naked woman's ass included. So, seeing that is sacred. And this worship gets twisted just enough to be poison, coated with contaminated sexuality and the lessons of abuse. But the divine is there. Great beauty, worship, love.

You need revolutions in your thinking. It has become fossilized, ossified, and stenotic. There are bone spurs and obstructions. There are also rats' nests in your mind. So foul inside and looking benign from the outside: encapsulated rot and infestation.

Your problems are your lessons. Do your own homework — do not pray to have your homework done for you. This calls in bad spirits who will cripple you with their help.

The Real is not what you expect. Surprise is a name of God. You cannot figure out the Real, but you can open and receive us. The Real is not an it — it is an us.

Volume 13

A vision: **An insectoid queen's battleship**

An interstellar battle cruiser with many protuberances. It is like an insectoid queen. It sends out hordes of snake like beings that look like shackles and chains. They attach very strongly to humans and to the planet. These shackles and chains are vivid: heavy black metal, the shackle, a circle open like a mouth, the chain like a reptilian body. Areas of the planet are deeply infested. The queen moves close, sucking the life force from all those connected to the shackles and from earth herself. These areas form depressions, concavities, sores in the energy body of the earth. Sores and worse. They are trying to link up, to globalize to suck the planet dry. This will take thousands of years and create a vortex or black hole of pain that will contaminate this region of space for eons.

Fight hard, my son, but this warfare is not military. It is fought with love, only love. This is not literally clear, but it is spiritually Real. There are also cosmic-scale forces for good that combat these colonizing starship queens. No one is perfect, 100 percent fighting for the good. You, too, my son. You — we — have defeated one queen cruiser. Now it is a dangerous booby-trapped hulk. But there are many; do not get proud. Fake retreats are a favorite strategy of the dark ones. Do not trust "victory." The normal human response to victory is terrible — flaccidity, drunkenness, and spoilation. Revenge and vaunting. This is the dark ones, not victory. A good response to victory is grief, love, and compassion. Your very words and language are colonized by darkness, so it is hard to be clear.

A mother ship comes and gathers in the queen cruiser.

It was really just a scout, a probe seeing if it is worthwhile to farm the noosphere of your planet, to enslave you all. You have done well in helping make this unprofitable for them. Inadvertently they are great trainers for you. The globalist one-world dream of domination would allow them to rule your world. Beware. Everything you have witnessed so far is skirmishes in a peripheral and relatively unimportant sector. Your mind is not big enough to comprehend the scope of the struggle or to imagine the beings who lead it. It is way beyond you. Externally, you are small and easily overwhelmed; internally, not so.

Love your body. Love it. Your excellent self-care can be tweaked into hate-based punitive behavior easily. Look with love at all the week and flabby places in your body and all the rats' nests in your mind, the fear holders, the ambitious ones.

Your pride in your work as a healer sets you up for trouble. You can be entangled. You are even proud of your humility! You can be seduced and manipulated by your pride. Under your pride is a core belief in your worthlessness and unlovability. Focus here. Do not try to hand him off to spirit — he would experience this as rejection. The two of you come to us together.

When you lose curiosity with another human, you have failed. Go slower, especially when you feel the urge to go fast. Pause when you feel offended, shamed, or scared. Listen. Do not gloss over. Turn toward. Rushing can prevent all healing. Learn.

Symptoms are rarely the problem; they are usually an attempted solution gone wrong.

The interruptions and lessening of inner work and prayer times distress me, Lord. Please help.

You need faith. Work is occurring that you are unaware of. You're aware of less than one thousandth of 1 percent of your inner world. Much less. And yet your effort is crucial and meaningful. Stay steady in your inner work and have faith. All is well. Accept help in your work.

Great spiritual leaders almost never write books; they write directly on their disciples' hearts. This is more Real, more enduring.

Proceed in joy. This will feed and nourish you. Turn toward your worry and fears with love. Comfort them. You have crushed them like a conqueror. So of course, they are still there, only more deeply hidden. Welcome them now. They are noble beings with great gifts.

Learn with joy, teach with joy, not with hate, no matter how justified. **Resentment is hate: a picking at a festering wound, an obsessive trichotillomania of the soul.**

There is a reservoir of grief, defeat, loss, despair, abandonment, and suicide. The beings trapped their cry, "Just stop. Make it stop." A reservoir, not all yours — an ocean of defeat. Dark parasites all over this and in this feeding hungrily.

Yes, evil exists as an active, intelligent group of beings. At their cores, there are sparks of light, but this will be a moot point for eons to come.

Night terror is an old problem — many lifetimes, a classic attack point for the dark ones.

Sometimes we let people's managers fill them with clever words to keep them busy while we work undisturbed in their depths.

More silence. Attentiveness. Listen deeply. Be still and know. Make less noise.

The grieving process converts shit into gold. Transmutes suffering into compassion, pain into love. This is grief. When it is aborted or prevented, the hurt is converted into bitterness, hate, and self-righteousness. Each loss is a fork in the road. **Where you are bitter, look for what you have not grieved.** There is never a Real external reason for bitterness. Look inside. No matter how terrible the outside event, bitterness is our internal reaction — poison you make which makes the injury worse. Look at the worst and stay there with love. Joy emerges, a crop of plenty from this plowed and watered field. Invincible joy, great joy. Nothing is worth hate; it is addictive, soul-destroying, and seductive. It appears falsely powerful. It is a terrible weakness.

Effort or surrender?

This is largely a false dichotomy — at any rate misleading. They work together like day and night, inhale and exhale, the tides.

Real power is from the inside, and it radiates out, giving gifts of freedom, openness, and recovery of joy. Fake power is gathered (stolen, usually, although some may give it away eagerly) from outside and hoarded. This hoarding turns it to poison, a toxic soup. People in your world have been seduced into competing to increase their hoards. This turns blessings — curiosity, intelligence, energy, conscientiousness — into curses. This prevents love and friendship.

Whatever happens to you, always look in the mirror: what does this teach you about yourself and your inner depths? **Even as you fight an opponent, learn from the struggle. This — not victory — is the purpose of the struggle.**

Help!

(Gentle laughter) You could not tolerate or endure much more of our help. We love you; all is well. You are a shining star with some shit still dripping off of you.

You have a cage full of trapped beings inside of you... some are animal, some alien or insectoid. Stinging. Cursing. Poisons, Infecting... and the only way to clear this is to set them free. Most will not know you helped them; there will be no gratitude. Do it anyway.

Defeat can be our greatest victory. Like hitting bottom in the 12 steps. You are too foolish to tell the curses from the blessings. You humans often exert your greatest energies to destructive causes. Pause. More listening. Deep listening. Be still and listen.

Jung called inflation the greatest danger of working with the archetypes. This is pride. The danger gets bigger and bigger the closer you are to us, to Spirit. The dark ones use your pride to try to snatch victory from the jaws of defeat. This pride creates monsters of theocratic certainty and self-righteousness. Beware. Be aware. Feeling bliss and power and radiant love is wonderful and dangerous. If you try to own it, it will destroy you.

You need the opponent to struggle and wrestle with. Your body needs gravity for you to gain strength and the ability to discern up from down.

From us, love radiates out in all directions to the good or bad, the lazy or the hardworking. Some can receive it; most cannot.

Your mind cannot figure out love. Intellect is almost useless here. Feel your way in with curiosity, gentleness, awareness, kindness. Quiet calm. **Peace can open a way where the great warriors could not.** Forget about trying to figure out what love is. You cannot think your way here. Recognize it as you would recognize an old friend. Greet it as a dog greets its master home. Not with serious looks and pen in hand to take notes.

When you wrestle with the pigs, you are down in the shit with them. This means they have already won. They have seduced you into their world, into paying attention to them. Do not be seduced or provoked. Do not engage at their level.

You are here to learn love. Do not be distracted. It is a constraint-release process, kenosis. Focus on the blocks, the exhaustion, anger, and unlove. How can you love people who are actually being assholes and worse?

I cannot, I reply.

Find a way and you will be free!

Don't I need to detach, and doesn't love mean to attach?

Love is not attachment. It does not cling. Give it away with no expectation of return. Give it — your great treasure — away freely, even indiscriminately, like rain. Love is not attachment. It is more like a state of being.

Your identity as a serious scholar must go; it is tainted. It prevents joy, delight, and splendor. Playfulness and freedom. Even scholarship can be tweaked into something toxic — pomposity, rigidity, one-up arrogance. Every virtue has near enemies. Your passion for learning can be used to harm you. You can become so busy taking notes and tabulating results that the heart slowly shrivels and dies. Learn in order to be changed.

Scholars in divinity schools are unlikely to find me. They are armored against me by their very ideas. They strengthen the armor that keeps me away in the name of seeking me. Very sad.

Your desire to be recognized as a Holy man by this world is dangerous. This is an attempt to twist your great longing into something small and toxic. This more subtle trap is nearer the castle, the spring, the source.

Am I a lost dog sniffing my way home?

Yes, my son. Dogs and humans are much more similar than humans and gods. You cannot comprehend us at all. You exist in three of four dimensions with five or seven or twelve portals, senses. We exist in an infinite number of dimensions. Our sensory modes have transcended portals. There is no longer a wall to have doorways through. Vast spaciousness. Your words fail… You are being watched with love.

The greater the virtue being tweaked, the more toxic or poisoned it becomes and the harder it is to recognize. You are an eternal being of Spirit, and it is good to remember this. **All your actions are done for eternity — they are irretrievable and permanent. This makes even the most seemingly trivial actions — physical and mental — deeply meaningful. Each moment matters — treat it with respect. They are all lived for eternity, from eternity, and in eternity.**

Joy, beauty, splendor, ease. Nothing to do. More emptiness would help.

You need to accept unknowing here. You do not know this territory. Do not put your boxes on it. Open all your sensory modalities. Listen calmly. The last few days of distress were birth pains. There are many births lined up waiting for you, for your womb. You are both a mother and child in these Spirit births. Learn to enjoy them or at least be curious. Notice how much fear and contraction this evokes in you. There are many births to come. Your death will be a birth and just a beginning — one after another. You literally cannot imagine. So don't try. No theories, no boxes, no container. None. Open. Observe. Curious. Learn. It was your loss of faith and curiosity that really hurt you, not the birthing process itself. Your clamping-down managers were clamping down harder when they needed to let go.

Deep joy is a guidepost. Fanaticism is never joy-filled — a telling sign. A failure of humor is a telling sign.

Theories and mental boxes are antithetical to learning. They are a rear guard parading around after the war has passed by. They busy themselves organizing specimens of deadness. Real learning is moist, fresh, and alive, full of imagination, excitement, and joy.

You are more the battlefield than the warrior. You are a witness, and your witnessing changes the reality it witnesses, just as in quantum physics. You participate in this fundamental way. Be curious. Observe, witness, learn. To learn, you must be open. To be open, you must be fearless. You are an immortal Spirit. Remember this — an immortal Spirit.

Distraction is an attempt to tweak the great virtue of curiosity itself. See what parts of you are attracted by the shiny, glittering thoughts and objects that dark ones dangle tantalizingly. These parts need your love. Do not manage them — love them.

Your pain is tuition. You are paying for a lesson. Learn. Be a curious student and explore. Go around the pain and peer and peek in a kind and respectful way. Do not be Sherlock Holmes.

Dissolve and expand yourself so that you can receive our love. The attacks get more subtle and stronger. The opponent must be strong to help you get strong. Be curious. The stronger you get, the more the attacks will be covert and hidden. A few of you getting free is a huge problem for the dark ones. This is like the hole in the dike that will cause the whole seawall to fail.

Do not put your boxes, your theories, on your new experiences. You will not see them right if you do. Look for what does not fit with what you know. Look for the anomalous. This opens cracks to the Real. Do not put your precious new experiences into old boxes, old theories, old formats. This kills the life in the new experiences and cripples the growth in you. It freezes you at the size of your current box. Not enough, my son, not enough.

You will not lose us. We are always right here with you. Your faith and awareness will wax and wane; we are here. Simple faith in this will sustain you.

Just as the hole dug by a mole or ground squirrel can cause a hillside to collapse when the rains come, so a few individuals gaining freedom can release the ocean of life force. This is way bigger than individuals or soul groups. You are like cells or organs in the grand human Swedenborg described. Humans are an image of the cosmos, not the other way around.

All is not as it seems — not even close. Phonies, hypocrites, liars, and salesmen rule your world. If they were merely sold material goods, it wouldn't be so bad, but they are selling enslavement, soul death, and Spirit blackness. They pander to the worst in humans — envy, greed, hate, fear, pride, disgust, lust — all the perversions of love. And there are perversions, counterfeits that poison their holders. They sell to the power-less wanting power, the abandoned wanting company, the lazy and greedy wanting unearned moral superiority. It is loud and flashy. High-speed, glamorized. All we offer is the still, quiet voice of the Real. They insist lies are truth, slavery is freedom, total dictatorship is total freedom, hate is justified, and it is paraded as a virtue. Real grief could have transmuted all this suffering into love. Domination structures hate grief because they need fear and rage to fuel them.

We give you so much, and your gratitude is mostly for these words — a small thing, really. Every moment, we give you great gifts — breath, life, consciousness, more. You take all this for granted and focus on these words. We love you. All is well.

Your pleasure when you do a good healing session with a client is tainted. The joy in relieving their suffering is good, but your self-satisfaction and sense of being special and self-aggrandizement are not good, not at all. We gave you all of this, your intelligence, your heart. We guided you on your way. Yes, you have worked hard, but be not proud. This inflation is a form of pride. It can destroy you. You get intoxicated by your own success and the desire people have to be with you. Very seductive. Be aware.

Everything is a teacher sent from God. Look at all this way and you will flourish and be indestructible. Almost nothing will irritate you any longer, and the irritations will be valued as teachers from us. This is the pathway to impeccability and exponential growth. Beware of your pride. Because of your pride, we have had to send many teachers to you disguised as students. People who disagree with you are great teachers. Be curious about your irritations — they too are sent from God. Study them as a Holy text.

Your father was a monster, no father at all. He was eaten away by dark ones. So, you have had no lifelong leader, teacher, mentor, guide. We sent you many who took you partway. The lack of a single one has left you more open; it has given you a healthy distrust and outsider perspective. But it has also left you feeling alone.

Reincarnation exists but not as you think. Group souls reincarnate, not individuals. The relationships among parts of the group's souls change and evolve over many lifetimes. Your cells die and are reborn thousands of times in the life of your body. Your body soul dies and is reborn thousands of times in a group soul. The group soul dies and is reborn thousands of times within a civilization. A civilization dies and is reborn thousands of times within a culture. The culture dies and is reborn thousands of times within a species… the species… the ecosystem… the planetwide life dies and is reborn thousands of times here and on other planets. And so on, and on — many other levels you cannot even imagine.

Your civilization is dying: decadent and moribund. Keep at your inner work. You can save much. Create holes to let in the living waters. Something can escape and be born in another plane, dimension, or world. You literally cannot imagine.

We love you. Rest into this. You often fill the space with your words and theories. It can be effortless. When a scrap of what we offer in abundance gets through to you, you make so much noise about it, and have all these theories, love your ideas and comparisons. This self-generated noise you make in your attempts to receive actually blocks reception! This makes it so hard for you to learn. The dark ones have tweaked one of your great virtues — sincere yearning, stretching, working, perseveration — and perverted it. Your analytic managers are so hyperactive, they turn the presence of Spirit into something to be analyzed. It isn't. It is something to be lived. Something to be baptized in. To wash you, to flow through your veins.

Your Real contribution is preparing your bodies, physical and spiritual, to be a vessel for us. Analysis is not integration. It often is a killing of the Spirit and a chopping it up so it fits into your old boxes. Instead, feel your way in. Feel. Sense. Explore. Can you hear and see differently? Open new paths and new voices. Listen. We are here. Hear us. Live into this.

Let go. You have to let go to learn. Melt, empty, purge. Empty the fetid, stagnant, smelly, foul oceans of toxins. As you do this, the reptiles of the mind who live there will be crowded together and start to war. The stronger will eat the weak. A few will survive. It's all persons, Bob — there are no objects. Even the fetid gases are persons.

As you empty the reservoirs and swamps of hate, your vision becomes clear. Keep your eyes open. Keep open. There is much more.

Learn, love, learn and love. "You are here in this life to grow in the ability to love." This is pretty close, but it's a kenotic, emptying process: you grow in love by draining hate. So, this is a dirty, smelly business. Go to the last places you would look for love. Dredge up those murky, muddy parts of the ocean floor. The things which provoke your hate and contempt. These are the gold, the path. Be curious about your own hatred.

For you and most of your world now, Real reverence is very hard, and worship is impossible.

Each action, each thought, each feeling state is laid down for eternity. Each moment is therefore supremely important and meaningful. There are no empty moments or boredom. It is all in your attitude. Eternal meaningfulness is here and now. Each act, thought, attitude, and feeling.

We are helping you; our help does not make it easier.

Look squarely at your hate; this is the doorway to love. Hate lets in the dark ones who come roaring in and obliterate your mind, shut your heart, and scatter your parts. All this happens so quickly, you don't even notice.

The betrayal trauma, the way of the snake, is far more soul-destroying than the physical pain of abuse. There are great oceans of this in your species.

Your fascination with the hell realms and the beings who live there is both good and dangerous. It is good if you go there full of our light, radiant and pure. It is dangerous and toxic if you go there hungry and looking for pleasure or power. Even healers can be seduced by this very easily. It eats many of them alive. Be aware. Your desire to teach is good, and it is not pure. It covers a multitude of sins with the clothes of good intent. Be aware of your arrogance, your desire to be the center of attention, to be valued, your willingness to trim your sails to be popular. Be aware. Your fascination with the hell realm beings is a form of curiosity; remember that all great qualities have near enemies and can be tweaked and used against you. Fascination can become obsession, then entanglement and over-involvement. Send the dark ones on. You are on a good path. Open all your senses, inner and outer. You are flawed, and we use your flaws to good ends.

Treat everything and everyone as a valued teacher. Always, especially when you don't want to. You will learn more, and people will feel better for being with you. Everyone has something great to share. Everyone.

Purification is expansion. Removing the intrusions makes space, which allows radical expansion. Even this optimal form of expansion leaves you vulnerable like a newborn. Each expansion will be counterattacked by the dark ones immediately. Count on it. There are many grades and levels of this ahead of you. It is good; the counterattacks are confirmation of the value of this process. To purify is to grow, even when it looks like annihilation and total destruction. This is kenosis. Whatever is a burden — dead wood — must be burned away. Expansion is constraint release. Removing shackles and chains. Leaving prisons we have chosen to live inside. Waking from our conditioning and trances. Empty your treasure chests. Death is necessary for growth. Dissolve to expand.

Most refuse the gifts of Spirit and choose poisons instead. "My yoke is light," it says in the Bible. The double meaning is intentional. It is not heavy, and it is the opposite of darkness.

Where do I go?

You feel indigenous nowhere, so you must become indigenous everywhere. Expand the tribe you live in to include all people, all living things, all nonliving things, all Spirits. Beings from the past and the future. There is much more than you can imagine. Keep expanding, growing, learn to enjoy this process. It is very difficult even to be indigenous in your own body or your own mind.

In the therapy world, there are all these schools, each with its own name. Their organizations are squeezing and controlling; they sell a brand. There is climbing and elbowing aside. All of this is small potatoes, but it is also very toxic. It is like those old-fashioned sticky strips they use to catch flies. The dark ones proudly display their catch. This hoarding, grasping, controlling, and squeezing destroys itself with its own success. The dark ones howl with laughter.

Knowledge is a two-edged sword, wonderful and dangerous. If you remember it is all tentative in your world, an appearance of truth, an appearance of a finger pointing at the moon, then you are safe. Understanding is a process, not a state or a thing. There are no things — none. No settled doctrine. No fixed corpus of ideas.

The quality of your attention is more significant than the object of your attention. We are everywhere and because your attention is warped, you see us not. Your quality of attention is a narrowing and focusing. You need to widen, relax, and exhale. Listen deeply in active love. Only this satisfies. Flitting, inconstant attention always produces boredom. Your culture works to keep you bored and dissatisfied. In this state, you crave entertainment. The dark ones can use entertainment to install propaganda and brainwashing. This is a profound and basic emotional racket. Like all emotional rackets, it has the fundamental structure of addiction. A false god (entertainment, alcohol) is offered instead of a Real God (deep attention, Spirit). This is idolatry. It creates more boredom, then fear and disconnection and the need for more. This is addiction.

The dark ones are close to locking down your world. Addictions are parasites of the Divine, near enemies of Spirit connection. Addiction and enabling addiction are the dark ones' core methods.

It is only from sensitivity to the still, quiet voice that deep satisfaction can come. Then you will be impervious to the blandishments of the dark ones. Notice that all addictions always need more — quicker, faster, more intense, stronger — each step on this path makes the deep listening needed to hear the still, quiet voice harder and harder. When you become acclimated to the world of glitter and speed, the Real is no longer of interest and you are lost for a long time.

Whatever emotion you cannot feel runs your life.

How can I be in contact with the feminine Spirit?

Slow way down. I can talk to you using words near your own speeded, glitter-distracted mind. She is much more still, quiet, and

calm. Almost no movement from your perspective. Pervasive being. A fog engulfing a glade of trees. So gentle. The words and noise and rushing and clocks and flashing lights, all foreign to her. You are glutted with the surfeit of old stimulation. You are crammed full, bloated, obese with gaudy, moving images of sex and violence. There is no room in you for the silent mist, the living water, the deep, empty listening, ripening into contact. The gentle freshness you really need. You suffer from a food addiction of the spirit, an obesity of the soul.

I want to belong.

You do belong; Nothing can stop this. It is the feeling of belonging that you crave.

Many things you worry and fret over are ephemeral problems of human thought structures and not a concern in the Real.

Parts and wholes. This is a mystery; contemplate it with delight and opening. Do not narrow it and nail the coffin lid of certainty down.

Most of the deepest spiritual work is done out of your awareness. Whether or not you feel us is not a good indicator of the depth of the transformations. It is important for you to feel us because it gives you hope and strength. These make you less vulnerable to the dark ones. Even when the dark ones seem to be in control, our work goes on. It never stops. Even when people are flying into hell at their maximum speed, we are still working with them. We never stop.

Every day, you need more forgiveness. **Your lack of forgiveness hurts you. It milks maximum misery out of any event.** Quality of attention. Stop, be aware, greet what is with curiosity. Offer deep contact. Open attention. Not your peevish impatience and busyness. Wonder. Delight. Fascination. Awe can result. Make time. Daily, moment-by-moment forgiveness. This will make the room you need.

You can learn much from relatively small upsets with people you love. If you do this, you will not need bigger losses to trigger you.

There are no irredeemable evil ones. There are some who do everything they can to become irredeemable — to maximize the pain they cause and maximize their own damnation. This creates zombies, almost robots of the darkness. This is based on their belief that no one would ever want them or value them. They feel abandoned and worthless. Negative drains on the world. This is the key, and it is a lie. No matter how hard they try, they cannot make themselves irredeemable. Spirit wants you. You are not an accident or an error. There is meaning, fascination, wonder, and delight.

As you learn, you sense more clearly the horrible slums you humans live in — cesspools of self-righteousness and resentment. These are addictions offered by sexy, gaudy, charming, popular salespeople. The whore of Babylon is the biblical image. It often looks as if the whore of Babylon and the robots of addiction rule your world. This hell realm can also be an extreme training ground for saints.

Your mother's psychotic episodes left deep wounds in you, Bob. Millions of children have watched their mothers die, be imprisoned, disappear, or go insane. Insanity, perhaps, is the most subtle and therefore able to reach deeper into the child's soul. The body is right there ,and yet the mother's spirit comes and goes. Almost to lure and tease you into empty hells. This tributary river of maternal insanity leads to the vast ocean of abandoned children's suffering. Most of them die, their souls howl, collapse into silence to wake and howl again. Your species does this. It leaves behind the parts who carry the grief and fear and pain and sickness unto death. Go back and comfort one; perhaps this could make a hole in the dike so that the earth dam will collapse and release the ocean of suffering.

The dark ones gather the bodies of their dead and wounded. Go ahead and let them. Treat them with kindness and nobility even as they sneer and try to take advantage.

The abandoned infant is inside the warrior. Do not look elsewhere.

The dark ones consider you an infection. An infestation that they do not want to spread. They want to stomp you out to maintain the darkness. But many small fires are starting all around. A conflagration of light may be imminent. The dark ones would rather destroy the planet than let this happen.

Take everything as a lesson. Study it as a sacred text. The world is a sacred text. Your body is a sacred text. Your life is a sacred text. The

attacks of the dark ones are a sacred text. **Even the betrayals, infections, and deaths… all sacred texts. We love you.**

Doubt is not bad; you need it to correct your course.

It is good that the dark ones find, attack, and make visible the pockets of hate within you. Even when you are 100 percent right (it is never
really this pure), hate is never justified. It poisons you, not the other
people. Some of them like it. The dark ones and the people they dominate love being hated. Whenever you feel hate, the dark ones are around.

Lord, help me feel your presence in me clear and strong today.

**No, Bob. You need to sharpen your orienting skills, to find us
when there is static and noise and confusion. It is not a time of clarity
right now; it is a time of navigating through haze and darkness.**

You need to learn new navigation systems to connect with us. Swim
through the fog and darkness to us; we are here, warm and serene. The
cold ocean can feel like a heat sink which will slowly drain your life force.
We are the warmth which fills and rests you. Peace— natural, great peace.
Navigate by this. The temperature gradient. The intensity of an aroma,
the breeze direction, the currents in the water, magnetic fields. Learn these
new ways with curiosity and delight. If we were fully here with you, you
would never get this lesson. Don't pout, child — this can be great fun and
exciting, too. You might orient to the subtle shades of gold and yellow in
the light… You may also learn to navigate by delight and joy themselves.
You can also swim upstream to where the flow is coming from.

Notice that you do all the things you accuse others of doing to you.
Amazing, isn't it. Use others as a mirror. No blame.

**Self-reliance and distrust of authority, which are great virtues,
can easily be tweaked into arrogance.**

The dark ones are always trying to rattle your cage. This can be good
because it helps you be more aware of the cage and escape from it.

There is still a baseline fear in you. It is the fear of all the abandoned
children dying alone. It is the fear of this fear that paralyzes you. But secondary fear, this fear of fear, is also the royal road to freedom. Love this part first.
Turn toward the heart of confusion, fear, and darkness. There is healing here.

You are leaving the IFS box and the psychotherapy box. It is time to go, once again. Do not get in the boxes — stack them up. They make a nice staircase. Climb up.

Spirit, please help me.

(Laughing) Get out of the way. Let us shine. Your cramping, clenching, constricting, and tensing prevent the light. The light is here already. Look for blocks and love them until they melt in ecstasy. (More laughter) That's an exaggeration. They melt in joy, delight, and warmth. The ecstasy comes later.

One way to avoid being snared by dark ones is to accept nothing you have not earned. Nothing — praise, fame, money, goods. Notice how advertisers know this trick — the allure of the unearned — when promised something free if you buy their product. A blatant, obvious lie, but it works over and over. Perversely in your culture, the ill-gotten gains are valued more than the hard-earned rewards.

You prepare your vessel; empty your home and clean it. A bond can be formed. All is well. We cannot give great gifts to the unprepared. They will not receive them.

Being with us is interactional and relational. You cannot think your way.

There is wave after wave of attacks by the dark ones, and with each wave you get freer and freer. Nevertheless, you are a low-level apprentice. Do not get proud.

The cure for exhaustion is wholeheartedness. It is not coasting or slacking off. It is uphill all the way. You cannot coast uphill. Learn to enjoy the climb. The Dalai Lama was once asked if monks ever get vacations. He could not understand the question, but when his translators finally succeeded in explaining it to him, he laughed and laughed and then said no. **Each death opens unlimited possibility, unlimited access to light. It also opens an abyss you could fall into.** The way gets steeper and steeper. This is why like monks, you get no vacation. Rest into me, rest into us. It is uphill — the air and water and food become healthier. You become stronger. Allies emerge. Each step brings more strength. This is a marker that you are on the right path.

When someone hurts you, pray for them. This will forestall your resentments. Pray for them.

Tell no lies. Tell the truth with kindness or keep silent. No lies. The first indication of a lie emerging from you is that you become unconscious. There's a blindness. Notice this darkness and do not lie.

Help can be a poison. It feels like relief, but it cripples you. It weakens you. This help can reduce you to a clinging dependent being drained of your life force in a coma ward of the soul. Do not take your parts to other people for care. They are your responsibility. Do not try to hand them off to us either — that lets dark ones in to feast on you. Hold and care for them and welcome us in to support you. More help than this would cripple you, as your mother tried to cripple you.

Many, many Spirits failed to launch at some stage. Young hawks often have to be pushed out of the nest by their mothers. There are thousands and thousands of these launches for eons ahead of you. Dark ones will always try to sabotage these, usually with fear and laziness. Learn to enjoy the process of launching.

Is there a reservoir of the suffering of unlaunched souls?

Yes, Bob, a huge one. In a sense, all the reservoirs of suffering are a refusal to launch, to move on, to graduate, to let go. Usually of pain, suffering, and resentment. This is a poison the dark ones farm and use to hose down your world with toxic sewer sludge. Any resentment is poison. They are harder to let go of when accurate and justifiable. Failure to launch. When a caterpillar is inside the cocoon to be transformed into a butterfly, the first stage is that its body liquifies. Its immune system fights this with everything it has until it is overwhelmed. The great difficulty youth have in launching makes them easy prey for political manipulators who tell them, "Just join our crusade and you can escape all of that."

Your life has made you study the dark ones. You know more about this subject that no one wants to see.

Some people have made themselves a well-defended cave in hell and think they are free. Barricading yourself in a psychic fortress is defeat disguised as victory. It is terror-based.

Study self-centeredness. It is the core of all addictions. This is not some sacrificial high-minded morality; it is practical self-care. The self-centered are always miserable.

You often feel more grateful for these words we give you than you are for your life. You trust the good intent behind these words, but the intent behind your life is the same. It is a hard school. These words are a dilution, a thinned-out version. There are blessings all around you. You swim in them and see them not. Drink them in and you shall be strong.

Do not repress the parts of you that hate. Get to know them; they are infested by dark ones and in pain. Do not let them sink out of awareness to form cysts and live on deep inside of you.

Safe, defended psychic spaces can be seductive traps that can keep you trapped for lifetimes like a fly on a sticky strip. Learn. Study these as you would study a poisonous snake.

Clean up your own side of the street. There's plenty of garbage there. Clean up with joy, celebration, and light.

Your life is built on the legacy of millions and millions of deaths and agonies. All those deaths and each agony meant something. Even the dark ones' greatest triumphs of destruction can be used as foundations and building blocks for something good and eternal.

People who resist the call of the Gods go mad. The "mental health" system is tweaked by the dark ones. It is a proud and well-defended bastion of theirs. It does not help those called by the Gods; it destroys them. It aborts the entry of Spirit into this realm. It crushes the most sensitive and visionary.

Your planet is hell; a deep hell. This can be a springboard, a launching pad for saints — for Holiness. There is a searing fire, high-heat smelting. Much dross can be burned off here. Weird and creepy things try to eat you from the swamps. The fire is safety, purity, and light. It burns inside of you. Go into the fire.

How do I "go into the fire?"

With whatever is most painful within you — be curious. Approach the suffering, turn toward, bring light, enter with kind curiosity, come blazing with your own light, our fire, our heat, and you

are everywhere safe. You can enter the deepest hells; we are preparing you for this.

Sometimes every human is fooled into being a blind servant of the dark ones.

Things done from Real love and kindness are always right. Love and kindness in all directions — including inward to yourself and your parts. Things done from hate always hurt you. Sometimes we can tweak them enough so they do good in the world, but they always hurt you.

Do I work to relieve suffering or save myself?

Both, they are intertwined; you cannot do either one alone.

Dissolve. This is key. Dissolve. You are way too small. Your sad little boxes, the prisons you choose to live inside, dissolve all of that and more. When all that is dissolved, the Real is what remains.

Your work is laid out for you. There are endless depths of beauty all around you. See beauty more. Every time you see beauty is a triumph of the Holy.

You are part of a soul group. You reincarnate in groups. You extend in many dimensions, to heavens and hells, into the past and the future. You are a node in the net that exists in many dimensions and many worlds.

Own your own hate more. Don't express it — own it. It does not matter if you are "justified." Hate welcomes in the dark ones, believing it is necessary for the fight because the opponents have armies of dark ones. All this is false. The dark ones are parasites; they always weaken the host.

Some invite in dark ones to perform magic to keep themselves safe. They end up living closed up in caves deep in hell realms, believing they are free. This is a blueprint, a wiring diagram, a master strategy of darkness. Remember all those idealistic Chinese youths waving Mao's Little Red Book, chanting and thinking they were free? An annihilation of Spirit. (Well, Spirit cannot be killed, but…) They jumped from miserable, stale, stuffy boxes of who they were into what appeared clean, fresh, and noble. It was a more severe prison: less human, more metallic, more insectoid. A disaster of the Spirit for so many.

You are here in a body for a purpose. All the suffering is meaningful. The price is huge, overwhelming, and unbearable — it is only this which opens the gates. The unbearable can set you free. Do not despair, do not give up. All is well, even in the deepest hells.

You live in a world that tries to make everyone either one up or one down to you. Find equals.

Whatever part of you manages to align itself with your sexual energies will have the power to seize control of your system. All the parts work to capture this, to partner with it. You also need this energy for Spirit. Your sexual energy needs cleaning. Still there is contamination, adhesions, and splinters deep inside it. Land mines of the soul.

Everyone is capable of mystical experience. Telepathy, remote viewing, ESP, and more are all natural for you, but you need more purity and cleaning, or the power surge would burn you.

The prison walls are closing in on your planet. The poison infiltrates through the intellectuals and political leaders. They are the plague carriers. The fleas on the animal. Tools of the dark ones.

You must develop your own independent navigation system. Good enough to stake your life on and the lives and souls of others whom you love.

You are an eternal being. Who you Really are is eternal. You have vast psychic powers, and when you are pure, you can access all the knowledge in the library of the mind of God.

Light is the great metaphor for Spirit. There are false lights. Some people would set up false lights on shore to lure ships to wreck on the rocks so they could loot them and enslave the sailors. There are fake messiahs all around clamoring for attention. And the light is Real, important, central. We love you, little one. All is well.

The dark ones and the domination structures on your planet love the pandemics. They love crisis and terror. As long as they get to tell everyone what to do, any means seems justified to them.

You are an eternal being. Say this to yourself several times a day. This is a good basis for a navigation system.

The dark ones have almost totally succeeded in corrupting academia and the professional intellectuals. The word soul is taboo. So is prayer. So, they talk of meditation. They shit on all that is Holy and sacred, spoiling for a fight. Do not fight this battle. Develop your navigation system. You are an apprentice sweeping the shop clean; watch and learn.

Spirit, I need you today.

Let us hold you. You always need us — today you are just more aware of it. This is a good thing, but painful.

Do not think of yourself as a Spirit warrior. Beware of pride. You are safer as God's garbageman. If you got major recognition now, even this late in your life, it could destroy you.

You are approaching a core experience. Lonely, cold isolation. It is easier to fight the world than to be with this. There is a vast reservoir of this pain — all the infants who died of abandonment and all those who froze to death. When they sense yet another being going down like this, they gather around. Body warmth is so important, but it's more than that; there's a subtle interpenetration of radiant energy fields. It's a kind of food in a good way. Many groups work this way. Much of the healing is not what you thought you were doing at all.

It is so hard for you all to sense Spirit now, to sense the Real. This has always been hard, and it's much worse now. This is a triumph of the dark ones. The idea that the unseen world does not exist is perhaps the greatest core lie of the modern world. Western culture is mechanomorphic, antihuman, insectoid, antibiologic, and antilife. You have added a sauce of hate with these words, but the reality is there.

Take every lesson inward. How do you recreate the terrible tyrannies of Mao, Stalin, and Hitler inside yourself? Who are the internal dictators? Who are the willing agents, the generals and bureaucrats who seek total control? Who are the suppressed and regimented? Who are the outlaws?

The tapestry, the flow, the expansive history even just of your planet, has terrible suffering. There is splendor too, but it is soaked in blood. After a great battle, the sun rises over piles of the dying and the dead. There is a groaning, a wailing… and the splendor is there. Grief, joy pain, joy.

Reject nothing; turn toward. Take every lesson inward. Spirit's tears water this planet; let your tears water your life.

When you really know something deep in yourself — clear and clean — you do not need to prove it to others.

The lonely, abandoned boy within you was frozen by other parts to keep him hidden. He was too full of pain to be in this world. He sneaks out at night, overwhelming or bypassing your conscious mind. Welcome him more; you have rejected him harshly. Your rejection redoubled his pain, coldness, and isolation.

Body contact is so important and needed, both the living warmth and the radiating, interpenetrating energy fields. In many ways, this is more important than genital sex and a major reason for, and benefit of, sex. In the womb, you are surrounded by this living warmth. You still are, but it is attenuated and different now. Harder for you to recognize. This is a reason to be in nature. To walk off of pavement. To be inside a forest. To touch the earth with bare hands. The interpenetrating fields vibrating, humming, resonating mutually strengthen and reinvigorate each other. Shake off encrustations. Reawaken the memory of who you really are — fields of shimmering, eternal force. Your idea of eternal is way too small. Eternal does not mean stasis, frozen, or solid. Movement as well as stillness may be eternal.

The hatred in you is fear, really — fear you cannot yet tolerate directly.

When you judge someone as less than you, poison enters.

You reincarnate in soul groups. Your soul group was attacked and shattered like a Jewish shtetl in Russia being raided by Cossacks... like a sledgehammer hitting an apple and splattering it widely... like Divine sparks of light spreading out throughout the cosmos and forming shells to survive. Take off your shell — let the light shine. Be the beacon, sound the ram's horn, the shofar. They will come. I see a glimpse of bedraggled and wounded people slouching homeward, the light of dawn or dusk. Some are filth-covered, some deformed, some raving. The return will be hard. It means giving up the security of anonymity and the safety of being scattered. This is not physical; it is more Real than that. Call them home, inside, and out. Calling your

soul group home. This joining, this reunion is a deep threat to the dark ones, the critters. They live by creating isolation. They thrive in isolated creatures. They create separation and distrust, distance and division at every level.

Pay attention. Enjoy the learning. Do not rush past. Open all sensory modalities, the conscious five and the many unconscious ones. Be as aware, as open as you can be, to the porosity of your mind, to the transliminal. When this is open, you will not be limited by sensory modes — you will know.

You need your robot, your ability to make behaviors and responses automatic. This frees your mind for thought and exploration. You could not walk or swallow or ride a bike without this robot. Like every great virtue, it has toxic near enemies: thought loops, habits, addictions, ruminations, and perseverations.

Develop your own navigation system, a navigation system in a world of lies. We are weaning you off our guidance in these dialogues. More and more, you sense the Real directly. There are no logical rules for you to follow. There are so many dimensions you live in, unaware. **Your current system based on logic and the five senses is totally insufficient — like trying to see in complete blackness or trying to smell underwater.** Yes, this is another launching. You would not learn this unless we pushed you; it's too hard. It can be scary or exciting, depending on your attitude. You will fall, but we will pick you up.

I'm afraid to lose this connection.

Yes, that's understandable and you will be rewarded with a much better connection, more sure and certain and deep. More will be able to flow through. A river, not a stream.

Words and writings are all around you, Bob. It is almost an addiction. The words don't need to go entirely; it is your attitude toward them that must go. Your idolatry of verbal ideas, images of God instead of God, dialogue instead of direct contact. We will never abandon you. Direct sensation and knowing, nothing less. More global. Words now only a tiny part. Feel your way in — do not analyze. You are proud of your words and understanding. They are training wheels — remove them.

Whatever you do, do it with kindness. If you need to end a relationship, do it with a scalpel, not a bludgeon.

Your fears are at root false. You are an eternal being; everything else is weather.

When you get any dark one or entangled energy out of your system, do it freely. Do not ask for any reward from them. Getting them out makes more room in you for us. This is more than an adequate reward.

Love, learn, let go. Kindness all around. Simple. Be open to the new, to surprise. Otherwise, you will only see what you expect. This would lock you in a boring universe. Stay open — there is much more. Wonder. Awe.

Volume 14

Your species was banished here because you were holding back the evolution of another solar system. You are, in a sense, a prison planet, an Australia of the soul.

You are excruciatingly tender about these dialogues. Notice this. Be open and curious. Your inner visions are going in totally unexpected, unwanted, and incomprehensible ways. Pay attention. Pause more. There are Spirits all around you. Pause and listen. Your depths open to you. Pause and listen. We are here. Pause and listen. The female Divine is here. Pause and listen. More space, less knowing, less opinions.

Learn to navigate with your eyes closed and your brain turned off. Pause and listen, then go in peace and curiosity. No matter what experience you are entering, it goes better when you meet it in peace and curiosity with full presence. Greet what does not fit, the anomalous, this way, and it will bring you great joy and great learning.

You need many less opinions than you have.

There is a control room in your mind that is kludged together out of many old routines. It is a compound legacy, not well designed. It is your interface with this material world. Various parts and Self get in and start driving your vessel.

There is more in the Real, the subjective realms, than parts, Self, and Spirits. Much more. You assumed it was all these three classes. You did not realize that this was a small, theoretical box you lived inside. You almost never perceive the boxes you live in — prisons of the soul — until you are ready to leave them. Do not get in the boxes. Stack them up, climb on top, and reach higher.

There is a desperate, terrified, frantic manager part in you, emaciated but with a beautiful face. She curls in and down. She is so desperate that she clings to the dark ones like a meth addict clings to their meth. The dark ones laugh as they keep her terrified and weak while offering her power. They keep her on the edge to harvest her misery. This manager is well-intentioned, and she does much harm. Deep, slow grief will heal her. Be kind.

You are more a battlefield than a warrior or general. And your cooperation and permission are crucial, a sine qua non. Not many let us work.

Most of your world is an anomalous mystery covered by a thin veil of theory and refusal to look. So, pause and look. That's all. And it's enough for endless growth.

There are more galaxies in your universe than all the grains of sand on all the beaches of your planet. You know so little. This is even more true in your inner world, your subjective realm.

How can I sense you, Spirit?

First, look for any parts, any rebels or ronins who do not want to sense me and love them. Focus on the unlove with love.

The whole universe is alive, from subatomic particles to galaxies and beyond in both directions. Alive and therefore flexible and renewable. **Life force is indestructible. It takes on new forms, that's all.** The dark ones hate this message. They know that if you truly absorb this, you are immune to them and beyond their reach.

When you get above a certain level, the dark ones can no longer see you, so they set out traps and trip wires and land mines of the soul.

To receive Spirit, do less, slow way down, focus inward and open.

(I got an image of Spirit in the form of a man standing behind me, radiating light in all directions. Some enters the back of my heart and then radiates out into the world through me. This image brings me peace.)

There is a long path ahead. Enjoy the trip — the pilgrimage — as much as you can. Keep going. Stay curious and you are invincible. This is the key. Persevere. One foot after the other.

Whenever you let a fear block you, it limits your life and will continue to weaken you until you can face it. Be curious toward the fear — go right into the center of it. We are with you; fear not.

The idea that you are made up of parts, Self, and others within us is a valid and very useful first-order approximation. It's all that's needed for most navigation. A ship on the ocean only needs to navigate to an accuracy of a quarter of a mile or so to find home port. If it tried to navigate to an accuracy of a foot or inches, it would encumber or damage the process. If it tried to get Real accuracy — millimeters and subatomic distances — its navigation system would be totally useless. More accuracy can be a problem, a seductive and crippling trap. You only need a rough outline of Spirit now. More would confuse and paralyze you. Learn how to navigate. You need direct experience of the resonance of the field. You do not even have words for this. Can you navigate without names?

Everything you have learned so far is preschool, an oversimplification, a first-order approximation, and much of it is wrong. The abyss is truth. The howling emptiness. We are here beyond, far beyond all you know.

You usually do not like Spirit's help. When we give it to you, you experience it as pain and react with fear and contraction.

Invite us in more, right in the middle of things.

The images and felt senses are given to you because this material is beyond what a rational brain can do. Any brain — language — theory — understanding would kill or imprison the life force. Feel your way in; invite us in. Be careful not to entrap or reduce or put it in old boxes. Open. Spread your legs like a woman about to be impregnated. Receive. This is the living way to receive and contain. It leads to birth and growth and more life. This is the opposite of rational knowing, which leaves things cold and dead and pinned to a board. Guard this vagina, this opening, with all your care, strength, tenderness, and love. It is more precious than rubies, diamonds, or gold. Treasure this.

When a part of you thinks of dying and wants to go home, give it a home in your arms while you have a physical body. Provide a home here and now.

When you get that time-out-of-time feeling — that bird's eye view of your life — enjoy it. When you realize that you know so little, this is a good thing, even though it hurts. It is a blessing. It brings you closer to the Real. Notice who is hurt, who is scared rather than excited. Love them. Whole new fields are opening up to you. Your belief that you know blocked all of this. Great, unimaginable things are possible because you are eternal. To soar above this lifetime and all the billions of lifetimes on earth. More vast than that.

Pray more. Open more. Let go. There is still crap all over you, sticking to you. Let it fall away. Cleaning yourself is serving us, not just a preparation.

It is good you are realizing that you know nothing. This is a big step toward knowing.

You can barely ascend high enough to view your own life as a whole… let alone see the billions of lives that led up to you, lives and deaths. Wave after wave, like at the seashore. Relentlessly pounding and massaging the coast so that what is strong and more Real can stand free. There is the Real — it exists. Everything you perceive in space-time is just a cheap headset, a training device. There is so much more. Most of the Divine is invisible to you because you have your space-time headset on.

Look over your whole life span. Get used to this height, this perspective. It is a small step toward your eternal nature. Mostly, you focus your attention on petty minutiae that won't be important next week. Flashes of the eternal knife down through all the clouds and strike you.

Listen to the blessings that you would have rejected as deflationary before. We bless you every day, and most of what we offer you, you do not accept.

To dissolve is to expand, even though it feels like death. Set aside everything you think you know and pay attention.

You view Spirit contact almost like fishing or hunting. You go looking for something — some experience — and then bring it home to feed on.

Is much of my writing an attempt to capture Spirit and put it down where it will hold still?

This is not all bad, and it's much more valuable to let us change who you are. Then you can come back a different person. Focus on being changed. Listen to be changed, especially when listening to Spirit. Much of being changed will be the stripping away of old stuff. There is still dirt, encrusted shit, boils, pockets of contained inflammation, breeding grounds for dark ones. Also, some deformities, twistings, scoliosis of the spiritual spine, blind spots, deafnesses, and more! Ulcers, sores, darknesses, obscurations, willful refusals, fear, and terror. If you had seen all of this earlier, you would have given up or not tried at all. There are many adhesions, some flesh to flesh, some dark ones to you, sticky. This is a significant word.

Spirit, can you bathe us?

Wrong metaphor. You want composting and metamorphosis. Dissolve and reassemble. Each sore, each pustule, can be a great and saintly teacher. **Purity is learned in filth** — in accepting and seeing and cleaning filth — not by running from it.

Yes, your visions are fairly accurate. There are beings who are farming human miseries, getting people's souls caught in inverted tornadoes of Hell, creating suffering which they feed on.

Turn confusion into curiosity. Confusion has fear in it. Uncertainty has less. Curiosity has none. It's a continuum. Learn to welcome more and more radical unknowing with love and delight. **Certainty is poison for you. You go to it for relief from fear.** Do not go to certainty. Go to love and faith. **The more unknowing you can embrace, the deeper you can grow.** Confusion is a state of grace. When you can value and enjoy it, you are there — all the rest is semantics. Certainty is an enemy of growth, and yet you seek it like the Holy Grail. Appearances of truth — hints, aromas — are all you can get on this planet, and they are enough to follow. They will stretch your abilities to the maximum. They will make you open, alive, and flexible.

Underlying all addictions, there is something Real. Something of the sacred. Sex addiction is the addiction to Divine connection. Alcohol to Divine energy. They are counterfeits of the Real, idolatries, and you can learn about Spirit by studying the fakes. They point fingers to the God-shaped hole within you.

Bob, you are still arrogant. This is why arrogant people annoy you. It slows your learning, it prevents you from seeing all the saints around you, let alone the angels. Your desire to be a teacher and an influencer narrows your field of vision drastically.

When you find delight in confusion, it becomes curiosity.

We love you, Bob, without reason or reward. This just is, like gravity. Soon, you will exert a similar gravity, love force, to all around you. This natural force pulls things together and creates complexity and individuality out of cosmic chaos and randomness.

There is a deep down, unsatisfied longing, a loneliness, a need. It has been sexualized and projected out into the world. You must connect with this part of yourself directly inside. We will help you. Fear not.

Pray more, think less.

Notice how your sense of hurry, your rushing, sets you up for fear. See how they go together. A great lesson. The dark ones often use delay tactics. A major purpose of this is to trigger you into rushing. Rushing is toxic — go slow.

Do this work to be changed, not to accumulate ideas and words — to be changed in who you are. This is good. Let go of the rest. Open; do not focus. Warm, soft opening is a cure for fear and rushing.

If you want to feel self-esteem, do not ever disrespect others.

Your protectors do not want to allow deep connection. It is too dangerous. It exposes wounds, raw tissue, organs, and guts. Slow down and open. Pause. The dark ones want to prevent connection, too. They provoke revulsion in you in reaction to the gored, wounded loving child in hiding. Yes, your love was gored, scraped, ripped with talons of hate, and fed on in a world of lies and gaslighting. This happened. Be open, be warm, be soft.

A collapse into fear is not all bad. You can clear away the rubble and rebuild on a sounder basis. The collapse into the ancestral ocean of fear is actually a blessing. That ancestral ocean can drain now.

Self is a slippery term, a shapeshifter. The witness. Separate the witness from all the ephemeral, transitory stuff. Then the witness is love and luminosity. Scrape the adhesions off of the witness. Burn the dead wood. Clean your sword. **This process is painful and harsh. Our blessings are not easy to receive.**

Focus on trust and faith. They are your surety, your invulnerable sanctuary.

Give love in all directions; doing this will break your heart.

The dark ones constantly attack now. They find any fear or resentment and pour poison in. The times you felt bad about yourself, your worries, each crack, they exploit. Each wound or sore they try to infect.

How do I best prepare myself to receive your gifts?

Look where you do not want to look. The irritations, the pettiness, the fear, all that you avoid.

Notice how you try to manage Spirit. You do this all the time. We have to sneak in.

The things you accuse others of, you do. Yes, the Western intellectual tradition today is hostile to Spirit. So are you in much more subtle and destructive ways. You manage us in the name of welcoming us. You filter our message and visions. You try to provide a channel for us, thereby domesticating the wild and undomesticated. Do you want a free mountain stream or an irrigation ditch?

The odor of sanctity covers the stench of self-hate. This will never work. It is like sticking an incense stick in a turd.

Go where you do not want to go and offer love there.

Instead of spending more time in prayer, let there be a prayerful dimension to all of your life.

Pause when you sense Spirit, beauty, or tears.

Soon enough, your body will fail and die. Prepare for this. Shift your values even more. Value the eternal, the other world — the Real — value us. Let us permeate and profuse your world. We already do, but you do not see it now. Pause; open. You are covered in something like latex gloves: tough, rubbery. They are the inner lining of the shell you live in. Take them off. They keep you a short distance from your life, from the Divine. Slow down; listen tenderly. Do not rush past or hush up. Go toward what's Real, eternal, and living.

Life is more eternal than things. You have this backward. Life is self-organizing. It is growth. It is the life that is eternal. Anything static will decay and dissipate and suffer a heat death of randomness. Eternity is alive, or it is not eternal.

Love is fierce, or it is not love. It is a butcher, a surgeon, a mother pushing her baby from the nest. Fierce, bloodthirsty, raving. She will eat you alive. Go to her.

Work on your fearful, terrified manager. He is a gateway, a plug in the drain of ancient fears. Now the ancient fears run him, and he tries to deal with them by controlling the external world. This can never work. The cause and the cure are inside. We need to go to the ocean of terror. Then, new depths will open to you. There will be vastness, soaring flight, and ease.

Give love in the face of fear and pain. Love without recompense. Just love. Grace. Almost no one will notice you, but your impact will be great. Send out love even to those who do great damage to themselves and those around them. They need it more than most.

Take on less. Slow down. Do not fill your life. Stay with your loneliness, your pain, and your fear. No amount of company can medicate these for you. It's almost like you try to lure people in to be with the parts of you that you cannot stand. Almost. It's not that harsh or black and white. **Heal yourself so your very presence heals others.**

Uncorrected errors propagate to infinity. They dig in and compound and fortify themselves and gather allies.

You unconsciously and automatically work to be impressive when you are with people. They don't really like it when you are impressive. If they believe you, they feel one down. If they don't believe you, they think you're a phony. Instead, interact with others to be changed. Slow down. You are caught in whirlwinds of your own making. Open, pause, listen.

Learning how to learn is more important than getting the answers. Your answer is not the answer. It is a provisional stepping stone.

Add the fertilizer of your attention to anything in your inner world and it will grow.

There is a killing in your usual way of knowing. Both personally and culturally.

You struggle to get others to admire you and to love you because you cannot — will not, really — love yourself or let us Spirits love you.

We, Spirit, are right here loving you. Let us in. Pause more, listen more. We are everywhere offering love freely. Very few will accept, and those who do only let in miserly scraps. In your arrogance, your illusions of knowledge and false certainty, you march right past us — self-righteous and forceful, missing everything. We call and sing to you, but you do not hear.

Curiosity requires not knowing. Cultivate not knowing. Be comfortable in it. It is only in this condition of not knowing, of being lost, of being a fool or helpless, that you can come to us. These are the conditions you spent your lifetime hiding from.

It is never a failure to have loved. Even when it costs you great pain. There is much bullshit and delusion done in the name of love, but the Real thing is always good. It can break through like the sun on a cloudy day — a piercing shaft. Much of your life is unlove and isolation, and compensations for the deficits these bring.

It's a staircase. Build a new stair. Each paradigm, each system, theory, and understanding. Each one is a nice box. Stack them up and climb on top. Do not get in the boxes. Look for what does not fit.

You can never see your blind spots directly. Doing this is looking for what you cannot see — an impossible task.

You are part of a multigenerational soul group. Join your Spirit family. You are part of something, a community, a larger organism, a tribe. Words are so poor. You belong. You are part of a Spirit community. There are more without bodies than with bodies around you. You are not the strongest or the best. You are not the weakest or the worst. We are not all equal. That's a ridiculous idea.

A vision: The shapeshifting woman and great love

I see a female with different flashing identities and ask Spirit, "Who is she?" He replies, "Ask her." I do, and I see her blush beautifully. I say, "You have gone through so many transformations. Some look very dark — and you seem so innocent and beautiful. Who are you?" She does not answer. She doesn't know? "Words cannot hold it," she says. I ask, "Do you want to be with me?" "Yes, she says." Looking down, shy and demure. Very sweet. I take her hand gently. It flashes. A young woman's hand, a starving Black child's shriveled hand, a clawed animal hand, now even an insectoid exoskeleton, crab claw.

Now that I have not flinched or rejected any of these, she also shows me callused, rough hand, a mucousy pseudopod hand, hands with sores and wounds, a stump. The images slow down briefly. Some tears in her. She looks up at me shyly and insecure. I still want to be with her. She seems to settle. But the identities flicker past quickly. Then she exhales and settles. She is a beautiful young woman, early teen then adult. Quickly, this flashes to an old hag, deeply lined witch. A sadness and a grief. She leans on me; I hold her gently. Thoughts of sex, but I have fear of her sexually. I do not want to hurt her feelings or hurt her. Spirit says, "You have our blessings." We kiss gently. I sense great passion. We settle back, holding each other side by side. I say, "I am glad you are here with me." She replies, "I have always been here with you, and you did not see me."

Is she a Goddess? She says she senses my fearful parts and says that we have been doing this dance for eons. There is time. She is now the stronger one comforting me. She shows me another flickering montage of identities. Spirit blesses us and tells us that each of us was the stronger, the leader at different times. Roles have changed. Rescuer and rescued. The healer and the sick. Master and animals. Prisoner and guard. But always the deep love was there. She watched as I was impaled and died a slow, horrible death. She was pregnant with our child. There's a wave of her great, loving soul that called others forth. This called more to it, like gravity. A reservoir or ocean of great pain and even greater love. Love at the edges of what is unendurable. Many went howling insane. Many turned mean. Many cast curses and caused destruction.

Spirit tells us that with the two of us reuniting now, much of this can drain. Peace, settling, rest. There has been a vast commitment between you two for centuries. This was a beacon, a lighthouse to many. A furnace in the freezing hells. It is time now to recognize, honor, to make conscious and reconnect. Love her with all your heart and being. I am afraid to recommit, but I do not want to lose her. She leads and comforts me.

In loving this flickering, shapeshifting woman, you have won a major battle, emptied a reservoir of pain and cleared many parasites. Invite in the sweet, warm energies of healing now. The only way to know who this woman is, is to love her. Love her without analysis. This love can open both of you to eternity and can cure the ancient fear and wounds you both have had from being lost to each other thousands and thousands of times.

Welcome the part of you that you saw covered with crawling insects. Do this and more of your Spirit family will appear. You have eternity. Fear creates clinging, which drives out Real love and connection. It creates a self-defeating cycle.

You cannot — structurally cannot — understand me/us/Spirit. You are just too small as yet. So of course there will be plenty of places for the nasty suspicions to work their way in.

There are parasites that can get into you and colonize your mind. They controlled your behavior and used you to spread their spores and young to infest others. You need to endure a purification, a delousing, a debugging. This is often strenuous and often releases a disgusting stench and visions of vile, slime creatures. Many refuse this, even though it is a spiritual doorway. After this, you can float free, away from this planet. You can be a blessing to the universe and not a disease carrier, a vector of infection.

The IFS and psychotherapy languages are breaking down for you. They are too small and rigid. Some parts have greater contact with Self — Spirit — than the person. The part can be greater than the whole. Feel your way in. Love. **To love is to know. Nothing can replace this — not the biggest concepts, not the best scientists.** You cannot endure our presence, so we send diluted rays of love and joy to heal you first.

Do not attack and expose the hypocrites. You will be splashed in mud and may be drowned in mud and shit. Take the high road; the air is better, and you can see much farther. In order to do this, you need faith and trust that the inner work is what's Real. When you want external world recognition, check your faith.

We often work to prevent you from getting external world recognition and rewards. We prevent this. This is one reason that when you pray your will, not mine, we often warn you, you won't like it. You are not strong or clean enough to enjoy the external world rewards without being contaminated and damaged. You would be more a Nero than a Marcus Aurelius. Sorry, but this is true.

Lord, clean me.

So you can succeed or so you can come to us?

You get into the belly of the beast best with prayer, not swords.

Do not trash people when they hurt you. Resist this urge. It will get you stuck to people who are intensely bad for you in negative intimacy. It is like the way the dark ones often provoke fights and war in order to get to stay in people.

When looking for faults and hidden hate, use a mirror, not a magnifying glass. This conserves energy instead of spending it uselessly in the world. Be kind, even to the assholes. You want evil and disrespect punished. This is poison for you. Get your mirror out. Use their energies to heal yourself.

You have tried to control us Spirits because you cannot trust. There is good intertwined with the bad. Strong drive to heal, speak truth and see clearly are tangled with control, desire to punish, and self-righteousness. Untangle this patiently with love.

No sneering. Sneering is a good sign of the dark ones. No more sneering, clever insults, self-righteousness, or riding in the one up position. All of these are poisons. Clean your own house and we will come.

Bob, you are so crippled, you know. Twisted and limited. Unable to move freely, bound up, tied up. Adhesions and scar tissue.

Spirit, can you lift this off of me?

Not yet.

Can you help me prepare?

Yes. We also are using you as an entry point into the coma farms of hate and the reservoirs of fear and shame. Are you willing to continue serving in this way, creating drains for the swamps?

Yes.

Then your own liberation has to wait. You will never see the results of this, and the ones in the future who will be most helped will not even know that they've been helped at all. There are others doing this work. They also remain unknown. You would not recognize them if you passed them in the street. You and they do not need to consciously know each other. For the work to progress, love is necessary. Faith is required. You do not control the process. That is pride and hubris.

You do not know who the saints are. No humans are totally reliable teachers, and yet we often speak to you through them.

You have become lopsided in your pursuit of knowledge so other things can unbalance you easily. This is a time-tested strategy of the dark ones. They get you to overemphasize and overfocus on one good quality so they can destabilize you with a counterpush. For example, celibacy creates rapists or internal self-hatred. Both are bad.

Truth is a conscious being, a beautiful woman. All the qualities are conscious persons; so are we. The ancients did not personify these — courage, beauty, truth, power. They recognized their personhood. It is you and your culture that scramble to strip all of this away. It is persons. All is persons. All is relationship.

The more unknowing you can welcome, the more we can give you. Open, unknowing, welcome, all senses open. Wonder. Surprise. Your knowing is a blockage. The dark ones encourage this ossification and stenosis. Let love be your form of knowing. It is a surer guide than facts.

Be honest. Be Real. There is great love and light in you. It is who you are. Let it out.

The pathway to feeling your strength is to know your weakness. We are bringing them to light. It is a well-disguised blessing.

Surprise is good; it is a sign of the Real. We can be with you more as you tolerate more surprise and more unknowing. You and your trauma response parts want to nail down your understandings. Spirit flees from this mishandling. You see this nailing down of ideas as milking every drop from what you are given. In some ways it is true that this is a way of valuing and respect. But there is much grasping and control within this. The dark ones, once again, exaggerate a good quality to turn it into poison. Sound familiar?

Often your understanding of something is butchering and cutting up an experience until it fits into what you already know — into your tiny, little boxes. Butcher the boxes instead.

Your body is a complex energy field. A system of energy fields, really. Constantly penetrated by many other energies and in relation to still more energy fields. Independence is a sometimes useful illusion, but you do have agency. You have agency, choice. It is through choice that you can learn to navigate — to captain your ship. You will be given bigger and bigger vessels as you progress.

The attempt to heal trauma by burying it makes it immortal. This is a triumph of the dark ones. Love the hurt itself. Do not shy away. You can do this. The dark ones want the wounds scabbed over so they can feed on them in hiding.

See if you can loosen your theoretical boxes. You could not see if they were gone completely — everything would be a blur. Do not nail things down. No certainty. Look for surprise. Take delight in anomalies. You can do this when you are safe. You are safe when you can sit peacefully with the worst wounds. The peace of life and tenderness, not the peace of certainty.

Do not attempt to manage Spirit. Would you try to manage a surgeon operating on you?

Each new knowing brings ten new ignorances. Delight in their abundance.

When I sense the dark ones are angry at me, I think I am on a good path.

This is true, but do not allow yourself to enjoy their pain. This could drag you down.

Do not take anything that is not yours. This will help make the ground firm under your feet.

Notice the abundance of blessings that surround you daily — beauty, food, good people, peace, a home, health. Mostly, you pay attention to the flies and gnats. Notice what surrounds you — it is mostly glory.

Grief is a blessing. You already sense this. There are oceans of it. It can almost be a reward, a washing, a gentle rain, a freshness. Welcome it.

Stay curious. Curious, fascinated, wonder, awe, ecstasy... Curiosity is the first step of the staircase. The exploratory impulse. Have the exploratory attitude, or better, the exploratory mind even, especially as your body weakens and dies.

Faith doesn't matter much when our contact is flowing in sweet; it matters when it feels dry and desolate, when the work is out of your awareness, or when your parts are afraid.

Your getting good feelings from the esteem of others is an addiction. It is an idolatry. It results from a lack of faith.

Pause and be still. There will always be reasons not to. Still. Pause and be still. We will lead you if you let us. Pause, listen, and have faith.

We are bringing you along as fast as we can, and this is hard on you. Earlier, you and I had to work so hard for each tiny shift. Now you open floodgates.

The human mind with its reason cannot comprehend or analyze the Real, but you can experience it. You can do this by loving it, not by analysis.

Natural great peace. Peace is the core of healing, the font, the spring. It can flow through you. Managers can all let go. Find this spring. Sit by it as it flows into the world.

You could feel much more gratitude. It feeds you, not us. Just as prayer helps you, not us. Gratitude, like prayer, can cure resentment. Resentment is a terrible toxin, and it is contagious. It is being farmed and intentionally spread. Resentment is an intentionally spread pandemic.

Gratitude is an experience, not an idea. When you are grateful, you will not get sucked down into resentment so easily. Pause when you feel grateful and open up. When you really feel this, it radiates out of you freely without effort. Like resentment, it is contagious.

With my weak faith, I want something totally unequivocally, trustworthy, and always right.

You want to abdicate your responsibility and flee from your deep freedom.

I always sneered at people who did this.

This was a clever strategy of the dark ones to keep you from seeing it in yourself. Go to not knowing. Let the abyss be your foundation. Can you stand on the abyss in gratitude and grace without clinging? If you try to grab us, it will not be us you get a hold of; it will be dark ones, imposters. This is why theology always fails — it is an attempt to grab us and nail us down, to have fixity and certainty.

You are like dry, rock-hard soil. It takes many wettings before you soften and open to growth. This is why so many messages are repeated over and over, so they can sink in. Your soul is softening into humus — humility. You will be able to grow things, to be fertile, to be teachable.

You will never find peace or rest in grasping or clinging. Never.

The dark ones attack children and child parts of you. They are more innocent, gullible, and less experienced. This is part of the reason your education system is so terrible. Domination structures and the dark ones want to create a generation of fools who will sell their birthrights for useless baubles.

Evil now has a slicker front — fashion designer clothes, big desks, five-star hotels, fine education. Very civilized, but the basics are still the same.

Every accomplishment and triumph of the human spirit is immediately attacked and perverted, even as it is being born. Constantly. This will make you strong. You will have an immune system that will allow you to thrive in hell. Fear not. Be open. Look. Receive. Stand tall. Do not grasp. You need nothing. Stand tall. Make yourself as big as you can, and we will make you bigger.

Pride and arrogance are a perversion, a slight twist that turns your God nature into a curse. This is a trap for the bigger fish who are closer to home. You are Godlike, a divine, eternal being, and pride will destroy you quickly if you let it in.

Reject nothing. It is all lessons, not obstacles. Be a student of everything and everyone, especially the people and things that irritate you the most.

Go with interest and fascination. This will lead you home to wonder, awe, joy, pain, and exquisite sensibilities.

Iain MacGilchrist estimates that it only takes a change in consciousness in three percent of a population to change the world. This is about right, but it really only takes one person to open fully, and everything is transformed.

The struggle is needed to strengthen you. It is not a mistake.

The dark ones are out there trolling; they have many fishing lines with many hooks and lures in the water. You bite on some.

You must go to your hurt parts and needy ones and welcome them home. You — not us directly. We operate through you. If you try to hand them to us directly, the dark ones will enter.

Pay attention. Pay attention. Attention is a moral act. It creates the world you live in — a mostly controlled and mostly shared hallucination. This is an ancient pattern. Imagine the mother's guilt and fleeing from that guilt, an inability to turn and face the Real. The great sorrow of the child. This is a hole in your human legacy that the dark ones exploit to enter humanity. It is an infestation point, a gaping wound.

Many of the abandoned ones armored up, got mean and competitive, to force people to pay attention to them. To make people care. This always fails to soothe the hurt.

Look within and radiate out.

You have everything you need, but you see it not, so you go out into the world from lack. This sets you up for pain. Turn toward the lack and pain within you and let us love you. All else is futile.

The ambitious people you feel disgusted by reveal what you do not want to see in yourself. Learn.

On the bad days, keep doing your inner work. Stay curious. A path without bad days would be a downhill decline, a seductive error.

Put your best out there. Your heart, your wisdom, your skills, your teaching. Put these out there as well as you can and let go. The attempts to sell and promote these ideas makes you ill.

Listen well to each discomfort. Learn from each, even the tiny ones, and you will not need the illness and incapacitation. Treat each discomfort as a valued and honored teacher. Bow to it. Slow down.

The fake retreat, fake conversion, is a major stratagem of the dark ones. Also, when they cannot resist a good development in you, they encourage it and work hard to make it extreme and unbalanced so they can attack again.

Each person you meet is a mystery beyond your comprehension.

Pain is more reliable than pleasure as a teacher. You cannot ignore it. So be curious about it until it is melted and gone.

You do not leak energy — you hose the world down with your judgments and attempts to control. You spray your energy vigorously all around you. This is not just a leak. When you do this, you are a magnet for shit, and then you complain it smells bad! Oh, Bob. You recall all the small affronts and play with them until they fester. Learn.

When you scan a room and judge the people as attractive or uninteresting, it damages you and them. When you judge someone as a reject, it shuts off all possible learning. Even calling someone or a part hyperactive is too judgmental. Any diagnosis is an error that prevents Real relationship. And it is all relationship. There are no things.

Listen deeply to your whole life, especially the difficulties.

Clinging and grasping are a lack of faith. As you let go more and more, there is less need for dementia to free you later.

Unwillingly, the dark ones are great teachers. Very expensive, but great.

You talk too much. It slows your learning.

Pay attention to the need for attention. It is often an addiction. Your culture is built around competing for attention.

We will never abandon you. Even if you go into the deepest Hell and curse us for eons, we are here, we are love unending. Rest into us and speak from here.

What you need and want is right here waiting for you — an endless supply given freely with grace. And you search elsewhere in gar-

bage and addictions, in young women's bodies, in fame, the attention of others. When you are full of us, you are immune to addictions.

To connect with us more deeply, your sense of being special must go. Hate and judgment and comparison must go. Lots of stuff that parts of you cling to desperately. You love them and let our love flow into you and through you into them. Do not hand them off to us.

Make offers — do not make commands. All commands take people's agency and power, especially when they want commands. No commands.

Real love expects no return. This is your safety.

Reuniting with the mother is complex, thorny, and difficult for you. It should be the easiest, most natural, and warm thing. The core of all subsequent relationships to people and wives and animals and Spirit and earthworms and, and, and... In you, it is a rotten cavity, a smelly black hole with jagged edges. Pus and vileness. Lurking danger. Seduction. Dark fluids. Abomination — the whore of Babylon. Death and destruction. The first step for you to heal this is for you to pray for your mother's soul.

Back in the old country where your ancestors ran a pharmacy, they were poisoners. It was very profitable. Some of the souls they poisoned have cursed your whole lineage: your grandfather who fled to America, your mother, and you. They vow to pursue this to the ends of the earth, to wipe you all off the planet. They are dark and have invited in the darkest. They would destroy the planet to destroy you. This is an opening for evil. Welcome and meet those who cursed you. It is dark ones riding on humans. Pray for the souls of the poisoned ones.

Love is more important than writing your books. Serve love everywhere, in all directions. When you expect no return, it is safe to love freely. This will free you.

Everything, everyone, every experience is a teacher, especially sent for you — all those you hate and resent and the difficulties, the disappointments, and the sadnesses, the losses — all teachers. Expensive ones, excellent ones. We want to give you more power and range. We want to open your crib and free you into a bigger world. So learn. You must learn or the increased power and range will damage you and others.

My words are not clear.

The language itself has the energy of the dark ones built into it. This is another triumph of theirs.

Build more pauses into your life. This is respect for the moment. Eternity is now. Failing to do this costs you the experience of the sacred. We are always here, and you rush past us in a bad mood.

There are some things, some beings, more important than suffering. Things and beings worth suffering for. The fixation on sufferings is a smallness, a rearview mirror navigation system. It is often a ruse for the dark ones. Alcohol, drugs, and escapes all reduce sufferings. Turn toward, open your heart, and love. The more you love, the more you suffer. Love more, give it away, grieve, and expect no return.

Volume 15

Your work now is to leave behind a trail of what you have learned on this planet. This is a time of summation. Treat it with that respect and remember that you are a beginner and that your job is to learn.

Your most difficult clients are great teachers. Study with them. Some of them are infested with critters who are eager to infect others or at least to provoke a fight. The therapy stuff is a necessary prerequisite. A precursor. You have to drop the sludge, scrape the shit off your shoes, before the Spirit work can be fully Real. This isn't accurate — they precede in tandem, in spirals, in a nonlinear multidimensionality. The therapy is the opening, but you cannot comprehend this fully. Know that if you do not do your personal therapy work, your spiritual work can be stopped and even reversed. You cannot comprehend the work of Spirit. The caterpillar has no idea of the butterfly. None. Its body resists the necessary liquefaction with all its might.

You puff yourself up when you feel small. This becomes an addiction, a way of life. You come to believe you need attention and praise to stay puffed up. This prevents you from ever looking at the deficits under it all. Then these parts feel even more desperate and lonely as you play your destructive, addictive game of "look at me." Be humble. Notice your failings. Welcome the lonely parts who feel small.

Pray for the people who hurt you and speak truth to them with kindness and fearlessness. When there is pain in the relationship, use the mirror more than the magnifying glass.

You are selfish, deeply selfish. This even infects your spirituality — it is primarily about your feeling tones and inner states. This causes you pain. In Al-Anon, it becomes clear that if you go into meetings focused on how others think about you, it feels bad. If you go into a meeting focused on how you can help others feel better, it feels good. You forget this simple truth. Even this is selfish — the bottom line is how you feel. This is not the Real bottom line. What is the Real bottom line? Splendor, radiance, vastness, and more. You become part of something immense, a valued creative part, an asset. No longer a sick one who needs care. You become a source of energy, a hearth where a fire can burn and give light. You do not yet comprehend selfishness. Stay curious.

Critters and dark ones are all around every opening to Spirit, to the Real. They offer glittering, gaudy alternatives like circus sideshows. Religions are often like this too — corrupt and eaten out. How can these things live? They all can; they all do. Everything has us in it, or it could not exist for a millisecond. Everything and everyone. Do not put these ideas into your preexisting boxes — listen and sense.

You are deeply beautiful and loved. The cracks and crevices and broken parts have great beauty — time out of time beauty. A battlement of old, a place of struggle. Be aware. Open. An old, scarred land. Many dead. Open.

Words are always in part inaccurate. They can also be poems that point beyond themselves. Each word in a sense is a little poem. It points to meaning — it does not hold meaning.

When you sense those underworld seas of pain and terror, open a streambed and then stand aside. Witness the draining of the ancient suffering. Do not empathize and let it flow through you. This would kill you and constrict the flow. Witness the flow. Do not minimize or skip witnessing.

Love in all directions. Focus more on others and their feelings. Be curious and build them up. You still try to be impressive. Look at this, it causes much pain. Alcoholics Anonymous knows this: the way to stay sober is to help others. This breaks the spell of self-centeredness and the resulting addictive attention-seeking. Build others up instead. Everyone is competing for this, so give it away freely. Your refusal to do this is a form of greed or even hatred.

The idea that God became flesh and incarnated about two thousand years ago in Jesus is meaningless unless it happens in you and happens over and over. Happens today, now. The names do not matter, but the Spirit in which they are said matters a lot. All names flawed, all names okay.

We warned you that you would not like it if we came closer. In the presence of Spirit, your life becomes more difficult, not easier. A spirit-filled life is not an easy life. It is very demanding, stringent. It is easy to fall — dangerous and worth it.

Ask more, be curious more. You focus too much on what you want to say. This is fear-based, unlovely, and unloving.

Your arrogant dismissal of some people as unvaluable and over-estimation of others as important prevents all love. It is unlove in both directions. Putting someone on a pedestal is not love at all.

A vision: The cord spinners

I see cord spinners — spider people. They are here to seize earth for their food. They are trying to surround the planet with a net. Many humans collude knowingly and unknowingly. These cord spinners are implacable because they are desperate. Their mission may well fail. Their leaders especially hate this because they will be held responsible, so they drive their underlings. Many underlings flee and become refugees among us. There are undercover agents among them.

Note well that the spinner orifice that admits the twine is separate from them. It is like a gun, a tool. It, too, is a life form, but mostly without intelligence or awareness. What mind they have has been hampered by their overlords. Free them and they will be faithful to you. Even though these beings are trying to enslave your planet, do not take pleasure in the prospect of their defeat. Do not allow yourself to enjoy the suffering of anyone.

Spirit, I sense a meanness in me today.

It is always there, Bob. Today, you are more aware of it. It hates you and will crush you if it can. It will gleefully claim credit for each pain you feel. It is a complete fraud. The answer is love, just love, only love. And this is enough.

Notice what dark monster is stirring in you. Notice. Stay separate. Observe. It is of your father's line. It is still in you, swimming in the depths. It came to the surface to try and bite and swallow you. Follow it down; do not let it escape again. Redeem that one. It is not happy hiding in the muck on the sea bottom. It burrows there in the slime, lurching up to feed on the unsuspecting. Redeem him.

How??

Love. Oh, my son, have you learned nothing? Love, love, love. You know this. He wants to scare you into hate. Refuse that. Go with love. This is the full answer of God. Love is the sword, shield, and buckler. We love you; let this flow through you. All else is secondary at best. Most of it is fake and toxic.

To serve us Spirits, become a conduit, a channel, a hose, a streambed. Open a way so we may come again. We love you. All is well.

Invite the monsters of the depths up with love. Most will flee, but a few will stay and be transformed. Offer — do not command.

The quality of contact is what satisfies. Sex is merely a biological metaphor. This is really a spiritual issue. The profound longing is for this contact; the opposite of this is isolation, which kills your spirit. When you can offer this quality of contact in all directions, even to the denizens of your depths who disgust you, you will be free.

You still reside in a hell realm. Do not forget this. When you start to hate someone, pray for the son of a bitch as quickly as you can. Pray for the son of a bitch inside you, too. See if as soon as you notice resentment starting its wheels of hate, you can pray for the son of a bitch right at the start.

A vision: The vermin of hate

The dark ones will use your good intentions to entrap you. Watch your motivation — if there is grandiosity, you are in trouble; if you feel superior to others — trouble. If you feel hostile — trouble. If fearful — trouble.

Straight is the gate and narrow is the way?

No, no that's puritan control, manager stuff. The path is wide, and the meadows are green. There are poisons being sold by the roadside — seductive, tasty poisons, popular poisons. Most people gather at these stands and give up the trip. Sometimes these crowds clog the roads completely. The more they feed, the coarser and grosser they become. There is less seduction in it now, more violence. Sometimes we need to backtrack and find another road entirely. I will open a way for you. Fear not. You are leaving a congested area. Step out into the fresh, clean wilderness. Do not cling to human approval or acceptance. Only this will bring you home to Real belonging.

There is big hate in you. It is coming up. Ugly, angry hate from deep undersea. I"s like a huge tar ball with solid things stuck in it. It is spitting and defiant. "You dare disturb me? Me?" it asks. "I will destroy you." It hid in the ocean floor wanting to be oblivious. You have reawakened it from its long sleep. It is in great pain; it is enraged. This being has done much harm and then hibernated and hid to conceal itself. He called in all the demons he could and blasted the world and those who had hurt him. Then he hid. It is good to free him. He will have amends to make. We will help him.

The dark ones have limited resources and limited numbers. They can only succeed by getting tornadoes spinning on their own, by creating self-sustaining addictions, and by recruiting humans to work for them.

You are an eternal being and part of the cosmos. This means that you will be okay even as your body is destroyed or your species is destroyed, or your planet is destroyed.

Rest into the phrase "if it be your will." This will help you if you let it.

It is not a vast, impersonal universe that doesn't care about you. No, not at all. If the wave has personhood, where could it get it from but from the ocean? I care deeply for you, and my values are very different from yours. We are bringing you along, shepherding you through this school. Your wealth, reputation, and position matter not at all to us. Your physical health and survival as a species are not so important. Your soul, your eternal essence, your light — this is what matters.

Do not lie, even in the smallest things. It weakens you and poisons you. You see how other people's lies damage them.

Do not diagnose anyone. It labels and dismisses parts and people as a disease process. It blinds you to the Real. Do not do this to yourself or others. It is institutionalized disrespect... a way for the frightened and insecure academic to go one up. **Diagnosis is a more subtle and socially acceptable form of hate.** Do not do it. Do not collude with it.

When something new arises, there is always confusion. Move toward it and let your confusion turn into curiosity on the sure basis of our love for you. This is solid, stable, and Real.

There is great effort and great surrender. You must clean your vessel. You open and clear the streambed. We are the flowing waters.

Clarity is good. Finality is not. Clarity is a beginning, not a solution.

Your work now opens a way and helps reservoirs of suffering to drain. Some of your clients especially open the way. There will never be any awards or degrees or recognition in your world for this. We love you; you have paid a high price to be able to do this. This is why you are here.

Spirit, help me receive, feel, and connect with you.

Okay. Open wide your legs. Is this Real? Yes. There's a cloud of critters trying to intervene and mess this up. To contaminate it and make it salacious. Passivity, openness, and reception are hard for you. They can be tweaked and perverted into masochism. Ecstasy and pain, there is something deeper. The dark ones are trying to flood you with sexualized ideas and images. They hate Real contact. This flooding takes a lot of energy from them. It seriously drains them. It will subside if you stay steady. Do not engage with them; do not become a prisoner who runs your own prison. When you really deeply receive our love, you become pregnant with Spirit. There will be a celebration, a gestation, and a birth. The children of this union, human and Spirit, have great power. Become gravid. Nurture and nourish. Care and tend. We are with you.

We love you. All else is commentary. Give birth to yourself. Be both mother and child. You are pregnant. Care for yourself in preparation. Make your heart a manger and we will come. No pride, Bob — this is what causes stillbirths. This pregnancy will test your arrogance. It will probe for any faults and call them out. There are many leaks in you now. It is good to find them. Hate is the biggest. You are punished by your sins, not for them.

When you are blocked in prayer or inner contact, do not become angry at the blocker. This is the secondary protector goaded on by the dark ones. It can tie you into knots.

Your nightmare opened you to the unlove, the abandoned, and the desperate. This is big energy, and the critters do not want you to empty this swamp. It is filled with rot and infestations. Toxic tadpoles and minnows by the tens of thousands, crawling and slithering. You feel brotherhood with the unwanted ones. Remember that critters feed here, and they work to prevent any healing.

You are now strong enough to experience the attacks by the dark ones as a reassurance that your work is good. They hate it that you feel this way. Do not allow yourself to enjoy their discomfort.

Parts of you were so hurt as a child that they cannot grow as most do. This is not permanent damage. It means that you walk another pathway, visit other rooms, other houses.

Let your language be more poetic evocation. You squeeze us very, very hard to reduce us into declarative, rational statements. This drastically limits you and your perceptions.

Fear of fear is the key. It amplifies fear into terror and creates panic attacks. It is good you meet this terror while you have a physical body. Notice how it globalizes and how critters use it to try and invalidate everything about your life, prayer, and inner work. They promise that if you abandon all that, they will give you peace. You know that this is a lie. Do not do it. **Real peace is found by going directly into the heart of the terror. Only there. It's a good hiding place, isn't it? So few look there.** Those who do are strengthened by the journey. This strengthening is the peace, gives the peace. Yes, this is mortal terror, infant starvation, abandonment, cold terror. Go into the very center of it for peace.

You went out from your family into the world with this terrible aching need in you — the need of a starving, cold infant all alone. You tried to lure people in. Some sensed this need and stayed away. You presented as tough and needless. A pain-filled life. Now, you let us see you. This is good.

We use your deficits for good, just as the dark ones use your virtues to harm you.

Be open and curious. Notice all the details of your experience. Do not retreat into already known theory and story.

Be as kind as a sharp sword, gentle as only the strong can afford to be.

You are on a good path. It winds and twists and doubles back on itself. Onward. The shortest distance between two points in the inner world is not a straight line.

There are dark ones with you who now want to return to the swamps and reservoirs of pain and suffering. Their long and mostly successful foraging expedition in your family and you is finally petering out. Do not let them escape; help us catch them.

Do not try to trick the tricksters; this would be descending to their level and give them a victory.

You sense massive underground detonations deep in your inner world. Something much bigger than you is taking place out of your sight. You did help trigger this; it is good.

Does it matter what I call you?

Not so much, as long as you call us. Spirit laughs.

Notice that most of the irritations that come to you are over trivia or things you cannot affect. This keeps you tied up in unproductive knots of hate. Your early rage at the denial of childhood sexual abuse was productive; you had a Real part in getting this recognized. The critters want your energy spent uselessly. They get to harvest the rage, hate, powerlessness, contempt, and sneering. They feast on your suffering.

When you open pus pockets — physical ones or spiritual, emotional ones — expect a stench. Do not be dismayed. This is good.

Do not enjoy the sufferings of others, no matter what they've done. Never, never, never. If you allow this pleasure, it opens the pathway to sorcery. She is a terrible, beckoning seductress. As you grow in inner power, you are offered access to magic. Be aware; stay away. It is a good test of the purity of your intent. See if you can give away your healing and expect no recognition or credit. This is crucial.

But Spirit, I cannot yet do this; I want people to like me. I want people to love me.

We Spirits are right here loving you right now, and you will not let it in. We offer; you must receive. You pray for us daily. We are here; let us in.

I'm trying, Spirit.

Don't try. Pause, let us flow through you. Focus on us, not on your efforts. Come to know the sensations, emotions, and felt sense of the sacred. You lock yourself in a tiny closet inside a vast mansion. Outside that mansion is a planet and a sky. So much more. Open, open. You cannot contain the love we offer. You must stretch and grow and dissolve and then reform.

A vision: Returning to the back of your heart

It's not that you have a blind spot — it's much more generalized. You are blind almost everywhere, with only a tiny area of perception. You could not stand the Real. In your tiny area of perception, the vast majority of what you sense is illusion — sometimes temporarily helpful illusions, but illusions nevertheless. When your eyes do open, there will be confusion. Turn your confusion into curiosity and wonder like a child. Not the dismay of a tired manager who just wants everything neat and quiet. Joy — surprise — excitement — adventure. These are needed qualities. Play and Real learning are very closely related. This joy is how you grow. It is not frivolous or a waste of time. This is a necessity for spiritual growth. Joy, delight, sparkling play. Joy is a great virtue. Invincible joy. Tyrants of all kinds hate this. They often attack and silence the comics and comedians first. Find joy and dance with her. Can you be a Holy fool or maybe just a fool? What tyrants and demons most want is to kill joy. Joy defeats them utterly. So, they murder millions and impoverish more, all to drown joy in seas of sorrow and suffering, to silence her pure voice. Joy. This is the virgin. No matter if she is raped hundreds of thousands of times, and she has been, there is still a fire of joy deep within the caves of her. It cannot be extinguished, only hidden.

Joy, joy, joy, joy. Joy can break your heart. She can seem harsh to the frightened rigidities within you. She is never truly harsh. She demands the best from you. Give her away, share her, and she grows. Joy will feed you. You allow so little in. It is all around you, and you refuse to breathe, and you shrivel from the lack. Some die from this. It does not have to be earned, just received. You can do the dirtiest work, clean sewers or worse, resentfully or joyfully. What if the core of the cosmos was a fire of joy? This is basically Real, but easy to get wrong. Because it is a great virtue, its near enemies are devastating. Joy is a problem for you. Do you notice the incongruity? The irony? As a child in your family, joy was impossible. You still do not know her. You get joy from teaching and learning. This is good — a doorway. This is caused joy, conditional joy. Can you find unconditional joy?

When you sense joy, pause for it. This is a start, a crack in the wall. Joy pain is a deep spiritual state and a treasure. You also need something more ordinary. The critters have robbed you and your culture of this. They work constantly to prevent joy and fill you with addictive counterfeits, the fake coins of striving and ownership. You do not need anything to be joyful. A dying person losing everything can be joy-filled and radiant. Everything you need is right here, right now. At least notice how you defend yourself from joy.

We Spirits are not unkind or unloving. Sometimes what seems a bitter absolute defeat, total uselessness, is actually a triumph, a graduation, and a reward for work well done. We have the kindness of a sharp sword. The love of a mother hawk shoving her baby out of the nest. We love you.

We do not work to settle you. You are much better off being unsettled and learning to enjoy this.

The world around you is filled with lies and glittering phonies. Do not try and expose them or confront them all. You do not even need to know who is who. You merely need to be true to yourself and speak with kindness. Truth without love is not, after all, true. Be kind as a sharp sword glinting in the sun.

A vision: Self-righteousness and the vermin of hate

Your civilization is destroying itself in the name of moralistic, self-righteous salvation. The woke stuff is a well-baited hate trap. Diabolically clever. Feeding ridiculous and toxic ideas to children almost forces many of you to engage with their hate, lies, and seething resentments. China and Russia and the insectoid, regimented dictatorships may well inherit the earth. A terrible disaster. This planet was an outlaw's outback hideaway with some freedom and independence. The whole planet might now turn into a tightly regulated maximum-security prison designed to kill the soul and all joy. The hatred of spiritual connection, joy, beauty, and the new creates a breeding ground of evil — a farm of suffering, terror, and pain that the dark ones can feast on.

Evil now wears designer suits. It lives in expensive houses and works from behind impressive desks. From these palaces of doom, it spreads out like gangrene or cancer to eat the living, the flesh of the good, the alive, the tender, the fresh, and the new. It does not matter how terrible this domination is nor how many eons it lasts, the living freshness will triumph. Fear not, fear not. If you express this, no one will believe you. Even your closest friends will not listen. You will be even more outcast and rejected. Do not, like Lao Tsu, retreat into the far mountains. Continue to write and teach, put your ideas out. Do not expect recognition. They do not want to hear.

Your whole culture is infested with the vermin of hate. Small minds, dishonest and lost, but certain of their foolish mistakes. They are entrenched and bristling with arms. They have got many glittering traps, clever pitfalls, tornadoes, and slippery slopes. Do not fight them. Go around their fortified lines. Build alternative structures. Very few lift their heads up from the trough and interrupt their feeding long enough to look, and they are usually quickly blinded. Selling their birthright for a bowl of porridge, and the porridge is poisoned! Even as your human world teeters blindly into slavery, lies, and implacable hate, all is well.

When you pray well, it strengthens you. The water flowing through a stream cleans, clears, and refreshes the way.

Deep hells breed great saints.

Keep on with your work. All the strain and suffering are giving birth. Vast suffering is needed to produce one clean soul — thousands of generations, cycles of descent. The dark times allow the evil to flower so it is no longer latent in the soil.

Explore inward and downward. Do not be distracted. The dark ones will be even more invasive and controlling to force you and others to pay attention to them. This reveals their deep emptiness, terror, and aloneness. They would strangle you and their own children, involve you in fights and hatred — anything so they do not have to look inside. So, look inside. Here you can make a difference, a Real difference.

Pain is an acid which strips away rust and impurities, and it is also food for critters. It depends on how it is received and endured.

The tree does not strive for beauty and symmetry. Each cell gropes its way forward, moving toward light or moisture. You are a cell. You cannot even imagine the shape of the tree. Focus on your next right step.

You are a much bigger being than you know. At the outer limits of your knowing, you can only sense maybe 3 to 5 percent of who you really are. This is like your external awareness with dark matter and dark energy. As above, so below.

Be curious, not vigilant. Be kind in all ways. This way, you will not get stuck or glued. If you feel stuck to someone or something, look for your own unkind parts.

You cannot really experience the greatness of Spirit or of other people until you find what is great within yourself.

Fear is all around you. You swim in it. Your culture is based on it. Media and politicians work to keep you all terrified. Remember the phrase "the fog of war"? The fog of fear is the war. It poisons you. You act badly. Then guilt and resentment do the rest. The driving wheel is fear. Turn toward it, be curious. Pray for whoever scares you. When you remember who you are — an eternal being — most of your fears dissolve. Be grateful for your fears. They put cracks in your walls and help your immune system develop. Being radically honest and never taking anything that is not yours can defeat fear utterly.

Allow yourself to be cleansed; allow the stripping away of everything that is not yours. Stand naked. All is well. Some day you will believe this and taste the peace it offers.

The virgin enters like a fog. You cannot pin her down. She is seeping in, pervading, entering silent and moist. Your intellectual, verbal, and iconic senses are almost irrelevant. Your emotions matter some. Your silent presence matters deeply.

(Laughs) This is like soaking beans overnight before you can cook them, but this time it is for many lifetimes. Gentle, persistent, moist kindness. Be present. Stillness. Be still and know.

Curses sometimes damage the person cursed, but they always hurt the one who sends the curse. Always. And even more so when the curses work. You curse people all the time with your negative thoughts and judgment. Each one is a little curse; even if you don't send them out, the negativity ricochets around inside your head.

External recognition is not a measure of value.

The most important things are paradoxes or mysteries. They cannot be analyzed or understood or nailed down, but you can form relationships with them, and you can love them.

We bless you every day; many of these blessings you experience as pain and trouble.

When you love all the parts of you who, out of their hunger, take the bait offered by the dark ones, negativities will not affect you. A hundred thousand an hour will be no problem. The rain of negativities — hate, self-righteousness, pain, and fears — can help you find any lonely parts and any parts with unmet needs.

Your inner world has great value. The images are clothed beings put on so you can see them and interact with them.

Be honest. Do not trim your sails to the prevailing breeze. Be kind, inside and out. Kind.

Be aware of what you are aware of. Know you are knowing. Meta-cognition is unblending. It is a path to freedom.

Gratitude opens the door to reverence.

The universal will is not blind or uncaring. It navigates by senses you cannot understand through dimensions beyond your imaginings.

Each moment when you are entertaining negativities drains you. More than that, they are moments when you could be experiencing the transcendent. You could be charged with divinity and love. Yet you fill yourself with judgments and hate about transient, ephemeral trivia. Oh, my son, my son.

You are learning how to help drain the reservoirs of pain and hate. The unattached burdens want to destroy you, so they spray you with temptations. They can be used to help purify you if you do not get sucked in. They hose you down with offers of justified hate and resentment. This is like spraying septic tank fluids over a man with open wounds. Hose them down with love. Ignore the provocations. **Your desire to teach them a lesson is not good. Unwilling students do not learn.**

Your culture needs a back door. Open a crack to let Spirit sneak back in. IFS provides this. The 12 steps provide this. A Trojan horse. If you come directly, you will be smashed. Hose them down with love, even as they brandish spears and invade your home. If you go to them with hate and conflict, they use it to harden their shells. This keeps you out, but even more, it tightens the prison that holds the tender light within them.

A vision: **Returning to the back of your heart**

The back of your heart has clogged and closed again. This is the place of betrayal. It is very good you have discovered this new blockage. It is draining now. This had kept our light from getting deeply into your heart and through you into your world. There are ugly, smelly liquids draining. There are still globs and clots and chunks inside of you. Note that an old place you had cleared long ago — the back of your heart — reclogged. The old trails became overgrown.

Clear the drainage ditches. Not pleasant or glorious work, but important. It is drainage failures that create the swamps. Returning to old areas is not failure — it is good.

Spirit, I sense a lurking, hulking being in there. He is sullen and wary.

Yes, you see well. Let's get him out.

We hose him down with love. He reminds me of Quasimodo. He enjoys being free and clean even though he feels much shame. He won't go. There are others inside he wants to get. It is his family. He does have love in him. He gathers them and as they huddle together fearfully, he gently washes the green slime off of them. Now he is ready to go. There is one straggler child who is angry, resistant, and unwashed. He takes him, too. This one is actually a boss critter. An undercover, well-disguised plant of the dark ones.

It had worked to keep all these beings and green slime inside the back of your heart. It will return to the darkness while the family will go on to the light.

The dark ones do everything they can to distract you from connecting with us, with Spirit. They raise a ruckus, make noise, wave flags, show gory images to distract you. They hate it when we connect. They know this connection spells the end of their feeding in you. Focus on beauty and joy. Pause when you sense them.

Do not be jealous of the gifts we give to others. What you are given is carefully crafted to mold and shape you. It is what you need at this time. Work with it right where you are.

When you were a child, the dark ones almost squeezed off your contact with us completely. It was a pincer's movement. Your parents' betrayal on one side and your dad's sadistic attacks as a man of the church isolated you from your spiritual traditions. This left you open to the pull of oblivion, the pull of the coma wards. They almost got you. Endless rest is not the answer. Military discipline is not the answer. What will be your new way?

When you are lost, stop moving. Be curious. Sit still with it. Dance with it. Hold it close. Turn inward.

There is a part of you who took in what is unbearable, flat-out terror. He held this and contained it. He was banished and locked in a basement. Held incommunicado. Finally, now, he can be welcomed back as the tragic hero he is. His courageous sacrifice allowed you to survive without becoming psychotic. You had your own terror of a raped and tortured child, but also your dad's fears and ancient ancestral fears got in. This is bigger than you. Your work now can open the way for an inland sea of terror to drain. You are on a good path. Notice how many around you work to install more fear. They are shrill, worried, and desperate. Turn toward. When you can do this with love, not anger, you are free. Turn toward, open eyes, open hearts. Do not lie.

Listen! Do not talk. Observe. We are right here. You have a manager who cannot let go — this is fundamental. Let go into the abyss, into terror. Practice dying. **You get into an infinite regress of anxious managers trying to manage each other.** You could call it a thought loop. This creates a tornado which feeds on itself. Critters laugh and howl in delight as your good intentions drag you down. Practice dying — let go. Managers structurally cannot do this for you.

Your focus and work are inner. Do not look down your nose at others whose focus is elsewhere. This is foolish critter stuff. This will hurt you and them.

You are entering a cocoon. Submit to it. There is a vastness opening to you.

You are old. Your sun is fading. It is sad. There is also a nobility in it if you face it well. Grief is also noble. Sit down and face your coming death. Slow down. More silence. Be less acquisitive of experience. You can hold onto nothing. It must all go. You get to choose how. Release it or have it torn away from you, as it is all taken away from you. There are more ecstasies to come. Bigger ones.

(High in the Bear Paw Mountains of Montana with some friends, I began to sense the awe and vastness of the place. I started to hate my companions because they continued their normal daily conversations.)

You started to hate everyone because they interfered with your precious experience of Holiness. Your own hatred is what interfered, not their chatter. You can sense Spirit anywhere. Do not blame others for your failures to sense us.

Words limit your spirit; you can start to move away from them. There's so much more awaiting you. Words are an old set of clothes you have outgrown, straining and stretching at the seams. This is true — just as true as the fact that soon as you will outgrow your physical body.

What could replace the words? Images, movement?

Not so much, my son. More just love, awareness, contact, and connection.

You see people much more clearly now. Beware, lest you judge them. We cannot give you more vision until this is clean. Critters try to hook judgment onto vision to poison the prophets.

A vision: **The birth of the ancient worm**

I see visions of a huge, slow-moving worm emerging from the back of my heart. It is ancient; it is aching and in pain but can still be vicious and lightning fast. There are many beings much bigger than humans.

You sensed this when you were high in the Bear Paw Mountains. Just let this ancient worm go. It suffers horribly in slow motion. Do not hate it despite all the damage it has done. Do not hate anyone, anything. This worm is ours now. The worm's coming out of you so painfully is a necessary birth. Just watch.

The vision of the worm continued.

You have come through a tunnel, an ordeal. The worm is out. We have him. In a sense, you gave birth to him. We love him, too; and he is very hard to love. He caused so much pain. You held him within you unknowingly. You were his mother, his womb, his succor. What a horrible job. You never would have done this knowingly. You gave your body and life to nurture a truly evil one so it could be born anew. A big part of your life was harboring the worm and giving birth to it so it might heal.

Hitler and many others harbored the worm and gave birth to it with vastly different results. His birthing the worm will be famous for thousands of years, and yours will go by unnoticed. Those who do notice will think you are insane. This birthing through you, and the emotional and physical pain you have experienced in the past three weeks, is the culmination of much work — some conscious, mostly unconscious. Even though you were unaware of all this, being in ceremony with the Crow people helped make this birth possible. The ceremonies were your midwife.

You are no longer connected to the worm. Leave it to me — do not involve yourself here. There are many worms in your species, many. Humans are riddled with worms. Most are dormant or sleeping, gorged with the rich food you offer of hate and pain and jealousy and greed. Self-righteousness is the lock on the door which keeps them safe. Humans are an unwitting worm farm. We have stirred them. They are emerging from their caves, tunnels, and hiding places. This is good. The worms themselves are not evil, but many have been parasitized and are controlled by truly evil ones.

Each moment of your life contains the eternal depths — every single one. No special time or place is needed.

It is defocus and forgetfulness they are using now to attack you. Beware of discouragement. Remember, the dry and difficult times are often times of deep healing out of your awareness. Your awareness is tiny.

Much of the mental health world is inhabited and controlled by critters, by dark ones. This vision is true, but what you do with it is a problem. You can only give you more insight when you use it better with kindness, not with hatred. We do not give clarity to all. Clarity is power. We do not give it to those who use it to increase the harm they do to themselves and others.

We always answer your prayers — always. Sometimes we shout and you still do not hear us.

There is a sucking wind, a tornado. Focus here. Notice the sharpness of it. It is precise and thorough. Let it clean you down to the bone and beyond. Let it take the meanness, the judgment and the fear, and any trace of hate, cruelty, or delight in the suffering of others. When you are clean, step into the fire, the glowing, incandescent, uncreated light. Let us clean you. It will hurt. Let us work.

Your managers want to help. Tell them no. Tell them to receive now. Release. There is no one in you who does not need cleaning. Help your managers let go. They did save your life, and now they need to release. They can grow bigger.

Some things we do in you will make no sense or even seem damaging. This is Real.

The sneering of fools is a wise man's glory.

You are small. Your life span, nearly done. Stay with this smallness so your spirit may soar.

You may need to dive into deep hell realms again. The trip is terrifying, and the purification is precious.

Terrible things are done all around you. Lies are believed and promulgated as fact. They are getting away with it. They gain wealth, power, and fame. Do not hate them. That gives them victory. Do not hate. You may need to kill, but do not hate.

Hate blinds you to the Real by turning your focus outward. If you follow this path, you will end up in hell fighting bad guys. If you do not clear this, it can entrap you in hells for eons. Clear this now with small triggers. When you want to hate in the outer world, turn inward. For you now, there is a protector with a helpless one behind him. This helpless one is a treasure disguised as a problem. **Look behind your hatreds — there is an unmet need. Unmet needs are how we grow and therefore treasures.**

We are helping you as much as you allow… which is not so much. Find the parts of you who are afraid of receiving, and love them. Love them in imitation of the way we love you. Real love expects no return.

You are part of a bigger organism, a conscious organism.

A vision: An infection of love

The insectoid Queen of the Dark Ones. She looks like the queen of a beehive. She tries to cripple her children so they will not launch and leave her. They will stay near her where she can feed on them. This infests human mothers. This dark mother attack is worldwide now. A major invasion at the mammalian roots of humanity. The worldwide web of the dark ones looks like many lines all around the planet connecting with nets, like a spider's webbing. The planet is almost engulfed. This is an infestation. Go for the queen.

When I do, she sends out an alarm to the worldwide web of queens, but they turn on her and amputate her to prevent her infection with love from spreading. The queen network retreats, fortifies its boundaries, and prepares new attacks.

Now Bob, you help the queen they amputated go into the light. This encounter left a gaping hole in their encircling of earth.

I sense there are also other holes. Later, these insectoid queens offered to negotiate. But quickly, there is a blast of rage and ultra-violent images, screams of "fuck you." We tell them, you can go back where you've come from — we will help. They reply, "You fool — we cannot go back. We were exiled, thrown out. We have to send back tribute, life force energy units harvested from your planet from your suffering and pain. Our families will be killed if we fail and worse." Some weird shit came up, and then I thought, oh fuck, I went up to the top. Let's send back a shipment of life force with an infestation of love. A highly contagious love infestation that will take over your home planet. Then you will be free, and we will be free. When they realize the shipments are contaminated, it may be too late for them to maintain dominance, or they may cut you off and refuse all further shipments. In either case, you are free.

Love is a contagious infection from the viewpoint of evil, domination structures, and the fear-based. This is truer than true. Be the Typhoid Mary of love. Give this away. Don't get arrogant or judgmental, or you will have blown the whole thing.

Joy is your food. You cannot yet take in much. You are an invalid sipping a weak broth of joy.

You are becoming more of a spirit warrior than spirit's garbageman. This is not a more noble job at all. Warriors have done much damage. Garbagemen have never done any. You will need more discernment. Do not get proud or gloat.

Do not grab for the sword. When it is time, it will be given.

Your affection for us is still blocked. Look again at who blocks it.

A major strategy of the dark ones now is to exaggerate your visions — to push them too far, make them dramatic and compelling. This will be used to discredit you, to expose you to ridicule, to have the truths and clarity you bring obscured and hidden and even defeated utterly. Beware. Look for the parts of you who have a taste for drama and heroism. Remember humility. Your desire to be a visionary easily became an inflation. If it makes you feel special, it is poison, a delicious poison.

Is affection a better guide than cool clarity?

A good question, my son. Affection is never wrong. Your clarity often is.

When you are choosing the work and tasks, there are two major enduring guides: does this work bring you closer to Spirit? And does it help you feel more affection?

Automata have been set upon you. Mechanized, industrialized farming of misery. Habits, thought loops, ruminations, and addictions of the soul. You can intercept those more easily now. Automata of evil.

All your petty resentments and hatreds can teach you. Learn. You are opening up another pus pocket, a stinky one. Open all your interior senses — do not analyze or figure out or interpret. Open to detail in all senses, in all directions. Analysis will take you away from the prize, the treasure. There is treasure here. Stay with this. **Let go and you are free. Cling and grasp, and you are in a prison, in a prison of your own devising.** Let go.

The inner and outer worlds are connected, joined, and intertwined. They fertilize each other.

Meanness and hate survive in you, in your species, in your culture. You are permeated with them, steeped in them, bathed in them. You were fed them with your mother's milk. They have penetrated your flesh, your tissues, even your heart. So sad. Your flesh is dyed with their toxins — gray, green, brown, black. There are more fluids hiding in the gloom. They envelop your planet. There's a metallic taste, like a handful of old coins. Deep, deep, deep inside your tissues, you need the ancient river to free you. Fire is also your friend. You have opened another pus pocket, another room, another ward. It is good. Stay curious. Often, it takes great suffering to crack the shells, to break open the walls.

There is another ancient pus pocket. Outright terror, need, desperation, the cliff of insanity and howling. Go there. It is good you have discovered this cavity, this cave under you. You could not build higher on top of it, it would collapse. Critters will fight desperately to prevent you from resolving this. Blind terror, desperation, that's the name of this realm. There are swamps of UBs all around you. Clouds of locusts obscuring the sun. A good training for you. The intense terror you experienced in the third-floor bedroom of your family home screams so loudly in our Spirit world that many other spirits who suffered similarly snuck in. Some bullied their way in. Some were welcomed like stray dogs. You were so lonely; you welcomed any similar terrified beings. A deep resonance of terror and pain and isolation. Let this all open slowly and gently. Warm it in your breast, your breath. There is a great learning here and a vast swamp, a very toxic swamp. It can begin to drain. It is way bigger than just you. You have stumbled into a major reservoir of the dark ones. The mother terror. It fuels many other reservoirs of hate and pain. Expect the dark ones to attack. As the swamp drains, creatures will be revealed who do not want to be seen or freed. They are dripping with viscous red-brown shiny sludge. The stench is horrible. Beware of self-righteousness. Hate is never justified. Love is always the answer, no matter what the question. Remember these and you are safe.

For you, Bob, the virgin goddess comes as mist, fog, and gentle breezes now. It is so good you've begun to recognize her again.

Listen to the sweet, still messages and we will not have to raise our voice and shout at you.

Your mind is way too small. Reality is way more fluid and vast. There are no rock foundations; there are no things. It's all process, movement, relationship, and persons.

Trust the contact with us Spirits 100 percent. The words that come from the contact, not so much.

When people waste your precious time and energy, remember it is your irritations with them, not their behavior, that does the damage. Use a mirror, not a magnifying glass. Pray for them and help your own parts.

There is a shitstorm of critter crap. They want you to get discouraged. Stay steady, sturdy, and focused. Have faith. With Real faith, you are never dismayed, even in the deepest hells.

Drop all your knowing. Drop all your clothes and come naked with us. Ask, what can I learn here?

Separation is only one half of unblending. The other half is establishing good relations with the part or being you have unblended from. As you go to pray, as you go to dance, unblend from all your parts, drop all your ideas, go naked inside, come to us naked.

Most of the spiritual battle is entirely out of your awareness. It is other dimensions, and yet how you behave can determine the outcome.

There is a part of you emerging now who has much energy he could not use as a child. The holy energy of exploration. Exploration was blocked because your whole family, your whole world, was a web of lies. The only way open for the energy of exploration was the thin crack provided by intellectual curiosity. Your fascination with non-Western civilization and tribes was formed by your need to stay far away from the fog of lies and terrible truths that were your intimate Real world. The truths were lurking under the surface of your family like terrible sea monsters.

When you are attacked inside, go forward into it, into its mouth, down its throat. Only your own fears harm you — only this. Go toward the fear-holding parts with love. Welcome them home. Your impulse, and the impulse of your world, is to silence them and lock them away. This works temporarily but causes great long-term damage and creates food and attachment points for the dark Spirits.

Call on us more. Pray more. You have been handed a glittering sword flashing and bright. Use it well.

Afterword

What is this book? Channeling? Automatic writing? Or what?

We can think of various practices of connecting with Spirit on a continuum from total receptivity and passivity on one end to control and even manipulation on the other. On the receptive end, mindfulness meditation is perhaps the most prominent method today — just being aware of what's going on inside. Pure nonreactive witnessing. Dick Schwartz has clearly said that mindfulness meditation is a good beginning, but it's not enough. In IFS, we need to interact with and help the parts we meet. In the history of Western spirituality, there was a trend that has been called Quietism. Exemplified by Madame Guyon and Father Molinas, it emphasized total opening to the Divine and stated that once a person was in contact with the Divine, they no longer needed liturgies, or priests, or any intermediaries. Of course, both of these people, and many others, were persecuted by the Inquisition, and Father Molinas was executed. In terms of spirit possession, this end of the scale would be represented by possession experiences where the person who is possessed has no memory whatsoever of what happened while they were in trance. The medium in the famous Nechung Oracle of Tibet, the monk who is possessed, has this experience.

At the other end of the spectrum are the very active and even controlling kinds of spirituality. Shamans often worked very hard to become Masters of Spirits. They learned how to dominate spirits to force them to stop hurting their clients. Also at this end of the spectrum would be the many forms of deity yoga. For example, in Tibetan Buddhism there is the Blue Medicine Buddha meditation, in which the precise incredibly detailed image of the Blue Medicine Buddha is visualized and then invited down into the practitioner's spirit. More prosaically, many written prayers that are recited have a lot of this element of control and structure.

We could easily write a book exploring the implications of this continuum. What's usually missed is the middle realm. Let's call it the realm of dialogue. IFS is a form of dialogue with the parts of ourselves inside. Another great example in modern psychology is Carl Jung's active imagination. He opened his mind to whatever images emerged and then interacted and conversed with them. He did not just observe them passively, and he did not command them — he had a relational and interactive way of being with the beings he met in the depths of his psyche. Jung said there are three types of imagination: voluntary fantasy, passive imagination, and active imagination. He said that voluntary fantasy is trivial and of no interest. Passive imagination is either dreams or psychosis. Active imagination is a way to explore the inner world. IFS's insistence on dialogue and relationship with the parts from Self is quite similar. It's the interaction — the relationship — that heals. In Western spirituality, Saint Ignatius of Loyola, the founder of the Jesuits, spoke of colloquy — dialogue — as a form of prayer. He said it was perhaps the most intimate form of prayer. He suggested that colloquy could involve different forms of relationship, and he gave the example of two friends or a servant and a master speaking together.

The contents of this book are definitely from this middle category of dialogue or colloquy. This is not channeling or automatic writing. It is the result of an interactive, personal relationship. Because this book is a summary of thousands of pages of dialogues, the interactive, relational nature of these conversations can be easily forgotten. Everyone can develop this kind of relationship with Spirit if they choose.

About the Author

For over fifteen years, Bob Falconer has devoted himself full-time to Internal Family Systems (IFS) therapy. In that time, he has attended all the levels of IFS training offered, has been on the faculty of these trainings more than twenty times, and has attended many workshops and events with Richard Schwartz as both an assistant and a participant. He has helped train well over one thousand therapists and has offered courses and led workshops in Pakistan, China, Korea, Australia, Spain, Poland, Mexico, Canada, and the UK. He has also taught all over the United States, including the Fort Belknap Sioux and Northern Cheyenne Reservations.

He is perhaps best known in the IFS world for having coauthored the book *Many Minds, One Self* with Richard Schwartz. Bob's own history is one of extreme sadistic child abuse: sexual, physical, emotional, and spiritual. Both parents were addicts and offenders. His mother was hospitalized several times for mental illness, his brother committed suicide when they were teenagers, and his father was murdered when Bob was twenty-one. Bob's interest in therapy stems from his own determination to heal himself and then help others with similar histories.

In the '70s and '80s, therapists often pretended that child sexual abuse hardly ever occurred. There was no diagnosis of PTSD until Vietnam veterans got together and used political action to force the therapeutic establishment to recognize this diagnosis. Bob was one of the first men to publicly identify as a survivor of childhood sexual abuse, and he was very active in the survivors movement. For over ten years, he was the director of the Institute for Trauma Oriented Psychotherapy and, in this capacity, coedited a series of four books on childhood abuse with Robert Geffner of the Family Violence Institute. At this time, Bob also published an autobiographical account of his own abuse under the pseudonym Robert Blackburn Knight. A revised edition of this book under his real name will be released in 2026. Bob still consults with some complex trauma clients, but his focus has shifted to teaching IFS and now to exploring the others within us — our experiences of spiritual presence.

In his pursuit of healing for himself and others, Bob has explored many modalities. His undergraduate degree was in anthropology, and he has been fascinated by shamanism ever since. He had the great good fortune to study with Michael Harner and Sandra Ingerman, among others. His first love in the therapy world was Ericksonian hypnotherapy, which led him to Jack and Helen Watkins's ego state therapy. Since 1971, Bob has been regularly attending workshops and trainings at the Esalen Institute and has taken over 140 seminars there. The Gestalt therapy of Mariah Fenton Gladis and Christine Price made a deep impression on him. Bob also studied codependency and addiction with Pia Mellody in the '80s and '90s. He had the privilege of learning nonviolent communication from Marshall Rosenberg and studied expressive arts and dance with Anna Halprin, Stewart Cubley, Andrea Juhan, and many others.

Psychedelics have helped Bob's healing since he first became involved with them in 1967. He is very grateful for the current psychedelic renaissance and enjoys training people who know how to use IFS in psychedelic-assisted therapy. He also trains psychedelic providers in the fundamentals of IFS because he believes that even this very basic knowledge can prevent a great deal of unintended harm.

Bob offers a series of online courses teaching how to work with the others within us and spirituality in therapy. (Links to these courses on his website will be available soon.) He provides small experiential consultation groups on these subjects. His website also includes links to most of the over fifty podcasts he has appeared on, and a YouTube channel offers many free lectures and demonstration sessions.

Website: https://robertfalconer.us
YouTube: https://www.youtube.com/@bobfalconer
Facebook: https://www.facebook.com/theotherswithus